A HISTORY OF
THE CROATIAN PEOPLE

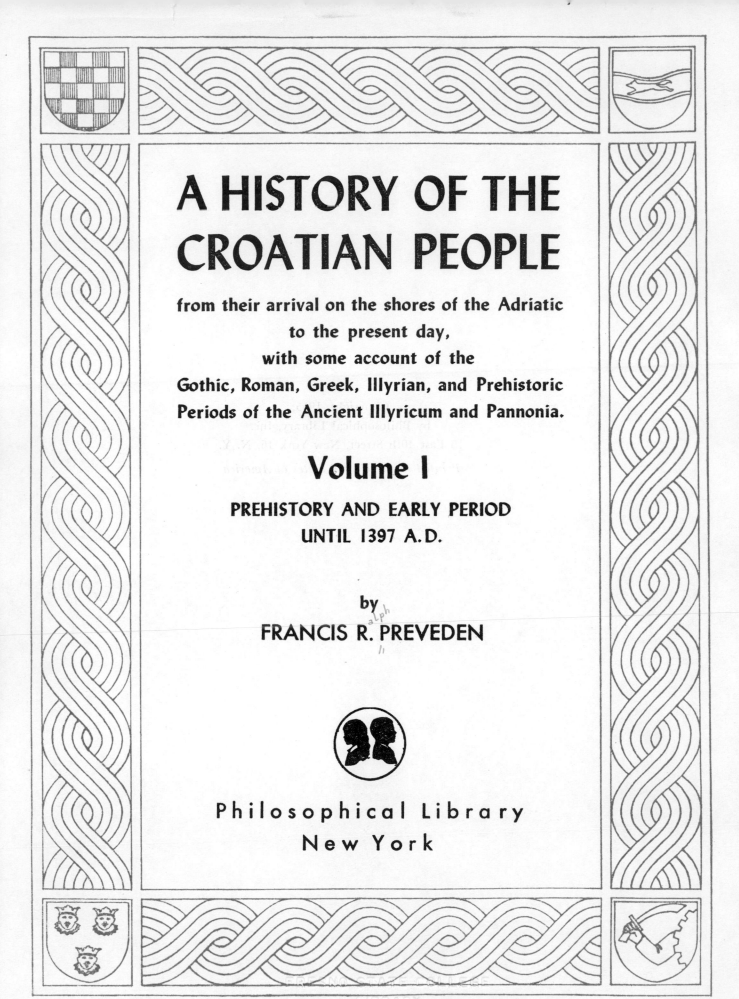

A HISTORY OF THE CROATIAN PEOPLE

from their arrival on the shores of the Adriatic
to the present day,
with some account of the
Gothic, Roman, Greek, Illyrian, and Prehistoric
Periods of the Ancient Illyricum and Pannonia.

Volume I

PREHISTORY AND EARLY PERIOD
UNTIL 1397 A.D.

by

FRANCIS R. PREVEDEN

Philosophical Library
New York

In fond memory of my father, JOSEPH PREVEDEN, *the black-smith of Kamenica, Croatia, and my mother,* CAROLINE whose love for Croatian folklore and stories of the Croatian past first led me into the paths of Croatian history.

TABLE OF CONTENTS

ILLUSTRATIONS:

Plates 1-12. Geography: terrain; water masses; vegetation.

Plates 13-15. Prehistoric artefacts.

Plates 16-23. Roman antiquities.

Plates 24-40. Diocletian's Palace.

Plates 41-54. Medieval Cathedrals.

Plates 55-58. Pictorial concepts of historical events.

Plates 59-64. Popular costumes and racial types.

Non Platoni, sed veritati.

What country, friends, is this?
This is Illyria, lady.

Act I, Scene II.
—SHAKESPEARE.   *Twelfth Night.*

The Croats, one of many Slavic tribes, left their Transcarpathian homeland and came to the shores of the Adriatic in the first half of the seventh century. The territory they occupied was the Roman Illyricum with its various provinces such as Istria, Liburnia, Dalmatia, Praevalitana and the southern part of Pannonia, with an adjacent district called Bassantes, later Bosnia.

In this territory they established three political and administrative organizations called White Croatia, Red Croatia and Pannonian Croatia.

While in their Transcarpathian homeland the Croats, like other continental Slavs, had lived the simple life of shepherds and peasants on the level of Homeric civilization. On their arrival in Illyricum, exposed to a culture which was still not so very different from that which had prevailed in the great days of Greece and Rome, they made rapid progress in the arts and ways of civilization. They did not destroy this culture, but absorbed it, adopted it, cultivated it, even as they absorbed and adopted the native population of the area. Soon they had adjusted to the ways of the western civilization to which they cling to this day. The Croat of historic times therefore has been culturally very largely the product of a Roman, Grecian, Illyrian past, even as physically he must be considered an admixture of Greek, Roman, Illyrian, Avarian, Frankish and Turkish elements with the old Slavic strain.

Therefore it has been thought proper to discuss at least the chief monuments of the Roman and Paleaeo-Balkanic civilization which existed before the coming of the Croats into Illyria. This task is attempted in the first five chapters of the book.

With the coming of the Slavs into the Balkans the Roman names, or, more accurately, the romanized Palaeo-Balkanic names, in part yielded to a new historical nomenclature. For example such names as Noricum, Pannonia, Dacia, Moesia, etc. have been lost, and the land renamed after their present inhabitants, Serbia, Bulgaria, Roumania.

Elsewhere, particularly among the Croats, the old names were retained, and are retained to this day, in spite of the change of population and its ethnological charateristics. Incidentally, such names as Istria, Dalmatia, Bosnia, Macedonia, and a host of river names, all reflect the word-coinage of some prehistoric populations. These old provincial names were retained by the Croats and began to assume an ethnographic significance, replacing the old tribal names of the new settlers. So in place of Croats, we got Dalmatians, Islanders, Istrians, Bosnians, Slavonians, Syrmians, etc., very much after the manner of the ancient Greeks, who were Thessalians, Boeotians, Athenians, Acarnanians, Arcadians, Lacedaemonians, Ionians, Cretans, Sicilians, etc., but all of them being at the same time Hellenes.

The provincial attitude, enhanced by the broken-up terrain, was frequently the opportunity for attempts to obliterate the national consciousness and ethnographic unity of the Croats. The most powerful efforts in this direction were those of Napoleon, who planned to create an Illyrian kingdom by effacing the national characteristics of the Croats and other southern Slavs. The plan was espoused by some ambitious politicians in Croatia, but failed with the collapse of Napoleon's power.

A new attempt to absorb the Croatian nation by the false complex of an inter-racial unity came later through the zeal of the youthful and wealthy Bishop Joseph Strossmayer and his associate Francis Rachki, both of alien origin. Belittling the power and cultural capacity of the Croatian people, they deprived the cultural institutions established in Zagreb of their Croatian names and characteristics, by overhauling them with the artificial name of Yugo-Slavs. With a group of youthful adherents they carried on an intensive propaganda, subordinating the reality of Croatia to nebulous Yugo-Slav ideals. Thus they prepared the ground for two dictatorships, one of a monarchistic-military vendetta, and the present communist dictatorship of Yugoslavia, both of which have been directed against the sovereignty and independence of the Croatian people.

However, even in the darkest hours of Croatian history, when the shreds of Croatian territory were called "reliquiae reliquiarum olim magni et gloriosi regni 'Croatiae'" (remnant of remnants of the once great and glorious kingdom of Croatia), the ethnic unity of the Croatian people could not be destroyed, surviving the

calamities of the moment, and striving stead-
fastly toward freedom and independence. There
has been no let-up in this struggle, even at the
moment in the face of an imported and imposed dictatorship.

One last word, and a most important one, remains to be said. It is the purpose of this work
to present the history of the Croatian people in
a completely objective manner, without bias,
slant or prejudice of any kind, in accordance
with the most rigid disciplines of historical
science.

Chapter I
THE PHYSICAL BACKGROUND

HISTORY is imbedded in geography," said Immanuel Kant, "for it must develop from the soil." In fact, geography is the most important component in the prolonged existence of nations, for it affects the life of countless generations in many ways. Moreover, this influence is constant, uniform and deep enough to form habits both in the ways of an individual and community. Thus it creates the traditions and ethnic characteristics of a nation as it proceeds on its march through the centuries.[1]

It is fitting therefore that we provide a proper geographical setting for an historical narrative. For, Croatia is the country which the ancient Greeks attempted to colonize, before they settled down in Sicily and other points of the western Mediterranean. Eager for the possession of the eastern Adriatic coast, the Romans sent their legions here from the time of the first Punic War, and it took them over 250 years of fighting to conquer the coast and its hinterland. They romanized it, but could not hold it longer than a few centuries, in spite of its proximity to Italy. The Croats took over this Roman heritage, kept it nearly a thousand years longer than had the Romans, and thoroughly slavicized the Adriatic seaboard, with its adjacent areas. This they did in spite of the fact that they were an isolated and remote Slavic branch, over a thousand miles away from the bulk of the Slavic populations. These historical phenomena, and others of equal importance in the 14 centuries of Croatian history, are explained in part by the extent and configuration of the terrain occupied by the new settlers.

Except for the islands of the Adriatic archipelago, the Croatian territory consists of a single tract extending north to south from the headwaters of the Sava River in the vicinity of Ljubljana, founded by Augustus in 34 B.C. on an ancient site connected in legend with Jason of the Golden Fleece, approximately to Kotor, which we of the west know as Cattaro in the bay of the same name. West to east it reaches from the Adriatic Sea, including the western shores of the Istrian Peninsula to the edges of the Pannonian plain. Thence if we should extend a line from the great bend of the Danube southward to

Cattaro following in general the course of the Drina River we shall have roughly drawn the eastward and southern boundaries of the Croatian land.* The whole area is in the neighborhood of 50,000 square miles, or the size of England. Its pre-war population was estimated at between 6 and 7 millions. Due to enormous loss of life in the last war, it seems now considerably reduced.

Politically the land was early divided into Dalmatia, Bosnia and Herzegovina, Slavonia, Croatia, the Mura district, and southern half of Istria. Some of these provinces were hotly contested by the neighboring states, and the disputes arising in consequence, are a part of historical record.

The mountainous coast of the Adriatic and the adjacent highlands are the product of the earth movements which took place in the Tertiary or Alpine age in southern Europe. Thus, they belong to the group of the young fold mountains, the center of which are the Alps. Curving from southwest to southeast the Alps run out in several branches: southeast through the Apennine peninsula, and further east, along the Adriatic coast into the Dinaric Alps. These run parallel to the Apennines and enclose a large depression, which in time became the basin of the Adriatic Sea. The northeastern branch of the Alps forms in a graceful arc the Carpathian mountains, while another branch running straight east between the Sava and Drava rivers, either failed to develop fully, or was split and dislodged by subsequent earth movements which left in their wake a broken chain of hills known as the Croatian Zagorye (Tramontane), Mount Moslava, Ivanchitsa[2] and the Slavonian hills, including the range of Frushka Gora (Frankish Mountains) in the enclave between the Danube and Sava rivers.

Thus between the Carpathian mountains and the Dinaric Alps another large depression was contained. After the thawing of the snow and ice-masses of the Glacial age, this hollow became filled with water and formed an inland sea, the

---

* North to south from 46⁰24'17" to 42⁰6'20" north latitude. West to east from 21⁰3'15" to 18⁰7'13" E. longitude (Paris Observatory).

1

level of which was higher than that of the Pontus[3] or present-day Black Sea. Through the weakening of the southeastern Carpathian barrier, the rocks of the mountain range separating this inland sea from the Wallachian plain and the Pontus, cracked up and were washed away. Thus a deep gorge, the Iron Gate, was formed through which the high level inland sea drained through the Wallachian plain into the Pontus. The vast Alpine area surrounding the Pannonian depression was the fountain head of new streams of water which are still being drained by a large network of river beds. They all empty into the Danube, which in its turn, still drains through the Iron Gate into the Black Sea. This process took place in the Diluvial age,—rather recently,— yet the lapse of time has been long enough for a huge river system to spread its rich deposits, and cover the area with soil from the uplands making it one of the most fertile agricultural areas in Europe.

The southern part of the Pannonian depression, extending south of the Mura, Drava and central Danube, forms the northern Croatian territory, rich in all manner of farm produce, and a center of modern industries.

The most characteristic part of the Croatian territory, however, is the mountainous Dinaric area, with its parallel folds of mountain ranges running mainly in a northwest-southeast axis, but here and there, under the pressure of past volcanic disturbances and tectonic shifts, turning sharply toward the sea.

The most important mountain ranges in the north are the Velebit mountains skirting the seacoast and occasionally dropping down to the water's edge from considerable heights. They are separated from the open sea by the long Morlachian sound and the island archipelago. Both the sound and islands are probably of the same origin occasioned by the sinking of the coastal mountain ranges. As a result of this change the hollows were flooded by the sea, while the ridges and high tops emerged from the water in the form of numerous islands and cliffs.

At their southern end the Velebit Alps merge with the Dinaric highlands as they issue from the Alpes Ferreae of old, or the Large and Small Chapel (Velika i mala Kapela), their present names. In between the Velebit and Kapela mountains there is a high plateau, dissected by a number of furrow-like ridges, most of them running parallel to the Kapela range. From the merging point of the Velebit and Kapela systems the Dinaric mountains run parallel to the sea coast in a southeastern direction toward Neretva river and Mostar, capital of Herzegovina.

East of the Kapela and Dinaric mountains a number of parallel ranges form the Bosnian highlands. These extend as far as the Vrbas River, east of which is another solid block of hills extending to the Drina. Beyond that are the hills and mountains of Serbia. The Bosnian mountains reach their greatest height in the south, while in the north they slope gradually in gentle terraces toward the Sava valley, which makes this area easily accessible from the north. Moreover, the broad valleys of the Sava tributaries, Una, Vrbas, Bosna and Drina, provide convenient avenues in the heart of Bosnia. A number of accessible valleys leading from Bosnia southeast to Macedonia, and on to Constantinople, have made its communications with the Orient easy. Both the northern terraces and the southern valley-roads affected the history of Bosnia in a most dramatic fashion, for they predestined it to serve as a buffer-state between the Ottoman Empire and western Europe.

Like most other Alpine ranges formed by earth-folding in the Paleogene period of the Tertiary age, the Dinaric Alps are of limestone formation, except where the limestone strata were dislodged by the ancient rock shifts and volcanic eruptions, which sometimes wrought havoc to the original stratification. Thus in Bosnia considerable blocks of igneous rock form the body of the central and eastern hill groups. In these hills numerous minerals are found, including iron ore, tin and silver. In antiquity the Romans mined gold in this area. Later gold mining was abandoned, either through exhaustion of the matrix, or because the sites had been forgotten.

The characteristic and desolating aspect of the Dinaric Alps is the abundance of karstland, extensive areas of dry and barren hills and plateaus devoid of soil and vegetation. The hard limestone which is the main structural substance of these mountain ranges prevents the absorption of rain- and snow-water through the surface, and the water drains through joints and cracks underground, forming subterraneous streams, lakes and rivers. When such underground channels are broken by some fault the water finds its way into the open in the form of

a spring, stream or river, such as the Buna near Mostar. Some of these underground streams drain directly into the sea, and frequently emerge close to the seashore as does the Ombla near Dubrovnik. Thus, the underground waters are a total loss to the countryside. The surface is left bare, barren and craggy, with holes, deep sinks and caves. Mostly there is no humus, and consequently no vegetation to clothe the stony surfaces. The Adriatic area is typical of "karst-lands"—hence the universal adoption of a name which is locally used in that region.

The waters of the Dinaric system move in three directions: eastward to the Black Sea; westward to the Adriatic and south to the Aegean. The streams of the Pontian watershed flow toward the Danube, as the main artery of the Pannonian basin, through its two great tributaries, Sava and Drava, issuing from the Slovenian highlands. The Sava River has 84 tributaries, the most important of which are Kupa, Una, Vrbas, Bosna and Drina on the right bank, and Bosut, Lonya, Krapina and Savinya, on the left bank. Each of these commands a network of tributaries of its own.

The Drava has 24 tributaries, the most important of which is the Mura, forming with its own tributaries an enclave known as Medji-murye, which enjoys a superb landscape and momentous historical past.

Another Danube tributary is Vuka, draining from the hills of Frushka Gora in the prosperous province of Syrmium (Sriyem).

The waters draining into the Aegean Sea through the great artery of the Vardar River, issue from and pass through Serbia and Macedonia, and hence out of the sphere of our discussion.

While the streams of the Pontian watershed flow through a gradually sloping terrain offering convenient valleys for the riverbeds, the rivers of the Adriatic basin are short, precipitious, rushing over rapids and waterfalls, and entirely unsuitable for navigation, except in their estuaries. Their scenic beauty is a chief attraction for the tourists. The most impressive is the lower course of Krka, with its terraced waterfalls near Skradin, 321 feet in height, and somewhat resembling Niagara Falls. Similar are Tsetina, with a cascade of 330 feet, Zrmanya, Trebizhat and Ryechina (Fiumara), near Fiume, with waterfalls and rapids dropping 570 feet on a stretch of 12 miles. Unforgettable is

the sight of the 15 Plitvitsa lakes, terraced one below the other and connected by a series of waterfalls. The most important river in Dalmatia is Neretva, the Roman Narenta, cutting through a deep canyon in the mountains of Herzegovina, and passing through its capital Mostar.

The Adriatic Sea

Of course the greatest hydrographic asset of Croatia is the Adriatic Sea. A partly submerged mountain chain now represented by the islands of Mlyet (Meleda), Lastovo (Lagosta), Palagruzh (Pelagosa) and the hilly Gargano peninsula on the Italian coast, divides the Adriatic into two basins, northern and southern, with separate and distinct characteristics.

On its northern and eastern coast the Adriatic Sea is encircled by mountains belonging to the Julian and Dinaric Alps. Their main branches run along the sea, usually receding a few miles from the water's edge, but sometimes dropping into the sea, or breaking up at its fringe into numerous islands of varying size. This forms an archipelago of 914 islands, with a total surface of 2,504 square kilometers. The maximum depth of the northern basin is 780 feet, while that of the southern is 3,780 feet. In the north the bottom is covered with yellowish sand containing microscopic remains of sea fauna and grits of oyster shells. In the southern basin the bottom is overlaid with soft, yellow silt.

There is a sequence of two tides a day, their duration and height depending upon the winds. Difference of height between tide and ebb is over three feet.

There are both permanent and variable currents. The permanent currents move along the coast from the Otranto straits north to Trieste bay, then turn west and return along the west coast to Otranto bay. The variable currents appear only under the influence of prolonged strong winds, when they affect the permanent currents by increasing their speed or changing their direction.

The highest temperature of surface water is in July, with 80° Fahr., and the lowest in February with 50° Fahr. The salinity of the water is highest in February with 38.5%, and in April it drops down to a 37.8% low.

The temperature of the air in shade reaches 104° Fahr. in July, and drops to 40° Fahr. in January. Rainfall is abundant. The rainy sea-

son throughout the Adriatic is the Fall of the year. July and February register least precipitation. Snowfall is very rare.

The magnetic declination is western, with a 5°W. high in the north, and a 3.5° low in the south. The magnetic inclination is northern, with 60° N in the north, and 56° in the south.

The whole eastern coast and the adjacent islands are studded with lighthouses and beacons reducing the navigation hazards at night.

In the Adriatic there are 360 kinds of fish, of which 85 kinds are used for food. There are also several kinds of edible molluscs, oysters and snails. Industrially important are the corals and sponges. Fisheries provide an important source of livelihood for the local population.

The Croatian Climate

Lying between the valley of the Danube and the Adriatic Sea, the eastern Alps and the Balkan highlands, the land of the Croatians is within the zones of three climates: sub-tropic, sub-alpine and continental. Along the narrow coastal strip from Trieste to Cattaro bay and the adjacent archipelago, it enjoys the mild climate of Italy. The towering heights of the Velebit and Dinaric Alps protect this strip from the cold northern and northeasterly winds, so that the thermic amplitude is relatively small. Rainfall is abundant; the sun shines through more than 2,500 hours a year; summers are hot and dry; winters moist and warm.

These circumstances and the fertile soil of the seacoast have created a luxuriant Mediterranean vegetation, with olive, orange and lemon groves, fig, maraschino cherry and almond orchards, vineyards, magnolias, cypresses, plane trees, carobs, spicy flowering shrubs, rosemary and machia, enriched by a galaxy of beautiful and fragrant flowers.

While protecting the coastline from exposure to the rigors of the north, the Velebit and Dinaric Alps impede the eastward flow of the warm coastal air currents and winds into the nearby hinterland. So at a distance of a few miles the subtropic yields to the characteristic central European climate, distinguished by a large thermic amplitude, increased cloudiness, less sunshine, sharp winds and extensive snowfall. Through the wide valleys of the coastal rivers, however, warm air-currents penetrate inland, and on the eastern slopes of the Dinaric ranges there are fig and orange groves, although

their fruit does not have the sugar content of the coastland produce. This area is called Dalmatian Zagora (Tramontana).

Eastward in Bosnia, while the central European clime prevails, the thermic gradient does not follow the recession in the north latitude, but the elevation of the terrain. So the climate in the northern half of Bosnia is milder than in the south, where the mountains reach to considerable heights.

Along the southern edge of the Pannonian basin, in the valley contained by the Sava and Drava rivers, the climate is typically continental and central European, with hot summers, rainy autumns, and cold winters, therefore a wide thermic amplitude. This fertile steppe land is well suited for the cultivation of cornfields, but much of it is not tilled, and in places the river valleys are covered with extensive tracts of hardoak forests.

Finally the sub-alpine climate of western Croatia resembles that of Slovenia (Carniola), Styria and Carinthia, with cool summers and cold winters. Rain and snow here are abundant, making it a land of dense forests, grassy meadows and fields of grain.

In general we have seen that the compass of thermic fluctuation increases as we proceed toward the interior. This is, chiefly, the case when proceeding northeast from southwest, so that the northeast part of the territory has the most typical continental climate. Naturally, there is a certain graduation also in the area of the central European climate, variations in temperature arising from differences in geographic latitude, distance from the sea, absolute height or some feature of the local relief. The well-protected areas capable of keeping out the cold winds, have a much milder climate than other areas in their immediate vicinity lacking this protection.

The transitional zone from the Adriatic to the Central European climate is represented by western Bosnia and western Croatia, while the eastern spurs of the Alps, with the Mura district, form the transitional belt from the Alpic to the central European climate. Here there are some middle size mountains and hilly terrain which locally affect the climate, and further east the steppe lands are subject to their own local variations.

Rainfall varies over the different parts of the Croatian territory, as might be expected consid-

ering the wide variations in altitude. The rains are heaviest over the sea coast, and the yearly average gradually diminishes as we pass over the mountain ridges toward the Pannonian basin in the northeast. In some of these districts, summer drought is an annual problem. A curiosity of the climate is that the southwestern and southern districts have their rainy season in fall and winter, with maximum precipitation from October to December, while the northern and northeastern part has a maximum rainfall in spring and summer, the winters being dry. The mountains are covered with snow four to five months of the year.

The rainiest of these lands is also the sunniest. In the northern half of the coastal zone the sun shines on the average from 2,100 to 2,400 hours every year, and in the southern half the average goes up to 2,750 hours. The mountains are generally cloudy, and the cloudscapes of these regions have an impressive beauty of their own. The eastern lowlands, as might be expected, are sunnier than the mountains, but not so sunny as the Adriatic seaboard.

Since there is a barometric depression over the Adriatic, and high atmospheric pressure over the eastern part of Roumania, the winds in the southwestern part of the country come from the northeast. From the Papuk mountain in Slavonia and the Bosna River, northern and northwesterly winds spread over the lowlands toward the Tissa.

In July the wind directions change twice a day, causing considerable difference of temperature at certain hours. In the morning, the wind comes from northeast spreading along the Adriatic and sub-Alpine area. East of this area western and northwesterly winds prevail, with occasional intrusion of air currents from the south and southeast. In the afternoon the directions of the winds are reversed.

The most noteworthy are the Adriatic gales "bora" (bura) and "scirocco" (shilok) the latter corresponding to the Mediterranean wind known in France as the mistral. They are both winter gales, the bora being the stormier and colder, while the scirocco brings moisture and a rise in temperature.

Bora comes from the karst plateaus and highlands to the seaboard, announcing itself by short and powerful gusts as a northerly to east-northeasterly wind; it is produced by the great difference in the temperature and atmospheric pressure between the Dinaric ranges and the sea. The bora spreads from Istria to Albania, but its worst fury is spent at the foot of the Velebit and Biokovo mountains, again in the neighborhood of Dubrovnik and south of Cattaro. At its worst, it may bring navigation to a standstill, and it usually causes extensive damage.

Whenever the barometric pressure drops over the Ligurian or Tyrrhenian sea, while southeast in the Mediterranean a high atmospheric pressure develops, the scirocco comes as a result. From warm and humid regions it brings, on its journey north, a sharp rise in temperature, heavy clouds and short, but frequent showers. However the scirocco is not an intense and destructive gale, as the bora is.

Vegetation

We have already discussed the rich and florid vegetation of the Adriatic seaboard. We found it to be Mediterranean, while the vegetation on the eastern slopes of the Dinaric Alps, which are open to the airs of the seacoast, shows a Mediterranean character with signs of transition into the continental zone.

Dense forests of oak, beech, birch, ash and alder reach inland to the steppe of the Pannonian basin. Along with the forest areas there are vast tracts of meadow and farm land. There are vineyards and orchards including varieties of cherries, plums, apricots, peaches, pears, apples, almonds and walnuts. There are the favorite garden crops. The most common grains are wheat, corn, rye, barley and millet. The more important industrial crops are hops, hemp, flax, sugar beets, tobacco and medicinal plants.

The deciduous forests do not reach to the top levels of the mountain sides, and the heights are clothed with conifers. As we ascend still higher only the dwarf spruce, shrubs and low mountain plants thrive, while above that is the area of moss, lichens, and the eternal snow.

The steppe lands provide a rich harvest of grain, especially wheat and corn.

Fauna

Because of the wide variances in climate and terrain, there is a variety of animal life in these parts, the coastal zones, the karstlands, the Bosnian highlands, and the Pannonian basin, each having their distinctive types. Some have been locally stettled as far back as the Mesozoic pe-

riod, but most have wandered in from distant areas.

Out of 229 kinds of millipedes (diplopoda), 137 have been recognized as endemic, with 10 genes, which are believed to come from the cretacean period of the mesozoic. The mountain ranges are better suited for the development of endemic types, since they provide specific homes or biotopes, and protective isolation. The subterranean cavities and cracks of the karstland are the cradle of numerous endemites.

There are many regions harboring lower and higher endemic species such as grasshoppers, scorpions, snakes, lizards and fish. The chief endemic area is in the Velebit ranges, with its rich park of animal wildlife. Next come the Dinaric karstlands and Bosnian mountains.

At the beginning of the quaternary era, and up into the third diluvium, huge mammals lived in this area, as we learn from the unearthed fossil bones of elephants, mammoth, rhinoceros, cave bears and lions. They all became extinct before the dawn of the historical period.

Large and medium game animals that have become scarce in many parts of Europe still survive in the Croatian lands, as might be expected where there is so much forested and mountainous country. The European brown bear, the wolf, the wild boar and the roe deer are by no means uncommon. The red deer, which is present in fair numbers, and the chamois of the sub-alpine highlands, are undoubtedly the prize game animals of the area. The elk may have been present within historic times, since there exists a word for this animal in the Croatian language, but there are no modern records of its appearance.

The last of the once numerous African visitors to survive here is the jackal, found chiefly in the south of Dalmatia.

Wild animal pests, of the kind that would be known as varmints in the United States, figure prominently in tales of Croatian village life. Foxes and polecats prowl at night around the farmer's chicken coops. Badgers raid the vineyards just when the grapes are about ready for the picking. For centuries the Croatians have held country wide hunts to drive the animal pests from their fields and thickets, but the fox, the polecat and the badger hold their own.

Bosnia and Herzegovina have probably the heaviest concentration of vipers left in Europe.

Three species occur here. There is an important industry in Bosnia for the manufacture of anti-venom, the serum used in the treatment of snake bite. Bosnian villagers hunt the snakes and bring them to the factory in sacks. The Dalmatian Islands also have many vipers. They are particularly numerous on the island of Mlyet. In modern times the islanders have imported the mongoose from India to keep down the snakes, but with comparatively little success. Among the several viper species best known are: vipera macrops, vipera bosniensis and vipera meridionalis.

Birds

The Croatian lands abound in bird life. The sea coast shelters enormous numbers of sea gulls which hover and flock around the harbors and throughout the waters of the archipelago. On the mainland wading birds populate the swamps in large numbers. Some of these birds are hunted as game although the main attraction for hunters of waterfowl are the flights of wild ducks and geese. The herons and storks, thriving on the frogs and snakes which infest the boggy marshes, are counted among the blessings of the area.

The storks indeed are almost the partners of Croatian village life, and figure very prominently in the native folklore. In autumn they leave the regions of the Danube for the warm waters of Egypt. In spring they return, and folklore credits them with returning to the same nest they had left the year before. Their favorite nesting places are the chimney tops, the Croatian chimney being conveniently constructed with closed top and the smoke vents on the sides. They express delight by a clattering noise produced by their long beaks. When one stork has thus announced himself, the whole community takes it up, and soon the village resounds with this clattering from the roof tops, so familiar a sound that the villager hardly notices it at the time, yet is immediately filled with nostalgia for his homeland when again he hears it or is reminded of it far from his native soil.

The storks have a habit of bringing snakes back to their nests to be eaten later. But the snakes frequently crawl free of the nests and tumble from the roof to the ground. That creates an intense commotion among the dwellers of the yard; the dogs barking and running

in circles, the cats pouncing on the serpent; and children who have been told that storks bring babies, suppose that the babies, too, will come tumbling down from the chimney.

Adding to the charm of rustic life are the swallows, who also prefer to share a habitation with humanity. They build their nests under the eaves of a hallway or patio, delighting the children with their quaint architecture. After marking out the nesting place, both male and female fly to a nearby pond and return with a beakful of mud. They fling this mud against the solid background so that it will stick. After thus laying the foundation of the nest, they build the next layers in semicircular shape. By putting one on top of another, they soon close it in, leaving an entrance opening. Then they line the nest with feathers or lint and the female lays her eggs. The gracefulness of its shape, its building skill, and pleasant twittering notes make of the swallow a domestic genius like the cricket on the hearth.

Folklore favors it with a number of complimentary stories. It, too, is credited with returning to the same nest it had used the year before.

The return of the swallows from the winter retreat in Egypt is taken as a sure sign of spring. And the refuse from the swallow's nest is believed to have healing powers in diseases of the eye, especially cataracts. Throughout Croatia the swallow, stork and turtledove are the very symbols of the calm and contentment of a prosperous countryside.

The village picture is brightened also by fluttering butterflies and varieties of goldfinches and titmice flashing across the yard in pursuit.

The singing birds are also well represented. Early spring is announced by the wailing sounds of cuckoo birds and the beautiful melody of thrushes which the music of Franz Schubert often recalls, while Beethoven combined the singing of both in his Sixth Symphony. In summer one can hear the plaintive song of the turtle doves. Early in the morning the skylark sings on the wing, while at night the song of the nightingale blends enchantingly with the fragrance of the acacias and linden trees and the blossoms of idleberry.

Less highly esteemed by the Croatians are the jays, crows, ravens and hawks of the fields and village outskirts. Then there are the sparrows which the farm wife lures to a trap in the barn by spreading a trail of corn. And high aloft the eagles, surveying all that passes on the ground.

On the whole, the countryside reminds you vividly of the scenes depicted by Virgil in his Georgics and Theocritos in his Bucolics, the former commemorating the life of the Roman Campagna, and the latter pastoral Sicily.

Agriculture, Horticulture and Forestry

Plant life in this area varies with the climatic belts, relief, hydrographic conditions and composition of soil, and so does the economic life of the population which depends on the produce.

Where the Mediterranean climate prevails, the chief source of livelihood is horticulture. Olive groves cover large tracts of land, with vineyards and fig orchards coming next in acreage. The Dalmatian wine production was a pillar of the country's economy until the blight of phylloxera destroyed the vineyards at the end of the 19th centruy. Citrus fruit culture is unimportant, but almonds, walnuts and maraschino cherries provide an important source of income. Bee-keeping is a favorite occupation on the islands and along the sea coast, and the honey from the island of Sulet (Sholta) is said to be among the finest in the world.

Truck gardening has also developed in this area to the point of producing a surplus for export. The grains, including rice, are of lesser importance.

Small cattle, adapted to the climate, are generally raised. Sheep, goats, donkeys and mules find their own food throughout the year, but horses and cattle can be kept only on stored hay and grain in a land where the pastures are burnt to the ground each summer. So the cattle of Dalmatia are providently kept small.

In the Dinaric ranges conditions for intensive agriculture are poor. Soil is available only in the valleys or on gently descending mountain slopes improved by terraces. Here the orchards, truck gardening and tobacco planting provide the main occupations. This is an area where sheep and goats do well, along with the specialized small cattle. The shepherds and the cattle men move their flocks and herds from mountain to valley and back again, following the grass according to the seasons of the year.

On the higher levels, along mountain ridges, plateaus and on the sloping mountain sides, the soil is poor and suited only for limited raising of grain. Fruit trees are absent, but

coniferous forests are abundant. Here a flourishing lumber industry has developed, providing milled timber for export, and building materials for domestic markets.

In the Bosnian highlands also lumbering has become an important source of national income. The wealth of building materials is evident in the Bosnian country-houses, where the lofty gables exceed the height of the lower structure. The grassy meadows have encouraged and made prosperous cattle raising and dairy farming. There are extensive and heavy bearing plum orchards, whose produce provides an export-delicacy for central Europe in the form of dried and filled prunes, plum jam (pekmez) and the popular shlivovitsa, known to the GI's of the Second World War as slivovitz or plum brandy.

The Pannonian plain, irrigated by the waters of Mura, Drava and Sava, with their tributaries, is a fertile country suited for intensive farming of grains, sugar beets and industrial plants. Truck gardening also thrives. This is a classical land for cattle raising, dairy farming, domestic animals and fowl of all kinds, including hens, turkeys, ducks and geese in large numbers. With the gradual clearing of the forests, the hillsides are becoming covered with vineyards. The main crops, however, are wheat and corn. The extensive oak forests in Slavonia shelter large herds of hogs feeding on acorns and roots. In Syrmium, the eastern enclave of Slavonia, the orchards and the vineyards are of chief importance. On sunny hills of Frushka Gora sloping toward the banks of Danube and Sava, Roman emperors planted the vine over large tracts surrounding their palatial summer residences. Plum, cherry, apricot, mulberry, and grape brandies are important items of domestic consumption and export. The mulberry tree, a nuisance in many parts of the world, is planted here along the edges of banks to prevent erosion. Its leaves are carefully gathered and used in the feeding of silkworms. This is a popular home industry in these areas, carried on mainly by the village women, and many a poor family finds it a helpful source of income.

Wine Industry

Viticulture is a growing industry along the southern banks of the central course of the Danube, and throughout the enclave between the Danube and Sava rivers. Before the ravages of phylloxera, viticulture in this area was a simple affair. Select vine shoots were planted and in a few years the stock would develop a maze of climbing vines entangling the stakes and wires and even the fruit trees nearby. Thus the plum orchards of Pannonia gave a double yield of plums and grapes in the same growing season. The plum brandy was and is well known throughout Europe under the name of "shlivovitsa," while the grapes of the region produce the good, full-bodied wines known as Syrmian and Karlovitsi. Such was the situation before the onslaught of the phylloxera scourge in the second half of the 19th century.

While the plum orchards remained unaffected by the blight, the vineyards were utterly destroyed and this branch of the national economy cut off. However, as in France and elsewhere, a remedy was found in the blight-resisting American vine. The introduction of this hardy stock and its grafting with the local *vinifera* eventually made possible the restoration of the Croatian vineyards. Today the *plemenka* grape produces a wine reminiscent of French *Chablis*. The heaviest bearer of the region is the *mirkovača*, which produces the vin ordinaire of the country. The Riesling grape here produces a superlative wine which at its best will stand comparison to the products of the Rhine and Moselle.

A type of claret (shiller) is produced from the very popular black "Portuguese" grapes (Portugizer), rich bearers and producers of the most popular wine in central Europe. Another popular black wine, with pleasant taste and bouquet is derived from a cultivated and improved variety of the Indiana grape.

White and red muscatel, and less familiar varieties are also grown, as well as malaga grapes especially cultivated for the table and raisins. Thus, for the pleasure of the emperors of Rome while vacationing in Syrmium, was founded an industry which has been an important part of the local economy ever since.

Locally, the grape is cultivated all over Croatia, but the wine-producing centers, besides the Danubian area, are located in the hills of Zagorye, northwestern Croatia, and Dalmatia, with the adjacent islands.

Fisheries

The waters of both mountain and lowland are full of fish. The trout of the mountain streams were celebrated even in antiquity. Bass,

pike, sheat-fish and fine varieties of river sturgeon are abundant in the Danube and the network of its tributaries. Among Adriatic fisheries the most important is the tuna, caught when the great schools of tuna from the Mediterranean swarm to the Adriatic coastal waters for spawning.

Mining and Industry

Along the island of Pag and the peninsula of Pelyeshats there are extensive installations for evaporation of salt water and drying of salt. Cement plants at Split and on the banks of the Danube at Beochin provide cement for the domestic market, with a considerable excess for export.

The limestone areas have extensive bauxite deposits, which are mined and exported for use in production of aluminum. The waterfalls and rapids of Krka, Tsetina, Zermanya, Vrlika, Pliva and other rivers and mountain streams have an enormous potential of electric power only a fraction of which has been harnessed to date.

Bosnia and Herzegovina are rich in ores and minerals. The most important are bituminous coal and iron deposits in the valley of the Bosna river. After the First World War a number of small coal mines and iron ore mines were opened in this area. Later a modern metal industry developed, with foundries and steel mills. During World War II the steel industry was greatly advanced by the German Krupp Works. At the end of the war the plants were destroyed in the fierce fighting of various groups for their possession.

Other Bosnian ore deposits include manganese, chromium, copper, ferrosulfide, aluminum, antimony, arsenic, lead, zinc and mercury. These deposits are small, however. The silver mines near Srebrenitza have been worked since the Roman times. The salt-mines near Tuzla* are also ancient but their output is low.

In Slavonia and Croatia industry is at its highest. It is chiefly a consumers' industry engaging in the manufacture of goods derived from the agricultural products of the area. Flour mills, packing houses, canneries, silk, linen and wool textile factories, leather tanneries, shoe factories, breweries, cement plants, alcohol refineries, sugar plants, match factories and lumber mills are all found here. In consequence Slavonia and Croatia are industrially the most advanced and prosperous of Croatian lands.

* This name is the Turkish translation of the original Croatian form *Soli* (salts). The Turkish form reproduces the plural form of the original by *tuz-lar,* with apocope (dropping) of the final consonant.

Chapter II

PREHISTORY

FROM the formation of the Alpine system in the eocene, the fauna of the Dinaric highlands and adjacent areas developed in the direction of higher vertebrates headed by birds and mammals. The warm climate of the preglacial periods contributed to the growth and differentiation of species coming from the old and less developed stock. By eocene and pliocene, herds of elephants and groups of mammoths were roaming over the spacious plains of Slavonia and Croatia. Huge dinotheria and rhinoceros lived along the banks of the Sava and Drava rivers, with their network of tributaries. Forests of palms and deciduous trees with rich grassy meadows provided an ideal habitat for the giants of the proboscide (elephantine) and rhinocerotide families.

Scientists have thoroughly explored this area and discovered many fossil remains of the vertebrate giants of the post-alpine period, together with many interesting plant fossils.[1] The past existence of Dinotherium giganteum in Croatia is attested by discovery of six teeth of this giant near Brdovets, about 20 miles northwest of Zagreb. Skeletal remains of the hairy-skinned mammoth are met with throughout Croatia and Slavonia: near Petrinya, Srb, Bribir, Vrbovsko, Brod on the Sava, and in the Drina valley. Two kinds of mammoths have been identified: Mastodon Arvernensis and Mastodon Borsoni. Remains of elephants proper are the most numerous of all. These fossils all come from the upper pliocene.

Four species of rhinoceros living from the pliocene era up into diluvium have been identified in various parts of Croatia and Slavonia. The most valuable are the Krapina finds, among which there is the whole skull of a fully grown rhinoceros, and fragments of the skull of a young individual. Obviously the Krapina man was fond of rhinoceros for he hunted them and barbecued them in his cave as some burnt bones indicate.

In his classical work on life in diluvial times in Croatia,* Charles Goryanovich-Kramberger lists 18 species of mammals, one amphibian and

* Goryanovich-Kramberger. *Život i Kultura diluvijalnog čovjeka iz Krapine u Hrvatskoj* (Life and Culture of Diluvial Man from Krapina in Croatia), 1913.

fragments of various kind of singing birds, gallinae (hens) and eagles. Chronologically he places this fauna in the older horizon of diluvium possessed of a warm climate, therefore in the third inter-glacial (Riss-Würm) period of the diluvium. Besides the elephant, rhinoceros and cave bears, the more important mammals identified by the Dr. Goryanovich are the wolf, brown bear, wildcat, beaver, horse, wild boar, ox and three kinds of deer. However, there is no trace of fish, reptiles, saurians, insects or ammonites. The most surprising is the absence of primates (apes) which must have been symbiotic to the other species of a warm fauna.

Ancestors of Krapina Man

Before we proceed with the presentation of *Homo Primigenius* under the guidance of Goryanovich-Kramberger and other outstanding paleontologists, the question arises to what older stock we should trace his origin. Obviously the symbiosis of flora and fauna in the Tertiary age both in the Pannonian depression and Dinaric highlands, was perfect. It was marked by a wealth of living species, most of which were later extinguished by the rigors of the Glacial periods. However, in this tropical interim the Pannonian basin gives the impression of Mesopotamia at its best. In that case, were there any human or anthropoid contemporaries of Dinotherium Giganteum, Mastodon Arvernensis and Rhinoceros Schleiermacheri carrying on in this area or in some nearby region? If so, who were they? Since outstanding paleontologists claim existence of humans in te Tertiary age, do not the tertiary flora and fauna of this area offer a clue precisely to such existence?[4]

A question of this kind cannot be answered in the affirmative, because of a lack of archeological evidence in the form of skeletal fossils of such inhabitants, or their crude implements. However, this archeological silence does not necessarily rule out the existence of either primates or anthropoids on their way to evolving into finished humans. In their resistance to decay the bones of primates cannot compare to those of proboscides or huge saurians, and only coincidence can help them along to fossilizing and

preservation. It takes another happy accident to discover their repositories, sometimes deep underground. The implements, no matter how crude, are usually better preserved than their human makers, and they unfailingly mark the presence of man, even though his remains are not around. But it takes a great deal of luck, indeed, to discover such an underground station, without or with human remains.[5]

Thus the absence of the much desired fossils in this Pannonian Canaan should by no means prevent an attempt to visualize the series of generations that became conducive to *Homo Primigenius* in this area and throughout the world. This will again bring us to the interminable discussions about the origin of man summed up by A. Gatti in the following words:*
"From a primitive group of mammals, possessed of miscellaneous characteristics of the primates, three branches separated: the first branch became conducive to man, the second to lower (cynomorphic) monkeys, and the third to anthropomorphic apes. Each of these branches split into various species or races, to which, on the simian side, belong both the *"Pithecanthropus Erectus"* and the various high and lower-order monkeys, and, on the human side, the fossil and living races.

"Another obscure point is the much debated question, whether man is of multiple or single origin. The scholars are divided into two opposite camps: that of polygenists—and monogenists. The first admit that man appeared independently in several regions of the earth, while the latter believe that he comes from one single source.

"The monogenism is today generally accepted in preference to polygenism, which places too much stress on the anatomic difference observed in various human races . . ."

Thus, regardless of the line of development followed in the evolution of the ancestors of Krapina man, or what their original homeland was, the question cannot be answered either in the affirmative or negative.

But the question itself is surely most provocative.

Homo Primigenius, Var. Krapinensis

While there is much doubt about the human character of *Pithecanthropus Erectus* (Java

man), *Sinanthropus Pekinensis* (China link), and even Heidelberg man, finished human anatomy and high intellectual power were certainly the endowment of Krapina man and his congeners such as Neanderthal man and the dwellers of various caves in Britain, Spain, France, Italy, Germany, Central Europe, Russia, Asia Minor and North Africa. The best preserved skeletal remains are those of Krapina, and Chapelle-aux-Saints in France. However, the chief characteristics of these paleolithic stations are the variety and type of implements used and comprehensively called Mousterian industry.

Distinguished from the earlier Chelléan and Acheulean stone industries, the Mousterian implements show much improvement in workmanship and efficiency over their predecessors. The new technique simplified the old method of chipping both sides of the flint core by leaving one side smooth, and sharpening the edges of the ax. Other cutting or scraping tools were similarly treated. M. D. Burkitt supplies a list of such instruments, with explanation of their workmanship and use. His list contains awls, certain curved points, coups-de-poing or almond-shaped fist axes, discs, notched tools, small points, side-scrapers, gravers and scrapers, with characteristic blades.

Following in the footsteps of Marcelin Boule, Earnest A. Hooton has analyzed the skeletons of *Homo Primigenius,* and reached some important conclusions.

"The skull of the old man of La Chapelle-aux-Saints [the best preserved primigenius skeleton]* is very large, and of a bestial aspect. The brain case is very elongated and low, the supra-orbital ridges immense, and the forehead very low and retreating; the occiput is protuberant and bun-shaped; the long brain case gives the impression of having been flattened down. The face is long and projecting; the orbits are very large; the nose is short and very broad, the upper jaw strongly prognathous and the mandible powerful, but with only a rudimentary chin. Since both face and brain are intact, we are able to compare the development of the one with the other. Remembering that anthropoid apes differ from man particularly in that their faces are very large and their brain cases very small, let us examine the super-imposition of the profile of the Neanderthal skull of La Chapelle-aux-

* Gatti, A., *L'Uomo,* 1934.

* Burkitt, M.D. *Prehistory,* Cambridge, 1925.

Saints upon those of a chimpanzee and of a modern Frenchman. The face of chimpanzee is by far the most projecting and the outline of his cranial vault is much smaller, both in length and in height than either of the human outlines. The modern man has the straightened and least projecting face and the loftiest skull, with the highest forehead region. *Neanderthal man falls between modern man and the chimpanzee both in facial projection and in height of cranial vault, but the fossil human skull in both parts is much nearer to the modern human type than to the chimpanzee.*" [6]

In a minute analysis of the available components of the skeleton the author brings out many interesting details. He finds that the face is of great size, form of the nasal bones is very broad, and the nasal aperture very wide as in the dark races of today. This is an important admission in favor of those anthropologists such as Churchward who claim that *Homo Primigenius* was a Negro.*

"The spine of our specimen is short and massive; the vertebrae of the neck have long processes like those of the chimpanzee. The pelvis is very high in relation to its breadth. The arms are not long but extremely massive, with very large joints. His legs are more human than the arms which retain close resemblance to those of the ape. The foot is chiefly a supporting organ yet retaining the prehensile properties that are lost in modern man. It appears that he walked with bent knees. The specimen is of low stature, and could not have been taller than 5 feet, 5 inches."

The writer concludes his review with the statement: "We must picture him as a short, bull-necked individual with massive head and heavy projecting jaws. The head was carried thrust forward. The chest was deep and round, the arms of moderate length, the legs very short. The gait may have been a shuffling, bent-knee walk, in which the legs were not completely extended upon the thighs. On the whole, Neanderthal man must have been a rather gorilla-like type."

Exceptionally interesting is the evidence brought out from the examination of the cranial cavity, on the mental faculties of Neanderthal man. According to this, his psychic powers were in advance of the more primitive types, and of

*Churchward, A. *Origin and Evolution of the Human Race*, London, 1921.

a capacity of speech approaching modern standards.

On the whole, here is Hooton's conclusion:

"Altogether Neanderthal man's brain was a massive and primitive affair, but distinctly human. The intelligence of this type of man was certainly far superior to that of any anthropoid ape, and may have been little lower than that of some primitive men of today. We know that Neanderthal man was not only able to overcome the formidable beasts of prey of the glacial epoch and to oust them from their cave lairs, but that he was able to use his wits sufficiently to select as dwelling places the most advantageous natural sites available—caves. A cave is fairly warm in winter and keeps cool in the summertime. It affords satisfactory protection against the elements. In these caves Neanderthal man lived, used fire to warm himself, and buried his dead. He had already developed the manufacture and use of specialized flint tools of several kinds, which served as weapons, and for cutting, scraping and other domestic activities. These flint implements are often admirably made and the edges chipped to a degree of sharpness which makes them useful cutting tools even today. They indicate a considerable manual precision and some ingenuity.

"We cannot deny to Neanderthal man full human rank. We need not be contemptuous of his achievements or intelligence. After all, he had enough brains to carry him through the glacial period or, at any rate, through the greater part of it. He was able to sustain existence when climatic conditions and the predatory animal life of Europe demanded strength, hardiness, courage, and no small intelligence, as requisites for survival."

The Krapina Cave

The paleolithic station of Krapina represents a cave hollowed out in a soft miocene sandstone block along the bank of a creek, the bed of which is now 75 feet below the entrance of the cave. But in prehistoric times the creek must have been almost at the cave level. In the pleistocene era the creek flooded the floor of the cave and deposited there a stratum of muddy yellow and gray sand nearly three feet deep, covered with a layer of gravel. The cave is about 25 feet high, and in time became filled with sand, clay and detritus. Here the remains of diluvial man, his animal contemporaries and objects of his

industry were found. From the bottom up, every layer contained some remains, including fireplaces found in several spots on the same level. From these strata about 500 human bones belonging to 10 or 11 individual were unearthed, and a supply of 1,000 stone and bone implements. A multitude of animal bones, some of them burnt, indicates that Krapina man's favorite quarry were elephants, rhinoceros young and old, oxen and beavers. All four of these animals are very difficult to kill, while the rhinoceros and the elephant are very dangerous. But the cave hunter found ways to kill them.

His industry is typically Mousterian, and consists of implements made both of flint stone and animal bones. The bone implements were made of the large bones of extremities, femur and tibia of oxen and elephants.

To the stone objects listed by Dr. Burkitt we may add here knife-shaped scrapers, saw and borers. Among tools made of bones we find an axe, many sharp points, and a triangular point in the nature of a harpoon. There are also a very large number of stone and bone artifacts. While in most of them the Mousterian technique prevails, older types representing the early Chellean and Acheulean industries, are also present.

The Krapina man was not only a skilled artisan, but also a brave hunter and a true expert at building fire. On available evidence Krapina man hunted the most dangerous animals such as cave bear, rhinoceros, elephant and buffalo because of the ample meat supply offered by their carcasses, while their hides were useful to him as garments, and bones as material for tools. Obviously he had to resort to stratagem in order to overpower the huge and ferocious beasts.

Dr. Goryanovich found in the clay strata a short round wooden rod, one end of which was burnt and the other used as a handle. From this he drew the conclusion that the inmates of the cave twirled the rod in a hole in a log, until it caught fire.

The condition of many human bones, especially skulls, femurs and tibiae, was such as to indicate that the individuals from whom they came had been victims of cannibalism. A portion of the skull was burnt, while femurs and tibiae were split in order to remove the marrow, a delicacy of the cave man.

The scattering of human bones alongside those of animals was evidence that Krapina man did not bury his dead, nor practice any burial rites, but rather that he ate them up with the rest of his quarry.

In spite of the crushing and scattering of human bones, Dr. Goryanovich could discern two races among the Krapina cave dwellers. The more corpulent and robust individuals had high mandibles, while the others had low, but massive mandibles. The same characteristics were revealed by the extant maxillae, although he could not say definitely if they should be paired with the mandibles. Since the high mandibles and maxillae correspond exactly to those found at Spy in Belgium, he has designated their owners as *Homo Primigenius,* var. *Spyensis,* and those with low mandibles as *Homo Primigenius,* var. *Krapinensis.*

In connection with the theory of Dr. Churchward that the African Pigmy (original and primary man) and the Nilotic Negro spread throughout the world, and that these two cohabited, Dr. Goryanovich's discovery assumes a special significance. The broad nasal aperture of the Negro is precisely a characteristic of Neanderthal man whose osteo-anatomy, according to Dr. Churchward, corresponds in many respects to that of the Nilotic Negro. Since the latter is larger in stature than the pigmy, the two races show comparative characteristics similar to those which differentiated the two races found by Dr. Goryanovich in the Krapina cave. It is possible that this analogy deserves further examination.

This would give us a fair picture of *Homo Primigenius* with the habits, skills and industry by which he held his own amid numerous enemies in the animal world, and in the face of climatic changes which made his life very difficult.

Krapina is a town located about 25 miles northeast of Zagreb, and represents the only paleolithic station in Croatia.

Neolithic Stations: Butmir and Vuchedol

The chief Neolithic station of the area is that discovered at Butmir, near Sarayevo in Bosnia.

Considerable archeological literature in different languages has developed around this station. Radimsky, Fiala, Truhelka, Pigorini, Reinach, Hoernes, Szombaty, Virchow, and Munro have been the chief contributors in the field of archeology.

The surface of this area covers about five acres and consists of three strata: (1) humus, 12″ to

16″ in depth; (2) a dark bed of charcoal, ashes, clay, mould, etc., containing pottery, stone implements and other industrial remains, uniformly distributed throughout the entire mass, to a depth of about four feet; (3) under this a compact mass of reddish-brown clay, 3¼ feet deep. In this layer twelve trough-shaped hollows were found. They were filled with materials similar to those encountered in the upper relic bed.

Although no human bones have as yet been discovered at Butmir, bones of domestic and wild animals are scattered throughout the relic bed. They include four kinds of cattle, hog, sheep, goat, deer, and giant stag.

Among the vegetable remains analysts ascertained wheat, barley, lentil, brome grass, crab-apple, hazel-nut, silver fir and others.

Compared with the finds in the Krapina cave, the presence of grain here is a novelty. A still more important novelty at Butmir has been the discovery of clay objects, both pottery and idols. We find here ceramic products consisting of small human figurines or idols, one quadrupedal form, dishes, whole or broken, spindle-whorls and weights. The human figures of which there are 21 are rudely made. A head is well shaped, however, with traces of artistic skill. The likeness of a four-footed animal is also crude. Much broken pottery, with a few whole pieces, was found scattered in the relic bed. Some of these objects are of crude workmanship, but others are of fine quality, painted dark-brown or black, and polished. The pottery was decorated by incised straight and curved lines; by irregular patterns of spiral and meander forms.

The Butmir industry shows all the characteristics of the neolithic Danubian culture whence it probably came. By following up the Bosna river valley the settlers of the Danubian communities could have easily moved to the upper reaches of that river, near Ilidje, the very site of Butmir. From Bosna's confluence with the Sava river at the city of Brod to the site of Butmir is not more than 100 miles, and from Brod to either of the Danubian stations, Vuchedol or Samatovtsi, the distance is about 50 miles, altogether 150 miles from the two Danubian stations. Since the terrain between the Danube and Sava is a level plain, and the Bosna valley, with few exceptions, as readily passable, trade contacts between Butmir and the points along the Danube were readily established. So the ceramic finds at Vuchedol near Vukovar, and the stone implements of Samatovtsi near Osiyek, coincide fully with those discovered at Butmir.

Another neolithic station unearthed at Jakovo-Komardin near Zemun, is about 100 miles from Brod, again with easily passable lowlands. Thus, we find a whole neolithic region along the central Danube river and the network of its primary and secondary tributaries. Neolithic communities were thriving, no doubt, also along the Drava, Sava, Drina, Bosna and Una rivers, all being easily accessible. Serbia and Roumania is also well represented by neolithic stations, noted for their ceramic products with incised spiral-meander ornamentation, and clay idols.

The finds in these settlements show in the first place the early traces of a peasant culture, with domesticated animals and cultivation of wheat, barley, millet and flax. In the second place they give insight into the spiritual life of the early post-glacial dwellers, with their worship of the Great Mother or Mother Earth (Cybele), Father Saturnus, perhaps the hunter-goddess Artemis, and the chief agricultural animal, the ox. The analogy would follow the matriarchal society, with the cult of the western Asiatic settlers and early Sumerians, who worshipped Ishtar and Tammuz, the life-giving deities in the early religion of the peasant. The man of the neolithic is no longer the parasite of nature, as was the hunter of the Paleolithic age, or the oyster-shell collector of the Mesolithic, but a *food-producer,* and this has vastly changed his whole way of life, his social organization and manner of settlement, his relation to his environment, his modes of thought and his religion.[7]

Age of Metals

The transition from the neolithic culture to the age of metals was slow and gradual. The eneolithic phase of this period is marked by the presence of a few copper implements found in the neolithic relic beds as a sign of transition from the use of polished stone to the adoption of bronze. Pure copper implements have been found in many countries of Europe and Asia. They mark an era when neolithic man had discovered the art of metal fusion, but still had to learn the more important process of alloying the metals and solve the problem of obtaining the necessary ores. Only the co-existence of copper and tin could solve this problem and make the fusion of bronze possible. Even though

bronze may have come originally from the East, Europe was to produce it in large quantity. It was the tin deposits of Bohemia chiefly, and of Thuringia, Spain and Etruria, that made this development possible. Gradually central Europe became a supply house of bronze manufacture, and the Danube with its tributaries, the Tissa, Sava and Drava, became the artery of a widespread trade in the age preceding the appearance of iron. This period is known as the Unetitse (Aunjetitz) culture, from its chief center, a prehistoric community located near Prague.

The only eneolithic or copper station in Croatia was discovered at Sarvash, with upper neolithic ceramics, incrusted with white, blue and red mass. However, the storing places of the peddlers who sold their copper ware to different communities are found throughout the country, especially in Bosnia.

Bronze stations are numerous and are found both along the Danube, with its tributaries, e.g. Dalj, Vukovar, Belgrade, Zuto Brdo (Serbia); Donya Dolina in the Sava valley (lake dwellers), with recovery of two prehistoric boats, 37 feet long; Ripach in Una valley (terra-mare, with pile structures containing two to three rooms); Kulen-Vakuf in Bosnia, etc.

The story of the bronze age is that of the beginnings of metallurgy with a few centers from which the manufactured goods had to be distributed over wide areas. This contributed to the development of trade and the exchange of goods, and invited the appearance of conqueror races which attacked and overwhelmed the neolithic peasant communities. The survivors took to the mountains. Mounds and primitive forts appeared with the typical acropolis on top of the hills. Social organization broke up into classes of warriors, craftsmen and peasants.[8]

The Iron Age

In spite of its great wealth in artefacts, the Butmir station represents a hiatus in relation to human remains. Thus neither the race of the Butmir dwellers can be determined, nor their burial rites. It is probable that the burial grounds are somewhere near the site of the settlement, but their ultimate discovery waits for the future. Wherever they may be, it is certain that they are neither dolmens, nor tumuli, but rather some cave ossuary or assembly of graves heretofore undiscovered, unless the "Mazdaic"

disposal of the dead was practiced, by which the bodies were left to the wild animals.

In sharp contrast to the archeological vacuum of Butmir are the numerous tumuli discovered on the Glasinats plateau near Sarayevo. When Dr. Munro saw them around the turn of the century their total number was estimated at 20,000—which he regarded as too conservative.[9]

"The builders of these burial-mounds practiced both inhumation and cremation," he writes, "the former being in the proportion of 60% and the latter 30%, while the remaining 10% were of mixed character, i.e., containing both kinds of interment."*

From the likeness of these tumuli to the Pontian and Transcaucasian kurgans, we may perhaps conclude that the burial rites were also similar, expecting that the Sumerian and Caucasian metal products will be replaced here by Pannonian bronze instruments. And in the tumuli of earlier date it is so. In those of a later age, we find the introduction of cremation, and an increasing percentage of ironware that has to be of Adriatic or Etruscan origin. Now if the ironware is indeed Etruscan, or from the head of the Adriatic—and the possibility of a local metal industry was ruled out by the Congress of Archaeologists and Anthropologists—it appears most evident that cremation of the dead was introduced into Bosnia from Etruria and upper Italy. The necropolis at Jezerine, near Bihach, a community situated closer to Liburnium and the upper Adriatic, reverses the percentage of cremations found at Glasinats, and shows a much higher inventory of ironware as well.

The interior of the graves, as described by Dr. Munro, sheds further light on the burial rites. "As a rule the remains of the body were found resting on the natural surface of the earth surrounded by a circle of stones; but sometimes a pavement of stones were laid on the earth, on which the body was deposited. In one or two instances the body was protected from the superincumbent mass by a rude stone cyst."

Before we look around for similar practices, let us investigate the pottery debris of the tumuli. "Pottery is very much broken, and few vessels could be restored"—writes Dr. Munro— "but nevertheless the fragments indicate a considerable variety of form and ornamentation—

* Munro. *Rambles and Studies in Bosnia-Herzegovina and Dalmatia*, Edinburgh, 2nd Ed., 1900.

the latter being formed, though sparingly, of concentric circles, semi-circles, lines and dots. There are vessels with round or flat bases, and some have small handles resting on the body of the dish, while others project from the side high above the rim." If we add that the rim of the opening was circular, with a large diameter, then the vessels, without the handle, will provide the patterns of the bell-beaker pottery that was widely spread along the western Mediterranean and the Atlantic seaboard, and found its way east to the banks of the Tissa.

A further clue to the nature of the Glasinats settlement, is the presence in the necropolis area of hill-forts (Wallburgen) broadly reminiscent of "Nuraghi" in Sardinia and "Brochs" in the northern-most part of Scotland, and the adjacent islands. "About thirty of them have been discovered through the Glasinats districts," writes Dr. Munro. "They are always situated on commanding elevations, more especially along the routes by which access can be had to the plateau from beyond the surrounding mountains. Their form generally assumes that of a circle, ellipse, trapeze, or rectangle, except when it is determined by the configuration of the site, in which case it may be extremely irregular. But, as a rule, it is a circular wall of small stones enclosing an area varying in extent from 33 to 330 feet in diameter, or sometimes much more. The height and thickness of the surrounding wall or rampart also vary much . . . So far as the the Wallburgen have been explored, 10% of them appear from positive evidence to have been dwelling places, as they contained relic-beds from two to five feet thick which yielded remains characteristic of the Hallstatt period."

This will fully vindicate an assumption that we have here the round barrow and beaker influences, with hill-forts of the Sardinian type. However, they are not megalithic in size of masonry like those of southern Portugal and Spain. The true megalithic culture did not penetrate into the Etruscan, sub-Alpine and Adriatic area, so that the Glasinats tumuli at first follow the Kurgan patterns of the Black Sea area—with an overwhelming quantity of bronze ware, and inhumation rites—while the later period introduces the hill-fort structures (Wallburgen), with funerary furniture of the Hallstatt industry, and cremation of the bodies.

That the two cultural periods coincide with the movement of the populations, can be inferred from the cephalic index of available skulls, which show that 76% of the inhabitants were dolichocephalic (long-headed) and 24% brachycephalic (round-headed). Whether the brachycephalic minority of the population belonged to the Anatolian race, or to the Bell-beaker people of southern Spain, remains an open question, but based on the analogy of Sardinia, where the tombs of Anghelu Ruju brought to light an almost parallel brachycephalic ratio (20%), under similar archeological conditions we may well have here a case of migration from the Atlantic region.

A huge supply of metal ware, both bronze and iron, was dug out from 1,000 graves representing less than 5% of the repository of the whole necropolis. Among implements, utensils, weapons and objects of general industry we find numerous cutting tools such as knives, double-edged axes, celts, iron spears and swords. Bronze needles, pincers, whorls, handles for various tools, also are present.

The most numerous weapons are iron lances of varying lengths. Bronze spears are also present. Arrow-points are of bronze and polished stone. Swords are of varying size, both single- and double-edged.

Defensive weapons are also well represented. A silver-ornamented bronze helmet is found, with bronze greaves and shields, buckles and girdles, all for military use.

A large number of fibulae or safety pins, with objects of personal adornment such as rings, bracelets, torques, pendants, beads and crude necklaces were found in profusion. The beads are of bronze, amber, glass, enamel, stone and bone, including perforated bear teeth. The presence of amber suggests direct or indirect trade with the Baltic provinces, the chief source of amber supply.

Commenting on the Glasinats necropolis, Dr. M. Hoernes stated at the Sarayevo Congress that 'Glasinats was merely rich in burials, but not exceptionally so, as he had seen them in equal abundance in several other localities as for example, in the neighborhood of Vishegrad, Focha, Plevlye, etc. At Imotski, between Mostar and Lyubushki, the tumuli were as numerous as at Glasinats, but larger and more difficult to explore. On the road from Ragusa to Bilek, Gatsko and Focha, they were also to be found on the barren Karst, but not in such striking numbers.

The Necropolis at Jezerine

The necropolis at Jezerine was discovered accidentally in 1890 and in a short time it had attracted the attention of the archeologists so that systematic excavations were soon started with the funds of the Bosnian government. Here in a square area of 190 by 100 feet, 553 graves were opened, in which 328 burned and 225 unburned interments were found. At five different points of the horizon, remains of funeral pyres were discovered, on which the cremation of bodies took place. Only three graves were found in the whole sepulchral area, in which the bodies had been cremated. The ashes of the cremated bodies had been collected and placed in the urns.

A large inventory of funeral goods was retrieved from the graves, including objects made of iron, bronze, silver, amber, glass, bone, stone and clay.

Cutting tools were made of iron. Among them we find swords, knives, knife-swords, spurs, along with fibulae, armlets and rings. Conspicuous in this group is the absence of lances.

In the bronze group we find needles, pincers and many varieties of fibulae, chains, pendants, ornamented pins, necklets, earrings, armlets, arm-bands, anklets, finger rings and other objects of adornment.

Amber provides disc-ornaments and beads, with a total of 1,288 pieces. This supply of amber indicates that the trade routes to the Baltic at this time were wide open.

Over 2,000 glass beads were found, enameled blue, yellow, white and green.

Bone was used in the manufacture of beads, discs and handles.

Stone and clay were restricted to four objects: two clay whorls and two stone discs. Also fragments of pre-Roman gravestones were found.

Unfortunately no objects were found from which we could determine the religious beliefs and worship of the dwellers of these settlements. Were they totem-pole worshippers? In that case their sacred poles have long since decayed. We find no temples around the sepulchral area. But the presence of a vast number of well-organized resting places for the dead reveals either belief in the life beyond the grave, and hence proper equipment for the deceased as viaticum for his long future journey; the worship of ancestors (Japanese: *shinto*, Roman: *manes*), a superstitious fear of ghosts returning to disturb the peace of those who refused proper burial to the dead body or all three together. How far totemism was spread among them, we cannot conclude from the funeral furnishings and grave goods so far unearthed.

Not more than fifty miles northwest of Bihach, three other iron age stations have been discovered: Prozor, Kompolye and Vlashko Polye, near Otochats.[10]

Chapter III
REMAINS OF THE HELLENIC AND ROMAN CIVILIZATION IN ILLYRICUM

NEOLITHIC and bronze age stations, together with sundry deposits scattered far and wide, are met with in numerous places throughout the Croatian territory. They are typical of the neolithic peasant culture of central Europe and the bronze age culture of the Pannonian Basin. The bronze industry of this area undoubtedly draws its origin from the eastern Mediterranean through the great trade artery of the Danube river and the Black Sea. The cultural shift from neolithic farming to the Unyetitse metal industry is best represented by the inventory of Butmir and Glasinats stations in Bosnia. These two are deeply symbolic of the origins of European civilization. Farming and metal work influenced—through interaction and mutual progress—the cultural development of the whole continent. But this development would have been painfully slow, but for a new factor, the navigation of river and sea.

Outside Europe the higher culture developed in the alluvial plains and great river valleys of the Nile in Egypt, Euphrates in Mesopotamia, Amu-Darya in Turkestan, Indus in India, and Yangtse in China. Fertile soils improved by irrigation encouraged a flourishing agriculture, with a stable social order capable of constructive effort in the crafts, trade, arts, architecture and science. It brought about great religious systems, city states, political unity, the art of writing and other manifestations of intellectual progress. All this was made possible through concentration and compactness of the population living in these productive areas.

Terrain and the woodlands made all this impossible in Europe. Impeded by dense forests and separated by numerous mountain ridges, the European population lived scattered in small clans and tribes separated from their neighbors. Hence the great diversity of regional life in the cultural history of mountainous countries such as the Balkans, Italy, Alpine areas, Iberian peninsula, and Scandinavia. Surrounded by mountains, each little valley was a microcosm of its own, with intense local patriotism, clannishness and small interest in the rest of the world. Until the science of navigation had been mastered, the same pattern of life prevailed along the sea where a coastal strip was separated from its hinterland by dense forests or towering mountain ridges.

But while Europe is a land of mountains, it is also a huge peninsula surrounded on three sides by the sea, which reaches deep inland through its great bays and the estuaries of large rivers. So where Europe was denied extensive alluvial plains on which to found a higher civilization, it was richly compensated by a matchless coastland, which in time became the stage of intense cultural activities. The cradle of higher European civilization is the eastern Mediterranean, with the island system and coastland connecting three continents. From this basin the Mediterranean culture will spread along the Aegean coast encompassing all of Greece; along the Ionian Sea connecting Peloponnesus and Sicily; along the Adriatic coast, and reach into the waters of the western Mediterranean.

The civilization of the eastern Mediterranean itself was not uniform, nor fully grown overnight. It also had its periods of development and fusion, for it sprang itself from various sources. The oldest branch of it is the Sumerian-Babylonian, which came from Mesopotamia; then the Trojan culture, itself an embodiment of continental Anatolian influences; the civilization of Egypt from its earliest dynasties, and chiefly the Minoan civilization of Crete, with its brilliant climax in the Palace of Cnossus. Through its advantageous location at the eastern third of the Mediterranean, Crete was the most important cultural center in the second millenium before our era.

Parallel to the Minoan, was the Cycladic civilization. It originated in the fertile Aegean islands with their rich deposits of minerals and established maritime traffic. The eastern coast of the Peloponesus was the recipient of both Cretan and Cycladic cultures, and developed its own splendid Myceneaen civilization. Toward the beginning of the iron age, Aryan invaders from the north occupied the mainland and coastal areas. Heirs to the Cycladic and Mycenaean cultures, they themselves created the superior civilization of the Hellenic world.

The growth and spread of Aegean civilization is to a great extent the work of the seagoing men who connected the great trade centers and trading posts of the Mediterranean and Euxine Pontus into one extensive cultural area. To the southeast lay the great centers of ancient civilization and to the northwest the vast area of barbarous lands, with which the enterprising Aegean navigators could carry on a profitable trade. The Mediterranean shipping could deliver goods to the ports of the Egyptian delta or Syria, from which overland traffic was busily carried on with Mesopotamia and inner Asia, and inversely, they could load goods in these ports for distribution north and west.

With the development of navigation the maritime trade was carried on with even greater vigor by the sailors and merchants of ancient Greece. After the decline of the Cretan state and its conquest by the Achaean Greeks in the 15th century, B.C., the sea lanes of the Aegean came into the hands of a new and virile race, which descended upon the southern coast from the northern mainland, attracted by the superior civilization of Mycenae, Tiryns, Crete and Cyclades. Achaeans were followed by the Doric tribes which established themselves on the mainland or settled down along the western coast of Greece. It took several centuries before the powerful Hellenic tribes occupied the whole Aegean area, with the Greek mainland. But once settled, they developed a prosperous civilization of their own, attended by the quick growth of population.

Between 800 and 600 B.C. this population, organized into City States, achieved a new momentum through colonization, expanding over the coastland of the central and eastern Mediterranean, over the shores of Hellespont, and even over the eastern coast of the Euxine Pontus. Such expansion not only took care of the excess population of City States, but also intensified the trade and navigation between the new areas and the motherland. In time, it gave great wealth and power to the Grecian world which was thus enabled to carry its civilization to the remote corners of the then known world.

Greek penetration into the Adriatic came at an early date. Since this gulf is the northern extension of the Ionian Sea, the shores of which were inhabited by the Doric tribes, it was natural for the sailors and merchants of Greece to sail along its coast to the head of the Adriatic.

There they met the amber merchants from the Baltic, and purchased ironware from the foundries of Hallstatt and Picenum. In this way the Greeks developed the carrier trade between prosperous Sicily and points north along both Adriatic coasts. They were following the example of the Phoenician traders who had visited the Dalmatian shores and founded their colonies before the coming of the Greeks.

The City State of Corinth was the first to establish colonies in the Adriatic. Even before founding the city of Syracuse in Sicily in the 8th century B.C., the Corinthians had established a colony on the island of Corcyra (Corfu) near the Strait of Otranto.

The Dalmatian Coast and its Hinterland

There is no lack of archeological remains throughout the Adriatic coastland and its archipelago that antedate the coming of Greek colonists. Both chipped and polished stone implements have been found scattered on nearly all the larger islands and in various places on the seacoast. But these finds are far behind those of Butmir and other places in Bosnia in the abundance and variety of implements discovered. This would indicate that the coastal area and archipelago were not in step with the neolithic civilization of the interior, and that farming was not developed among its aborigines. Held to the narrow coastal plain by the high mountain ranges of the interior, it could not participate in the busy life of the fertile river valleys of the Pontian watershed, and subsisted on the periphery of European humankind, engaged in fishing and the collection of oyster shells.

Such a dormant and backward life was the lot of the Adriatic aborigines until the fruits of the Sumero-Babylonian and Egyptian civilizations were brought to them by the Cretan, Phoenician, Cycladic and Grecian sailors and traders. Naturally this process was at first slow and attended by many difficulties. But by the era of intensive Greek navigation and colonizing, the old barriers had been beaten down and the vast physical, cultural and intellectual treasures of the ancient East and classical Hellas were introduced into this area, never to leave it again. For during the Greek and Roman times Dalmatia became a torch-bearer of civilization, and it remained true to its noble mission throughout the Middle Ages, even though by that time

it had acquired a different racial foundation. Dalmatia became a leader in high intellectual pursuits, and teacher of the fine arts in all Croatian lands. Moreover, the Dalmatian cities, in company with Venice, made the Adriatic for many centuries the queen of the seas and a world center in trade and traffic between the Moslem world and the countries of western Europe— thus contributing its share to the growth and progress of modern civilization.

Greek Colonies In The Adriatic Area

The oldest settlers in the Adriatic were in all probability Phoenicians.[11] They were followed by the Greeks, especially after colonizing the Korkyra island at the gateway to the Adriatic.[12] A systematic Greek colonizing began in the 4th century, chiefly with the aid of Sicily. It resulted in a number of Greek colonies such as those on the island of Issa (Vis), Pharos (Hvar, Lesina), Corcyra Melaine (Korchula), and probably others of lesser note. On the coast they established Lissos (Ljesh, in Northern Albania), Epidauron (Tsavtat), Narona (Vid), Iadera (Zadar), Tragurion (Trogir), Epetion (Stobrech), Salona (Solin), Asseria (near Benkovats), and Heracleia, whose location has not been identified.[13]

The most interesting archeological materials from this period come from the Greek tombs discovered on the island of Issa (Vis), Pharos (Hvar) and elsewhere, the relics which are now exhibited in the museums of Dalmatian cities. There we find impressive vases and vessels of elegant appearance, with painted decorations. The Tanagra figurines of clay are spacious in these collections. Most of these products originated from the Greek centers in southern Italy. The fragment of a marble statue personifying "opportunity" (Äiros), discovered in Trogir, represents the work of an accomplished sculptor.

So prosperous were these colonies of Issa, Pharos and Corcyra that they issued coins of their own minting. But some of the native Illyrian cities, Rizon in the bay of Cattaro and the tribal seats of Daorsi, also minted coins of their own. This would point to trade relations between the Illyrian aborigines, Greek settlers and occasional traders from abroad.

Ample light is shed both on the life of the colonists and their relations with the native population, by a considerable number of inscriptions coming from Corcyra Melaine, Pharos,

and other places. An inscription from Corcyra kept in the archeological museum of Zagreb describes the founding of the colony and the distribution of land among the colonists. An inscription from Starigrad (Città Vecchia) on Pharos tells of a pilgrimage to the Delphic oracle. Another inscription from Pharos commemorates a victory over some Illyrian tribe from the mainland, and probably graced a public monument.

Substantial architectural remains of the ancient fortifications are still extant. They can be seen in Starigrad and near the locality of Yelsa (Jelsa) on Pharos, near Stobrech (Epetion) on the mainland, and in other places where the Greek colonists of the third century had to defend themselves against the Illyrian pirates and raiders.

The Adriatic colonies apparently did not emulate the monumental architecture of their mother cities in Greece, for traces of majestic temples, stadia or other impressive public buildings have not been discovered in this region.

Interesting side lights on the Greek trade and colonization along the Illyrian coast are found in M. Rostovtzeff's *The Social and Economic History of the Hellenistic World.* "The character and activity of the Greco-Illyrian trade are illustrated," he writes, "not only by archeological discoveries, but also by a casual literary reference. Strabo has preserved a statement by Theopompus that shreds of Thasian and Chian jars were frequently found in the river Naro. The Thasian and Chian wine came to the river Naro and thence penetrated to the interior as the finds at Trebenishte suggest, probably through the Greek colonies of Apollonia and Epidamnus (Dyrrhachium). It was doubtless to Illyrian trade that these two cities mainly owed their prosperity attested by the interesting discoveries of French and Italian archeologists in their excavations of the ruins of Apollonia.

"A systematic study of these [i.e. excavations of the ruins of Apollonia] will certainly throw fresh light on the vicissitudes in the history of Apollonia and probably of Epidamnus, and will provide an instructive picture of their trade relations with Greece, South Italy, and Illyrian region. The scanty evidence at present in our possession points to a striking development of trade in the sixth and fifth centuries. Later, in the fourth century, when Dionysius the elder founded his group of colonies on the

islands opposite the mouth of Naro (Issa, Pharos, Corcyra Melaine, Melite), he struck a heavy blow at the Apollonian and Epidamnian trade, probably replacing the products of Greek agriculture and industry on the Illyrian markets by those of Sicily and South Italy. Still later the increase of Illyrian piracy made trade relations with Illyria very hazardous. Here again, therefore, the fourth century was a period of steady decline for Greek trade."

Roman Civilization And Antiquities

Although prosperous and independent, the inhabitants of the Greek colonies along the Adriatic coast did not penetrate far inland, nor did they harbor plans for the conquest of that territory. Greek military power was entirely directed toward the Near and Middle East, and the invasion of countries of great wealth and high civilization. Alexander conquered Asia Minor, Persia, Bactria, India and Egypt, but the western part of the known world was outside his designs. Thus his generals did not lead the armies against Carthage, whose possessions reached to the Atlantic, nor did they attach much importance to the valley of the Danube (which they called the Ister), with its huge and fertile territory. Sicily and the southern third of Italy were settled and assimilated by the Greek colonists, while the cities of Massilia (Marseilles), Nicaea (Nice), and Arles (Argyreia) were founded in southern France. But all this was the work of peaceful settlers, and not of the Macedonian conquerors.

However, neither the Greek colonists nor the generals were interested in the acquisition of the northwestern Balkans, the Pannonian plain or the Alpine area. Somnolent and dormant, this territory was inhabited mostly by Celtic, Illyrian and Thracian tribes still living in the neolithic and bronze age traditions of continental Europe. But for the Roman conquest, which quickened the tempo of civilization in this area, the neolithic farmer and bronze age warrior would have carried on in the old way for many a century to come.

Essence Of The Roman Civilization

The Roman civilization of the first two centuries of our era had two striking features for the student of history: 1) universal peace and security; 2) the building of towns and cities, with attendant development of agriculture, crafts,

trade, letters, commerce and communications on land and sea. Briefly this is the civilization of military camps (castra) and fortifications; of villages, towns and cities, inter-connected throughout the empire with a network of land routes; of ports and harbors, in effective intercourse through fleets of boats and merchant vessels sailing on rivers, along the seacoast, and across the deep sea. On country roads and highways, trains of ox carts and horse-drawn wagons were moving in all directions. Farming was attended to on clan-owned lands, in military hamlets (cannabae) and on large estates (villas) owned by wealthy Roman merchants, prefects and generals. City life was raised to a high cultural level through municipal administration, jurisdiction, forum, merchants' arcades, temples, schools (palaestrae), workshops, thermae (public baths with various social activities), theaters, exhibits of fine sculpture, and monumental architecture. This pattern was followed in nearly all the cities of the empire, and the natives contributed to it more than the Romans themselves.

Keeping these facts in mind let us now follow up the process of romanization east of the Adriatic, and lay bare its results in the form of archeological monuments, still extant, or disinterred. "In the second and first centuries B.C.," writes M. Rostovtzeff,[*] "when the military power of the Illyrians was broken forever (although some tribes still maintained nominal independence), large groups of Italian merchants and money-dealers settled in the more important maritime cities. When the Illyrian lands were finally annexed to the Roman Empire (in the time of Augustus from about 33 B.C., and under his first successors), the Romans transformed these cities into colonies. Senia, Jadera, Salona, Narona and Epidaurum, were first to be colonized.

"Colonization meant creation of almost purely Italian centers of urban life. To the colonies were assigned large tracts of best arable land. Many of the colonists became prosperous landowners and probably used the native population as tenants and laborers. We are able to follow the gradual extension of Roman land tenure in the territories of Salona and Narona. Some families, residents in these cities, were real pioneers in the new land. They built villas in the lowlands

---

[*] *The Social and Economic History of the Roman Empire.* By M. Rostovtseff. p. 221.

of Dalmatia, and introduced the capitalistic methods established in Italy and Istria. Lumbering and grazing were their earliest forms of activity. Later came the production of corn, and still later cultivation of vines and olive trees.

"Besides the cities, two legionary fortresses were established in the country, at Burnum and Delminium, as well as scores of smaller forts. In the time of Vespasian, however, the legions were removed from Dalmatia to Pannonia, though some of the smaller forts remained. These military establishments no doubt contributed largely to the romanization of the country. One of them—that at Burnum—owned large pasture lands in the neighborhood."

Another way of romanizing was through military service, which took 20 to 25 years. The recruits came from Illyrian villages, and when they returned home as veterans, they were granted authority and privileges which raised them to the rank of native aristocracy. As their numbers grew, many towns were formed with the status of municipality (municipium). This helped to break up the old tribal organization. The municipia were endowed with large tracts of fertile land which was taken away from the tribes and distributed among those benefited by the grant of citizenship. The residents were the native principes (tribal leaders), veterans and immigrants from larger cities. In time the cities amassed great wealth which they invested in local improvements and sumptuous edifices. Small localities established around the military camps and outposts were the cannabae, which also had the tendency to grow.

Dalmatia and neighboring Bosnia were also important mining regions that provided iron, silver and gold for the Romans. Especially important were the iron works, which supplied weapons for the legions stationed along the Danube.

The colonial policies which Rome followed in Spain and in Noricum and Moesia, she followed also in Istria, Pannonia, and Dacia. In Pannonia the important Roman arteries were the rivers Drava, Sava and Danube. Naval flotillas cruised on the Drava and Danube. Their naval base for this section of the rivers was in Mursa (Osijek), at the confluence of the Drava and Danube.

After various changes by his predecessors, Diocletian (284-305 A.D.) divided the Roman Empire into 101 provinces. These were grouped into 17 dioceses, all of which were subordinated to four prefectures. Two Emperors (Augusti) and two viceroys (Caesars), each of them assisted by a pretorian prefect, presided over the prefectures. Thus, the vast Illyrian province established by Julius Augustus was subdivided into four provinces.

After the Roman rule was consolidated in Illyricum, Pannonia, Moesia and Dacia, it continued in force until the barbarian invasions in the fifth and sixth centuries. In the meantime, momentous events took place in the area. Crushing of the great Pannonian rebellion under the leadership of the two Batons (6-9 A.D.), as well as the military campaigns of Trajan, Hadrian and Marcus Aurelius, show the importance which the Roman emperors attached to these provinces. An intense economic, social and intellectual activity had developed in the area. As a result numerous military camps, forts, towns, cities, bridges and aqueducts were built, manufacturing plants were established, quarries and mines exploited, throughout the Danubian provinces.

Many monuments of the Roman civilization are still on their ancient sites in the form of well-preserved structures and edifices, some of them ruined, others again buried on their sites, or scattered near and far. In our description of this archeological wealth we shall proceed by presenting mainly the edifices and monuments that are still preserved, then those standing in ruins, and finally the ruins buried in the ground and unearthed through recent excavations.

The Roman Antiquities Found in Dalmatia and Pannonia

The most valuable remains at the head of the Adriatic are found in the Istrian towns of Pola (Pietas Julia) and Porech (Parenzo, Parentium).*

At Pola the Romans built a huge amphitheatre on the sea shore. During the middle ages the Knights Templar held tournaments in this amphitheatre. Another grand edifice is the Temple of Augustus and Rome, with many fragments scattered around the temple. It was used by the Venetians as a granary. The back wall of

---

* The best pictures are on record in a book of A. Bernardy, *L'Istria e la Dalmazia*, 1915, in the artistic series of Instituto d'Arti Grafiche, Bergamo, and in the monumental edition of Cassas-Lavallée, Voyage Pittoresque, etc. 1802.

a temple believed to have been dedicated to Neptune is now being used as one wall of a modern building. These city gates are still extant: the Golden Gate, Porta Aurea; a gate with two arcs, Porta Gemina, and Hercules Gate which gives access through the city wall.*

Proceeding on our archaeological journey south, we shall find the cities of Nin (Aenona) and Zadar (Jadera) to be important sources of Roman antiquities. In Zadar two ancient columns are still standing on the public squares. Ruins of a triumphal arch and portions of the ancient walls erected by Emperor Augustus, are still extant. The museum of San Donato in Zadar contains many valuable ancient objects including stone inscriptions, statues, implements and glassware. Interesting are exhibits of glassware from nearby Nin (Aenona), but its more valuable objects such as busts of emperors and other art objects were sold to the Museum of Udine.*

City walls of the ancient Greek Asseria near Benkovats, southeast of Zadar, still can be seen.**

Yet none of these architectural remains can be compared with the palace of Diocletian in Spalato, and the ruins of Salona, the ancient capital of Dalmatia.

Diocletian's Palace and its Historical Significance

The imperial palace of Diocletian is still used for various purposes. Its mausoleum has been changed into a Christian cathedral. In the Middle Ages it was provided with a lofty campanile, which is the pride of the city of Split. The Temple of Aesculapius, the emperor's private chapel, was remodeled into a baptistery. Various premises are still used for stores, shops and private dwellings, while some of its arcades were converted into residential buildings. The aqueduct of the palace, nine kilometers long, was restored in 1878, and ever since has provided the city with drinking water.

* See pp. 218 and 282 in Rostovtzeff's *A History of the Ancient World*, Vol. II, for some monuments of Pola and a graphic reconstruction of a villa on Brioni, a small island near Pola.
* Attractive illustrations of Zadar and Nin antiquities appear in Amy Bernardy's book: *Zara e i monumenti, Italiani di Dalmazia*, Cassas' volume, and G. Kowalczyk's monumental work: *Denkmäler der Kunst in Dalmazien*, Berlin, 1910. (Plate 67.)
** A Greek votive altar from Trogir (ancient Tragurium) is pictured on p. 5 (Vol. I) of Cyril Ivekovich's *Dalmatiens Architektur und Plastik*, Vienna, 1910.

In the Middle Ages Diocletian's palace served as a citadel giving the population of Salona and the surrounding communities shelter against the invading barbarians. In those days it became the cultural and social center of Dalmatia. It gave birth to the city of Split, the largest and most prosperous city of Dalmatia. In the 16th and 17th centuries it was used by the Venetians as a fort against the onslaughts of the Turks.

Ever since its completion toward the end of the third century, Diocletian's palace has attracted the notice and admiration of later generations. A fourth century historian, Ammianus Marcellinus, mentions it. In the next century Sidonius Apollinarius describes Diocletian's tomb. In the tenth century emperor Constantinus VII, Porphyrogenitus, provides in his description of Dalmatia some details about the palace. He is the first writer to report on the conversion of the mausoleum into the cathedral of S. Domnius, a local martyr.

Numerous are the medieval Latin, Italian and Croatian writers who comment on the palace in the spirit of their time. In fact, every subsequent century produced new writers and new ideas on the value and significance of this grand edifice. Under the title: *Ruins of the Palace of the Emperor Diocletian at Spalato in Dalmatia*, Robert Adam, an illustrious English architect, published a monumental work in 1764 with beautiful engravings of the palace, such as he saw it and as he reconstructed it in his imagination. The work of Adam was emulated, or reproduced by many writers who have written since on Diocletian's palace.[14]

Adam's drawings were matched at the beginning of this century by the French authors: E. Hébrard, an architect, and J. Zeiller, an archeologist, in their splendid folio volume entitled *Le Palais Dioclétien*, Paris, 1912. Excellent work was done also by a scholarly German architect, G. Niemann in his *Der Palast Diokletians in Spalato*, in 1910. In G. Kowalczyk's *Denkmäler der Kunst in Dalmatien*, 1910, C. Gurlitt discusses the palace from both architectural and military points of view and arrives at the conclusion that Diocletian meant his palace to be a real stronghold and center of the Roman Empire, a plan partially carried out a generation later by Constantine, through the founding of Constantinople.

A number of distinguished English writers followed in the footsteps of Robert Adam. Wil-

kinson Gardner wrote about it in his *Dalmatia and Montenegro*, 1848; Edward Augustus Freeman, the English historian, in his *Subjects and Neighbor Lands of Venice*, 1881, and *Essays*, 3rd Series. T. J. Jackson, the architect who restored campanile of Rab (Arbe), ascribes to Diocletian's palace a revolutionary rôle in the development of ancient architecture by saying: * "In the palace of Diocletian at Spalato we have one of the earliest, perhaps the earliest step towards that departure in architecture which resulted in the development of style of modern Europe. . . . The palace of Spalato marks the era when the old art died giving birth to the new."[15]

The Plan and Layout of the Palace

Unlike the summer residence of Hadrian in Tivoli, which was merely the playground of the imperial family, the palace of Diocletian was a combination of military camp (castrum) and summer residence (villa), in which the aged ex-emperor could spend his last years of life in security and leisure. Like any Roman castrum, the palace is quadrangular, but trapezoid in shape. Two sides have the length of 647 feet, while the other two are respectively 543 and 525 feet in length. This dissymmetry is explained by the irregularity of the rolling terrain. The palace covers an area of nearly eight acres. The building is surrounded by protective walls on three sides, while the façade of the building was turned to the sea and did not need land protection. On an average the thickness of the walls was 6½ feet, while their height varied between 51 and 72 feet, in accordance with the elevation of the ground. In spite of its deterioration through nearly seventeen centuries of existence, the palace contained, at last report, 278 houses and 540 building structures with 3,200 inhabitants.

On the land side three gates provided communication between the wall-enclosed palace grounds and the suburban area. The northern gate opposite the main terrace of the portico was called the Golden Gate, Porta Aurea; the eastern gate facing Epetium (Stobrech) was the Bronze Gate, Porta Aenea, while the western gate was given the name of Iron Gate, Porta Ferrea. Each gate was flanked by two octagonal towers, while the corners of the walls were reinforced by four

quadrangular towers rising 13 feet above the wall. In between the corner and gate towers the walls were strengthened with an additional quadrangular tower. Thus, the total of towers was sixteen, since the façade of the building was protected by the sea. Out of the original sixteen towers, only three are preserved. Two of these are used as private residences, while one of them constitutes municipal property. Others were demolished during the siege of the palace, or in more recent times by the local authorities as bad risks.

The three interior sides of the perimetral walls enveloping the premises, were flanked with two stories of arcades resting on massive pylons. The arcades of the ground floor faced the yard, while those of the upper story were turned outside. The lower story was used for warehouses and the dwellings of slaves, while the upper story provided living quarters for soldiers and employees.

The interior space was divided by two transversal roads into four unequal parts. The road connecting the northern or main gate, Porta Aurea, with the vestibule of the palace, divided the area into two halves, but the transversal road connecting the western, Porta Ferrea, and the eastern gate Porta Aenea, allowed more space for the southern portion, for it had to accommodate both the mausoleum and the temple of Aesculapius and the huge imperial villa facing the sea. Thus we have five quadrangles on the lot: the first extends along the entire sea front, from the western to the eastern octagonal corner tower, and occupies the interior up to the connecting line of the first two quadrangular towers. This plot received the structures of the imperial residence. The villa itself was connected through an interspace in which we found the ornamental vestibule, prothyron and peristyle, and the service buildings, kitchen, servants' quarters and horse stables, with the huge mausoleum in the eastern half, and the beautiful Temple of Aesculapius in the western half of the area adjoining the transversal (west-to-east) road. In the area north of this road we have two equal blocks disposed on each side of the main road (north-to-south), one of them assigned to the staff office buildings, while the other provided quarters for the imperial guard.

From the above it is not difficult to see that the high and thick walls reinforced with sixteen towers, and the interior disposition of the

---

* *Dalmatia, the Quarnero and Istria.* By T. J. Jackson, Vol. I, p. 206.

enclosed grounds, served the purpose of a massive Roman castrum of the fourth century, when the Roman troops had to defend themselves from the onslaughts of barbarians, and had long lost their initiative of attack. Thus the security of the emperor and his family was the first consideration of the architect designing this palace. Whether it was also to serve as an administrative center of the empire, as some suggest, is another question, but the massiveness of the building and its commanding position over a network of military highways, does not rule out such a possibilty.

Because of its military purpose the palace at Asphalatus could not resemble the summer palaces of former emperors such as that of Hadrian on his sumptuous estate in Tivoli. In Hadrian's time there was no question of security and the architect's entire task was to create and introduce an edifice of beauty into the landscape. In comparison, the palatial residence of Diocletian was a simple and monotonous structure, only the façade of which was softened by the architect's resort to decorative technique in order to break the stiff geometrical delineation of the huge block. Hence the portico, and three loggias with their elevated arches as an ornamental part of it. Even that could not sufficiently relieve, in the estimation of the architect, the monotony of the long line of 42 arcades, and so he introduced rhythm in their sequence by raising the arch of the tenth arcade from the western and the tenth from the central loggia, thus providing two groups of ten and two of eleven arcades, supplemented by three loggias. This made the façade from the sea a pleasant sight which could satisfy the esthetic requirements of the soldier-emperor.

The six towers of the north wall, with the same treatment of the outside arcades similarly offered a refreshing sight from the road leading to Salona.*

Between the two octagonal towers of this wall there was a passageway leading through the main gate, Porta Aurea, to the vestibule (now called rotonda) and the reception hall or tablinum of the palace. The Golden Gate itself was an elaborate edifice with two rows of blind arches: two of them in the lower row and seven

* For the actual state and reconstruction of its ensemble and details, see: Niemann: Pl. VII, XII; Hébrard: Pl. I, II, VIII; pp. 61f, 64-67.

in the top row. The arches rested directly on capitals of the columns based on consoles, without the support of entablature as the classic style required. The same deviation from the ancient usage is observed on all the arches of the peristyle gracing Jupiter's Temple. This innovation has been held by many historians and critics of art to be the very foundation of Medieval art which found its immediate application in the Romanesque basilicas of the early Middle Ages.

Alongside the two roads were wide roofed galleries which provided cooling shade in summer and shelter in case of rain. Beyond the transversal (west-to-east) road, however, the main road was bordered on both sides with superb columns of the peristyle, the most attractive architectural decoration of the focal group. At its southern base the peristyle ended in a magnificent prothyron or main entrance to the palace, which again led to the vestibule and thence to the tablinum or reception hall. Thus, the peristyle and prothyron formed an architectural ensemble which brought to a focus all the beauty and grandeur of this exalted grouping of villa and temples. Transversely to the peristyle both Jupiter's Temple and the Temple of Aesculapius were flanked by arcades apparently more elaborate than the rest on this road.

Mausoleum (Jupiter's Temple, later St. Domnius Cathedral)

Thus the columns of the peristyle lined the precinct of these two sacred edifices: to the left when facing the prothyron, Jupiter's Temple, and to the right the Temple of Aesculapius. Entrance to the Mausoleum or Jupiter's Temple was gained through a gate installed presumably under the third arch of the peristyle. The passage led over a stairway first to the frontal arcade (prosthasis) of the edifice, and then through the main entrance and was connected with an arcade ring that encircled the huge octagonal building. Thus, another architectural ornament lent beauty and dignity to the massive and somewhat monotonous exterior of the edifice, giving it an appearance of monumental grandeur. The frontal arcade rested on eight columns and its tympanon or triangular gable front had a high arch which continued in a vault to the opposite end.* The arcades of the periptery rested on 24 columns supporting the

* According to Niemann. See Pl. XXV.

usual entablature. While portions of the periptery are still extant, the prosthasis was removed in the 13th century to make room for the campanile.

The temple itself is built with large stone blocks. Its walls are 11 feet thick. The interior is round but the exterior is octagonal. Each side of the octagon is slightly over 25 feet in length. The weight of the building rests on a substructure, likewise octagonal, and 12 feet deep. The internal space of the cella has a 44½ foot diameter and height of 75⅙ feet. Its columns and niches form an organic whole. Four semicircular and four quadrangular niches are cut deep in the massive walls. Between the niches and two feet away from the walls are placed eight large Corinthian columns, 30 feet high, which rise to the upper level of the walls where they hold on their cornices another row of 8 columns, 16 feet high. Both rows of columns have a broken entablature adjoining the circular walls. The lower columns are of pink granite while four columns of the upper row are of porphyry and the other four are of red granite. According to Bulich* and Hébrard** a large dark-red porphyritic sarcophagus was placed in the cella as a resting place for the mighty emperor, while the niches were occupied by the statues of various Roman gods. The dome has a height of 25 feet, and was covered with mosaic. On the outside it was protected by a roof.

Today, with the statues of saints replacing those of the ancient gods, Jupiter's Temple serves as the Cathedral of St. Domnius. Little is known of it in the western world, although after the Pantheon in Rome itself, it is probably the best preserved ancient Roman building that we have.

The Temple of Aesculapius

The Temple of Aesculapius, now the baptistery, is a jewel of classical architecture. This temple had an important function in the imperial household, and was accordingly surrounded with every mark of its august position. It faced the Temple of Jupiter from a distant spot in the sacred precinct east of the peristyle. There is a spacious patio between the Temple and peristyle where the courtiers lingered while the emperor was offering sacrifices at the altar. The

* Op. cit., p. 90.
** Pl. XII, p. 73.

Temple is built on an elevation which still rises 8 feet above the street level. The main entrance had a covered front structure (pronaos) with six columns terminated by antae. The cella is quadrangular: 33⅓ feet long and 30 feet wide. The outside walls have pilasters on the corners, between which the surface is smooth. The main entrance is 20 feet high and 7 feet wide, while the walls are 4 feet thick. The cornice above the entrance is supported by two consoles. The ceiling is vaulted and divided into cassettes with rich bas-reliefs. Under the ceiling sumptuous cornices line the top of three walls, while the entrance wall remains without such ornamentation.

Peristyle And Prothyron

The two sacred precincts lined with two colonnades of the peristyle are united by the gorgeous prothyron, which also connects the two column rows of the peristyle. This is in an excellent state of preservation, although desecrated by houses and shops that have been built between the columns and otherwise abused by decadent posterity. The peristyle itself is 80 feet long and 47 feet wide. Each side consists of six columns, 17½ feet high, chiseled from red granite. We have previously described how these columns support circular arches placed directly on the capitals of the shafts without the super-imposition of an entablature to support the arches. Here, on the contrary, the entablature rests on the arches giving the structure an aspect of arcade. In the time of Diocletian this may have been considered a daring innovation but the solidity of the structure to this day, and the history of the medieval edifices proves that this was a notable advance in architecture.

The prothyron is built on an elevated platform reached by five steps from the street level and rests on four Corinthian columns of pink granite. The two central columns support directly an arch which develops into a vault, as in the two temples, while each central column is spanned with the corner column by entablature giving the tympanum (front gable) its peculiar aspect. Above the tympanum a stone block 14 feet long was installed, probably to serve as a platform for a decorative statue group.

The Vestibule and the Palace

Through the arched corridor of the prothyron one came into a spacious round hall, 40 feet

in diameter, 57 feet high and vaulted with a mosaic-covered dome. This was the vestibulum or the front hall of the imperial palace itself. There were four niches recessed in the walls which probably housed the statues of the domestic gods, or large decorative objects. This part of the palace was in an advanced stage of deterioration when it was partly repaired. But it is still without its cupola and roof and has been exposed for a long time. From the outside this round hall was enclosed by four quadrangular walls. There is no doubt that this hall was richly appointed and luxuriously furnished.

An arched door opened into a still more luxurious hall, the most glamourous room of the whole imperial residence, which served for reception of emperor's friends, guests and high dignitaries of the empire. This was the sala regia or tablinum, the emperor's reception hall.

The length of the tablinum was 103 feet; its width 40 feet. The hall was lined with gorgeous columns, and its walls covered with white marble and alabaster of exceptional quality as the preserved fragments indicate. This hall towered above all the buildings and received light from above through elaborate stained glass windows. How luxuriously the tablinum was furnished we can merely imagine. Unfortunately, like all the other rooms of the palace, it was subdivided and made into small apartments by its occupants in the Middle Ages. The ornate southern door of the tablinum opened in the central part of the portico occupied by a loggia. On each side of the tablinum there was a set of guest rooms or xenia.

To the right of the tablinum, past the xenia, was a spacious and luxurious dining hall or triclinium. The rest of the space in the direction of the western corner tower was occupied by the gynaeceum or ladies' quarters. To the left of the tablinum and past the xenia, there was a spacious and rich library, 113 feet long and 50 feet wide. Farther on was the exedra, a sort of club room or drawing room and still farther along, extending to the eastern corner tower, were small apartments.

The location, size and purpose of these premises could be ascertained only after excavation of the underground structure had made sufficient progress at the beginning of this century. Hébrard's reconstruction of the main floor of the palace was based on these data. The underground premises proved to be desirable warehouses, and the local merchants are bent on clearing them all.

History of the Palace

Throughout the sixteen and half centuries of its existence Diocletian's palace has had a stirring history. From generation to generation it has fulfilled its essential task of giving security and safety to its inmates and the population of the neighboring localities. During the invasion of the barbarians it saved the lives of thousands of people who sought refuge within its solid walls. No enemy, Goth, Avar, Slav, Croat, Tartar or Turk, ever captured the palace. But housing the ever increasing masses of refugees created many problems. Some were transferred to nearby islands where they enjoyed relative safety, and some were accomodated in the arcades, towers, office buildings and barracks of the palace.

In the meantime, Christianity held sway. Pagan idols were replaced by statues of saints, and ancient sanctuaries were converted into Christian places of worship. We know that the palace still had many unoccupied premises in the 11th century. But gradually the two sacred edifices, Jupiter's Temple, which had become a cathedral, and the Temple of Aesculapius, converted into a baptistery, became too small and other churches, chapels and shrines were built or installed in some convenient spot. There were about 15 edifices of this kind, including a Jewish synagogue. In the 13th century when Spalato became Croatian, there was an increase of artistic activities. The most important monument of this period is the lofty campanile built at the main entrance of the cathedral which once was Jupiter's Temple.

The campanile consists of six superimposed towers: the three lowest are executed in the Romanesque style, the next two stories are Gothic, while the top is Renaissance. This last story is octagonal while the five below it are quadrangular. Construction of the campanile was completed only in the 17th century after numerous interruptions which were forced by the struggles of this turbulent era. Owing to its structural defects and the damage wrought by wind and lightning, the old campanile was torn down at the turn of this century and a new one built in a period of eighteen years (1890-1908). The present campanile is over 200 feet high.

The interior of Jupiter's Temple also underwent great changes. The emperor's sarcophagus and the statues of the gods were removed back in the sixth century and no trace of them has ever been found. In the course of time the Christian symbols filled the cella but in the thirteenth century most of them were removed, making room for a beautiful pulpit, an altar and some artistic objects. The native wood carver Buvina made the main door of walnut, and dividing the surface into 28 frames, he carved in them the main scenes from the life of Jesus. From the same period come the rich carvings of the seats in the cathedral. During the rebuilding of the campanile, the worn cornices topping the columns in the cathedral were replaced by exact replicas. In spite of all the changes it has gone through, the ancient temple presents even today a magnificent sight, rising in its grandeur as a true monument of the ages.*

Conclusion

As we study the remarkable engravings offered by Adam, Cassas, Niemann, Hébrard and Kowalczyk, and read the fascinating stories unfolded by Lavallée, Niemann, Zeiller, Gurlitt and Bulich, the reality of Diocletian's day appears before our eyes in all its magnificence. We are confronted with the indominable will and inexhaustible energy of the Salonitan Diocles, son of an obscure provincial libertine, who by his soldierly virtues was raised to the imperial throne. Diocles took over this Empire in a state of confusion, decadence and near-dissolution. He reorganized it, strengthened its administration and through a series of imperial edicts improved its economic life and raised the general welfare. He was also a builder of monumental edifices throughout the Empire. In Rome he erected the gigantic Thermae Diocletiani. In Antiochia, capital of Syria, he completed the imperial palace initiated by his predecessor Gallienus, and in Nicomedia, now the city of Izmit on the Marmara Sea, he founded a new capital where he built a palace believed by many to be the prototype of that in Spalato. In Nicomedia he abdicated, May 1, 305 A.D., and in the autumn of that year he was back in his native Salona and living in retirement at the palace. He had been there on a short trip also in 304, watching the progress of the great work that had been going on for more than 15 years.

During this time thousands of laborers, masons, quarry hands, stonecutters, artisans of all branches and men of the sea had been employed on the construction of this edifice. The stone slabs for the walls were brought from the quarries of Trogir and the nearby island of Brach (Brazza). The marble and granite columns were imported from Syria, Egypt and Aegean islands. The marble reliefs, friezes, ornate cornices and statues came from famous workshops in Greece, Syria and Italy, while the sphinxes gracing the embankment of the steps leading up to the prosthasis of Jupiter's Temple were brought from Egypt.

Hundreds of vessels were coming and going between this point on the Dalmatian coast and the foremost centers of culture in the eastern and central Mediterranean, in the full tradition of the maritime shipping which had played so great a rôle in spreading the high civilization of Mesopotamia, Egypt, Homeric Troy, Minoan Crete, the Cycladic islands, Mycenean Peloponnese, and classical Greece, each in its chronological sequence, all over the shores of the Mediterranean and its numerous seas. Thus Dalmatia, the most backward country east of the Adriatic prior to its colonization by the Greeks and conquest by Rome, became through sea-born trade a center of Roman and Hellenistic civilization and a leader in the arts. For neither before nor since, in the vast area of Illyricum, Pannonia, Dacia and Moesia*, had an edifice been built as majestic, immense and spectacular as the palace of Caius Aurelius Valerius Diocletianus, Imperator Romanorum.

The Medieval Successors of Diocletian's Palace

Regardless what the ultimate motives of Diocletian were, in building his palace on the Dalmatian coast, we must dissociate them from those of Hadrian, who put up a luxurious villa (summer residence) on his family estate at Tivoli. Hadrian's was a summer residence befitting the power and wealth of a Roman emperor. No hint at government activity or concentration of military power can be detected in it.

---

* For a detailed history of the palace up to our own days, see: Bulich, op. cit., ch. VI; Hébrard, ch. VIII.

* Now: Croatian territory, Hungary, Rumania, Serbia and Bulgaria.

In the case of Diocletian's structure, it was just the opposite. There the military moment, whether of defensive or offensive nature, was the prime consideration. The tall and massive walls of the camp enclosure, the quadrangular towers and octagonal bastions will bear out this statement. In comparison with the luxury and splendor of the Tivoli palace, the imperial quarters of Diocletian, even though fascinating by their classical beauty, were relatively simple and modest.

Thus the whole camp stands out as a field fortification dedicated to political and military assignments. In fact, it was used as a political center in the 6th century and an impregnable fortress throughout the Middle Ages.

For this huge administrative and military center it was proper to have magnificent temples for worship of the chief deities of the Roman empire. Hence the erection of the Temple of Jupiter or mausoleum, and the Temple of Aesculapius with their sacred precinct adorned with fascinating columns of the peristyle.

While the Temple of Aesculapius was a typical Roman or Greek temple, the mausoleum announced a new architectural style. The semicircular arches of the peristyle columns were the very challenge to the contemporary architecture. They opened up a new era of massive and decorative building taken over in the first place by the Christian basilicas.

The combined effect of these influences we see in the construction of the Christian edifices of worship, at first in the form of basilicas, and later of the massive and elaborate cathedrals, until their original Romanesque style combines, in the course of centuries, with the Renaissance patterns and the lacework of the Italian Gothic.

However, the persistent prevalence of the Romanesque style both in the exterior and interior of the cathedrals along the seacoast impresses us with the depth of influence exerted by the mausoleum, now Cathedral of St. Dominius, upon the architecture of the coastal towns.

No doubt that, besides the architectural attraction of Diocletian's palace, its fortified camp also impressed the citizens of the coastal towns, as well as those living on the islands of the archipelago. The most striking example of this influence we see in the defensive walls and bastions encircling the perimeter of the city of Dubrovnik. In addition, the sea front of the city's port performed its defensive function like the sea front of Diocletian's palace. Inside this fortified perimeter many residences were erected. As a result of such security and defensive measures, the city of Dubrovnik was never captured by an enemy, and only the ruse of one of Napoleon's generals, protesting friendship and good faith, duped the citizens of Dubrovnik into surrender.

Other cities, either forced by necessity or inspired by the impregnable bastions of Diocletian's palace, emulated the example. Such were the nearby Trogir, Hvar, Korchula, Kotor, Zadar, Rab, Shibenik, and others. So wherever there were massive walls and defensive forts, there were lofty cathedrals displaying both from inside and outside the influence of Diocletian's structures.

Even though restricted to a minimum of illustrations, the writer shows on the subsequent pages both the exterior and interior of Christian edifices marking a course of evolution both toward the Split cathedral, and away from it. Obviously, the chronological order of construction of these edifices is not adhered to in these pages, the variations of style being here the chief points of discussion.

Provincial Capitals: Salona, Sirmium, Siscia, and Other Cities

There are few places in Europe where the treasures of antiquity have been so well preserved as in Pola and Split (Spalato). Although other important cities such as Salona (Solin); Sirmium (Mitrovitsa); Taurunum (Zemun); Mursa (Osiyek); Aqua Viva (Varashdin); Siscia (Sisak) and many others still exist, their Roman antiquities are nearly all underground, demolished, scattered and dissipated almost as completely as the stations of prehistoric time. Considerable effort has been spent on excavating them and the yield of cemeteries and ruins has gone to enrich the museums of Croatia and neighboring countries.

Some Roman bridges and roads are still in existence, kept up and improved. They serve the needs of the traffic now as they did in the times of Trajan, Hadrian and Marcus Aurelius. Other roads have been grown over with grass and bush, and long forgotten. But in the years of the great migrations they were the highways of advance for the barbarian masses converging from many directions on the rich Roman cities. These roads were used by the hordes of Atilla,

by the Gothic tribes, the Avaro-Slavic raiders and the Croatians as they moved from their northern homeland to the warm shores of the Adriatic. In the Roman heritage of Illyricum and Pannonia we have to include the lines of communications which played such an important role in the history of the Dark and Middle Ages.

No Roman city of this area has aroused such a wide spread interest among archeologists as has Solin (Salona), for many centuries the capital of Dalmatia. Excavations on its site were conducted for more than a century, and an immense mass of archeological materials has been brought to light, much of it through the enthusiasm and energy of Don Frano Bulić.[16]

Siscia and Sirmium

If Salona, before the excavations looked like a shapeless mound of detached and scattered stones, Siscia (Sisak) and Sirmium (Mitrovitsa) do not have even that much to show of their ancient splendor as capitals of the province of Pannonia. Sir Arthur Evans, the famous explorer of Minoan Crete, visited the site of once luxurious Siscia on the upper Sava river in 1875. "There was a time," he wrote,* "when Siscia was one of the great cities of the world. She was a bulwark against barbarians, an emporium of commerce, a seat of emperors, a mother of martyrs, a gathering point for Roman-Christian saga . . . Siscia was a convenient point d'appui for Dacian campaigns; the winter-quarters for Tiberius in his Pannonian war; by Septimius Severus made the seat of military government for his world, and so benefited by him that she took the name of Septimia Siscia. Probably under Vespasian, a Roman colony had already been planted here, and Siscia became a Republic with municipal liberties modeled on those of the parent city. An inscription still recalls her Duumviri, who in Rome's provincial mirrors, reflected the two consuls.

"Later on Siscia became the chief city of Upper Pannonia; then, when Savia was made a province, the residence of the Corrector. She was the seat of an Imperial treasury, and it was here that the 'most splendid Provost of Iron-Workers' received the revenue from the Noric mines. Here, too, was established the Premier

---

* *Through Bosnia and Herzegovina on Foot in 1875.* By Sir Arthur Evans.

Mint of the Roman Empire; and Siscia shared with Rome herself the distinguished honor of first printing her name in full on the imperial currency. What numismatist does not know and covet that coin of Gallienus, or that choice piece of the Emperor who sprang from Sirmium, with the proud inscription 'Siscia Probi Augusti' —the Siscia of Probus? On it is to be seen the personification of the queenly city, holding in her hands the laurel wreath of the empire, while at her feet two subject rivers pour bounteously from their tributary urns."

After presenting a passage from Strabo on this city, and describing its commercial relations with Aquileia, Alpine towns, Upper and Lower Danube, Dalmatia and Italy, Sir Arthur describes an interesting relic found in Croatia, where on a gold plated chest the names of five most important cities in the Roman Empire were incrusted, and among them Siscia.

"The comparatively high state of Siscian civilization is also attested by her coins—those superb medallions of gold and silver—those gems of the fourth century monetary art that stands out among the poorer products of mints, Gallic and Britannic. But what distinguishes the Siscian coins as much as their workmanship, is their peculiarly Christian character. It is here that the first purely Christian type—namely that which alludes to the vision of Constantine, first makes its appearance."

Siscia survived well into the early Middle Ages. "In the dark period which followed the barbarian invasions, something of her old secular glory was still reflected in the Siscian Church. After the destruction of Sirmium by the Huns in 441, Siscia transferred her ecclesiastical allegiance to Salona. Her decline was more lingering than that of her rival (i.e. Sirmium), for her prosperity had rested on a more solid foundation. Her bishops survived the settlement of the Slavs hereabouts in the time of Heraclius. In the ninth century we find her the residence of a Slavonic prince,* but she suffered from the Frankish invasion, and in the tenth century was finally razed by the Magyars."

Sirmium

The capital of Lower Pannonia, Sirmium was also located on the banks of the Sava, not far above its juncture with the Danube. In its time

---

* Ljudevit Posavski.

it was the most resplendent city of these eastern provinces and the accounts of contemporary writers glow with its praise. On its site at present a prosperous town thrives under the name of Mitrovitsa. Of its ancient walls, majestic buildings, imperial summer residence, temples or statues, nothing is left on the surface. Most of it is still underground, and the objects that have been casually disinterred have all been shipped to various museums of central Europe.[17]

On the remains of Mursa Major, an ancient colony founded by Hadrian, with the surname of Aelia, and situated near the confluence of the Drava and Danube rivers, no reports are available. That it was a city of some importance we know. The governor of the country resided there, and it was one of the major naval bases of the Roman Danubian fleet. It is also a junction of roads leading from Aquincum (Budapest), Celia (Zell) and Petovio-Aquileia. Its present name is Ossiyek. It is an industrial city and the capital of Slavonia.

Roman Antiquities in Bosnia and Herzegovina

Roman colonizing began vigorously with the incorporation of these two provinces into Dalmatia. Military roads (viae militares) were built, settlements established and fortresses erected. As a strategic base Bosnia became a Roman outpost for the conquest and control of the lower Danube. Its roads provided a short cut to Moesia and the Moesian capital, Viminatium, whence the Romans controlled the lands north of Haemus and west of the Euxine Pontus. But most important of all were the Bosnian iron mines and foundries which supplied metal for the armament and equipment of the Danubian and Pontic legions. According to ancient writers gold and silver were here abundant, far more abundant in those days apparently, than in the Middle Ages or at present.

The natural route to the interior of Bosnia was along the valleys of the Bosna and Drina rivers with their tributaries. Thus procceding east to Moesia and north to Pannonia, the Romans created their military and administrative centers throughout the area. Even before the coming of the Romans there were, of course, roads and strongholds in these countries. The Romans adapted them to their needs and expanded them where necessary.

As in the case of the Pannonian Servitium and Cibalae, even the sites of many known Ro-

man settlements can no longer be identified in Bosnia. And where Roman architectural remains are found, the original name of the colony or its relative importance cannot always be ascertained. But there are numerous localities where the Roman strongholds and towns, roads and bridges have survived, in whole or in part, the destructive force of time.

The natural road for Roman penetration of Herzegovina, both military and economic, was the valley of the Neretva and its feeders—Bregava, Trehizhat, Rama, Buna and Listitsa, to this day a populous and industrious countryside. In the estuary of Narona there was a colony of the same name, the site of which is now occupied by the village of Vid.

The fragment of the ancient city walls provides the foundation of a large building called Ereshova Kula, built of stone relics of the ancient Greek colony. Other houses of the village were made of the same building materials. A considerable section of the city wall, a part of the Roman forum and scattered decorative pieces of architecture, are still standing above ground.

Along the banks of Bregava near Stolats, on a hill called Gradina strong walls can be seen which Patsch* finds to be of Greek origin. Near the town of Stolats the ruins of Roman houses were found, and in one of them an elaborate floor mosaic, with anthropomorphic figures of the four seasons. Foundations and walls of a Roman stronghold on the banks of Neretva, near Mogoryelo, between Mostar and Metkovich, show an arrangement of walls, gates and wall-towers similar to that of Diocletian's palace in Split. In the town of Konyitse remains of a Mithra temple were found, while a sacred grove with altars of Bindus, the native river-god, are still in full sight at the source of Privilitsa creek near Bihach.

From this wealth of Roman antiquities then, we draw the picture of a prosperous Roman province, with much freedom in self-government, and slowly developing the city culture of Rome. It did not have large cities as did coastal Dalmatia, but its numerous towns reflected the prosperity of the small towns of Italy. The same type of arrangement was found in both: a forum, surrounded by arcades and statues,

---

* Carl Patsch. *Bosnien und Herzegovina in Römischer Zeit*. 1911.

buildings for city magistrates, council-hall, thermae, basilicae, market halls and temples dedicated to the Roman gods. A large number of Roman coins, with an unbroken chronological series up into the sixth century shows that trade and commerce flourished here centuries after the Danubian provinces had been devastated by the barbarian invaders.[18]

Early Christian Architecture

In Dalmatia and Bosnia Christianity took root as early as the first two centuries of our era. A number of martyrs are known from this period. The first Christians appeared in the Roman towns and settlements and there built their congregation halls or prayer houses. Dr. C. Truhelka, who conducted excavations in many sections of Bosnia and Herzegovina, reports in his book on early Christian archeology,* several places in which he came across the ruins of the early Christian oratories.

He found such a structure in Vidoshtak, Roman Dalluntum, near Stolats; another in a place called Borasi in the valley of the Trebizhat in Herzegovina; one in Gotovusha, near the town of Plevlye. Two such churches were unearthed near the town of Skelani, along the Drina river, at the Roman mining town of Domavia. Similar discoveries were made near the localities of Shiprag, Varoshluk, Maydan, Dobravina and Zenitsa. This latter is the Roman Bistue, seat of the first Bosnian diocese. Later, during the barbarian invasions, most of these places were destroyed, together with their temples and churches.

* *Starokršćanska Archeologija.*

Chapter IV

DAWN OF RECORDED HISTORY

THERE is nearly a thousand years of historical record of the Adriatic area before the coming of the Croatians. The earliest known inhabitants of this territory were Thracians, who spread out over the Balkan peninsula in the first half of the Iron Age and reached the Adriatic Sea. They were pushed back by the Illyrians, who came from the northwest and settled in the western half of the peninsula. Some of them occupied the Julian Alps and descended into Lombardy, where they were known as the Veneti, and eventually lent their name to Venice. The Illyrians did not remain undisturbed for long in their new country, and in the second half of the Iron Age they were attacked by oncoming Celts or Gauls, who occupied the region of the central Danube and the Sava river. By the fourth century before our era the Illyrians found themselves confined to the territory that today comprises Albania, Bosnia, Herzegovina, Dalmatia, part of Croatia and the Julian Alps. The Illyrians had three powerful tribes: Ardians, Dalmatians and Liburnians. The seat of the Ardians was near Boka Kotorska, which we know as Cattaro Bay, and their country extended south and east of that bay. The Dalmatians, with their center around Delminium, a town in western Bosnia, inhabited most of Dalmatia. Along the sea coast to the north lived the Liburnians, a tribe known for daring in navigation.

As the Illyrians became well established on the mainland and the sea coast, the Doric Greek colonizers spread from the island of Corcyra (Corfu) along the Albanian coast to the head of the Adriatic. At the beginning of the fourth century they established prosperous colonies on the islands of Vis, Hvar, Brach and Korchula. Gradually they occupied also parts of the sea coast and founded Tragurium (Trogir), Narona (Vid), Epetium (Stobrech near Split), Epidaurum (Tsavtat) and other cities. With the coming of the Greeks the civilization of the Hellenic world was introduced, to blossom forth during the Roman occupation.

The Romans were not interested in the eastern coast of the Adriatic until the latter part of the third century B.C. At that time the Ardian branch of the Illyrian people developed a strong state with efficient armed forces and a fleet of warships, and Rome determined to curb the power of this vigorous neighbor. In 229 B.C., therefore, a strong army and navy was sent against the Illyrians, and after a year of struggle the Illyrian queen, Teuta, accepted humiliating terms. Soon after her death the Ardian power vanished. However, during the second Punic War, when Roman resources were depleted, the Illyrians organized a new state with its capital in Scutari and once again asserted their power on the Adriatic. This brought about a new war in which the Romans defeated Gentius, the new Illyrian king. The captured king and his family had to grace the triumph of the victor, Praetor Lucius Anitius, in 167 B.C.

Roman Conquest

After the destruction of the Ardian State, Rome soon came into conflict with the Delmatians (in Roman version, Dalmatians). After years of desperate struggle the Dalmatian capital of Delminium was taken by the Roman consul Publius Cornelius Scipio Nasica in 155 B.C. The Romans did not establish full control over the country, however, and the Delmatians joined with another Illyrian tribe, the Japudians, to offer a stubborn resistance to the Romans for another century. Rome undertook costly campaigns and more than once appeared to have conquered the natives, but as soon as they weakened their garrisons, the Delmatians would rise again and destroy their oppressors. Julius Caesar was twice in Dalmatia, without any intention of carrying on war against the Dalmatians. Since he was occupied with his Gallic wars, and later with his struggles against the Roman senate, he was not at first greatly interested in the Illyrian territory. After the battle of Pharsalus, however, where Caesar defeated his republican enemies, he sent Aulus Gabinius at the head of an army against the rebellious Delmatians and Japudians. This long campaign ended disastrously for the Romans when in the winter of 48-47 B.C. the Delmatians destroyed their army in a battle near Shibenik. What was left of the army fled and took refuge in the strong fortification of Salona (Solin), but the victorious rebels captured the fortification as well. A peace was soon

33

arranged between the rebels and Julius Caesar, but in the confusion following the assassination of Caesar the Delmatians again attacked the Roman legions with great success.

In 35 B.C. after stamping out the opposition of the republicans, Octavian planned a serious campaign to subdue the rebellious Illyrians. Octavian himself took command of the army, and was assisted by his best generals. The base of operations was at Senia (Senj), and the legions marched in the country of the Japudians. After stubborn resistance the Japudians lost their fortifications and the tribes west of the ridge of Kapela surrendered. The tribes east of Kapela continued the struggle and caused heavy losses to the advancing army. Octavian himself was wounded in a battle near Metulum (a place near Ogulin), which ended the heroic fight of the Illyrians.

After the submission of the Japudians, Octavian advanced against the neighboring Celts and their capital Segetisca (Roman: Siscia, Croatian: Sisak). The Roman army had to fight every step of the way. Segetisca was captured only after a siege of thirty days. From this point Octavian led his armies to Liburnia or northern Dalmatia. The people there were well prepared for the enemy, and the conquest of their territory took two years (34-33 B.C.). The Romans had to lay siege to several towns before they could crush the most stubborn resistance being offered at Setovia (Sinj), the last Dalmatian stronghold. But in the end Illyricum was conquered and Octavian celebrated his victory with a triumph in 27 B.C.

In spite of this conquest a great rebellion broke out in the Illyrian territory in 6 A.D. This was the most spectacular rebellion in the history of the Roman empire. It took Augustus three years to put it down. Since he himself was by this time an old man, he assigned the command of the huge armies to Tiberius, who was to be his successor on the throne. However, Tiberius' campaign was for a long time ineffective and his nephew Germanicus was sent to assist him in command. Augustus himself changed his residence to Ravenna during the campaign so that he could watch the military operations more closely. The Illyrians were put down definitely in 9 A.D., after three years of heroic struggle, known in history as "bellum Batonianum" or the war of the Batons, from the name of the two Illyrian leaders.

After the crushing of the Illyrian rebellion, the province heretofore called Illyricum was divided into two districts known as Pannonia and Dalmatia. As the Roman territory was increased in later times through new conquests, Pannonia itself was divided into four parts which were frequently renamed and redistributed. The capital of early Pannonia was Petovio (Ptuj) and that of Dalmatia was Salona (Solin). When the Roman Empire was divided after the death of Theodosius the Great (395) between his two sons, Arcadius and Honorius, the line of division between the Eastern and Western Empire passed through the Illyrian and Pannonian territory. The four Pannonias and Dalmatia belonged to the western half, while provincia Praevalis, containing parts of Bosnia, Herzegovina, Sanjak, and Albania, was assigned to the Eastern Empire. The more important towns in Pannonia during the Roman occupation were Aqua Viva (Varazdin), Andautonia (a place near Zagreb), Siscia (Sisak), Servitium (Gradishka), Aquae Balissae (Daruvar), Marsonia (Brod on the Sava), Mursa (Ossiyek), Cibalae (Vinkovtsi), Cusum (Petrovaradin), Taurunum (Zemun), Syrmium (Mitrovitsa), Singidunum (Belgrade), Bassianae (Petrovtsi) and Sopianae (Pechuh). In Dalmatia they were Tragurium (Trogir), Iadera (Zadar), Aspalatum (Split), Epetium (Stobresch), Aenona (Nin), Epidaurum (Tsavtat), Senia (Scnj), Albona (Labin), etc. The more important islands were: Crexa (Tsres), Corcyra Nigra (Korchula), Curicum (Kerk), Arba (Rab), Pharus (Hvar), Pamodus (Pag), and Ladesta (Lastovo).

After ruthlessly crushing out all opposition in a conquered country, the Romans consolidated their power by a number of military measures. The occupation was completed by distribution of garrisons throughout the territory, especially in places of strategic importance. In order to provide easier access to the affected area in case of revolt, the Romans built many roads and bridges throughout the country. Alongside the roads they erected patrol houses or military stations. The rivers were patrolled by fleets of naval craft. Fortifications were built in danger zones.

Pursuing their military policy, the Romans recruited young men in the conquered territory, sending them to distant parts of the Empire for military service. The service lasted nearly a lifetime and the recruits in most cases never returned to their homeland. Besides their task of

oppression and conquest, the Roman soldiers had other functions in the consolidation of the Empire. They built roads, bridges and fortified camps which were the nuclei of the towns that were built around them. They brought with them the Roman cults, usually deifying the emperors and the city of Rome. They were the pioneers of Roman culture by spreading the Latin language to the most remote parts of the Empire.

After establishing the Roman power in a foreign land, the conqueror set out on a course of colonial exploitation. The wealth and luxury of the Romans depended on the taxes they imposed upon their new subjects, and upon the variety and amount of the produce they could extract from a country. According to the Roman Law the land holdings of a province became the property of the Roman State, while the natives could merely rent the land by paying direct taxes (tributum) and an indirect tax (vectigal).

The foundation of the Roman tax system was laid by Augustus, who instituted a general census of the property and population of the Empire. The chief source of income from the direct taxes was the land tax (tributum), which was paid in money or in kind. The artisans and merchants had to pay income tax, while the serfs were paying head tax (tributum capitis). In the absence of legal heirs the property became forfeited in favor of the State (caduca), while 5% inheritance tax was collected when heirs took over the property.

An important source of income was duty on merchandise imported from foreign countries. In Dalmatia and the rest of Illyricum the Roman State drew its income from the mines. Gold mines were productive in Dalmatia and Bosnia, silver came from Bosnia (Domavia, now Srebrenitsa). Lead and iron mines were also exploited throughout Pannonia and Dalmatia. Marble and limestone quarries were operated in Dalmatia. In fact, the Roman State neglected no possibility in attempting to extract for its own benefit all the wealth of the country.

The population consisted of three strata: Greek colonists, who by the time of the Roman conquest became romanized; the Roman merchants and officials; the Illyro-Celtic population which lived in the country devoting itself to farming. The natives remained poor and on the verge of slavery, while the Greek-Roman population of the towns was prosperous. What

scraps of wealth the civil and military authorities left to the country after numerous levies of taxes and tributes, were consumed by the class of merchants and traders in the city.

The complex system of municipal administration and jurisdiction placed further obligations and burdens on the native population. In this way the proverty, insecurity and slavery of the Illyrian farmers served as a foundation of the wealth and luxury of the Greco-Roman cities. For a long time the countryside lived its own life, and it is not clear that romanization was complete even by the time of the fall of the Roman Empire.

The founding and improvement of the towns and cities were the chief Roman contribution to the civilization of Dalmatia and Pannonia. The cities were built after their Roman models. In every town there was a forum surrounded by the town hall and public buildings. It was decorated with the statues of the emperors and men of distinction. Temples and public baths, the water supply, which came from an aqueduct, added to the glamor of the cities.

The normal town or city was called municipium (municipality), while the name of great imperial cities was *colonia* (colony). There were two such cities in the Illyrian territory. One was Salona, assumed birthplace of the Emperor Diocletian, and the other Syrmium in eastern Pannonia. Both of these cities had imperial palaces, amphitheaters with gladiator shows, and arms factories. They also had large populations at the height of their prosperity.

Early Christianity and the Barbarian Invasions

Traces of Christianity go back to the first century in Dalmatia, but the new faith spread with full momentum in the third century of our era. The first bishopric was established in Salona and the first known bishop of this diocese, St. Venantius, died the death of a martyr in Delminum around 257 A.D. At that time the persecutions of Christians were frequent, but the worst of them came after the edict of Diocletian in 304. Many believers in the Christian doctrine were put to death, and St. Domnius (sv. Dujam), the bishop of Salona, together with many of his friends, met violent death. The martyrdom of St. Anastasius (sv. Ostash) also took place at this time. However, after the edict of Constantine in 314, Christianity made rapid strides all over Dalmatia and Pannonia. Many

bishoprics were established. There were bishops in Syrmium, Singidunum (Belgrade), Bassianae, Cibalae, Mursia (Ossiyek) and Siscia. In the fourth century Arianism took hold, as indeed it did all over the lands of the Eastern Mediterranean. This was the teaching which insisted on the predominantly human nature of Jesus Christ. Bishop Valent of Mursia and Bishop Ursacius of Singidunum were the leaders of the movement in Pannonia. Arianism was later denounced as a heresy and gradually died away.

By extending its frontiers so far from its Italian center, the Roman Empire lay open to attacks on a huge perimeter which it could not successfully defend in case of synchronous attacks. There were not only rebellions to contend with, but within the empire itself there were armed conflicts between the governors of various provinces or rival emperors. The attacks upon the empire came from two distant points: from Persians in Asia Minor, and from the northeastern parts of Europe where the various Germanic tribes pressed on the Roman frontiers with ever increasing vigor. Thus in the third and fourth centuries Pannonia became a battle ground on which the Roman empire had to fight for its existence. It was on Pannonian territory that the doom of the empire was sealed, as the westward movement of the European peoples took the force of a migration. After the period of the Marcomannic wars (166-181 A.D.) the Roman empire was on the defensive, and was forced into many humiliating and dangerous compromises. The Roman army itself became diluted with barbarian troops which changed its spirit and undermined its fighting efficiency.

Next the emperors, under pressure, permitted the eastern Germanic Goths and the Carps, a Thracian tribe, to settle within the confines of the Empire. The Carps settled down between the rivers of Drava and Danube in lower Pannonia, while the Goths were permitted to occupy Mesia (Serbia and Bulgaria). After a certain period the Goths moved on westward, invaded the present Croatian territory and by skirting the northern part of Dalmatia, continued their journey of pillage and plunder into Italy. The emperors, unable to curb them, took them as allies. The worst visitation was that of the Asiatic Huns, who established themselves along the course of the lower and central Danube. Under the able administration of Attila, a huge empire was formed that connected central Asia with northeastern Europe. In command of a large and efficient army, Attila invaded the Balkans, raided Italy and penetrated into Gaul, where in 451 A.D. at Châlons-sur-Marne he met Aetius, the Roman general. There he was defeated by the Roman legions and their allies in an immense battle which has been justly termed one of the turning points of history.

After the ravages of Attila's hordes, the empire could no longer regain its ancient power and vitality. The fatal outcome was only a matter of time, and, indeed, the last Roman emperor, Romulus Augustus, was dethroned in 476 A.D. by Odoacer, a Germanic chieftain.

The Coming of the Slavs

The power of Odoacer did not last long, because Pannonia and northern Italy were soon overrun by Ostrogoths under the leadership of Theoderic, a favorite of Zenon, emperor of Byzantium. Odoacer lost his life during the siege of his capital, Ravenna, 493 A.D. After this victory Theoderic was proclaimed king of the Goths and Governor of Italy, Dalmatia and Pannonia. Theoderic's ambitions were directed eastward and he consolidated his power in Sirmium and western Mesia (Serbia). This established the Gothic rule in the entire Illyrian territory. Theoderic was also an ambitious civil administrator and aimed to restore the old security and prosperity of his lands. While the military organization was exclusively Gothic, he respected the civil authorities that were Roman. His reign, 493-526 A.D., saw the revival of prosperity and hope.

After the death of Theoderic the Gothic State soon collapsed. Dissensions and strife in the family of the late king, and the ambitious plan of Emperor Justinian to restore his power over the Gothic territory, caused a bitter and sanguinary struggle that lasted for twenty years, 536-555. At the end of this war the Gothic power was destroyed, and the emperor regained the Illyrian territory. However, the Byzantine authority itself came soon to an end.

As the Gothic masters of Illyricum were engaged in a desperate struggle with the armies of Emperor Justinian, the mass of the Slavic population from behind the Carpathian mountains descended in a continuous stream upon the lowlands of the central Danube. From there they

continued their journey south and west, thus penetrating the Balkan peninsula and the eastern Alpine region. The moment was propitious as the warring factions were busy destroying each other. Moreover, both the Gothic king and the emperor of Byzantium sought the aid of the newcomers in the struggle. Thus the Slavs and Avars penetrated into the areas south of the central Danube and its tributaries. The struggle ended with the collapse of the Gothic State and the elimination from power of the Gothic element. Hence, the newcomers came under the largely nominal sovereignty of the emperor of Byzantium. This set of circumstances gave the Slavic tribes an opportunity to settle down peacefully on the chosen territory, or to continue their campaigns in alliance with the Avars, a Touranian people.

The cause of the Slavic migrations does not seem clear. There was hardly any reason for them to leave their prosperous households. They were either drawn by their military neighbors into the general westward movement of the period, or left their homes on their own initiative due to internal strife and clashes. From their Germanic neighbors the Slavs soon learned the arts of war, efficient army organization, use of better weapons, and especially the advantages of consolidating several tribes into a powerful unit under the authority of a prince (knez, knyaz, kuning).

The New Homeland of the Slavs

After the capture and destruction of the imperial city of Sirmium in 582 by the forces of Bayan, the powerful Avarian leader, a long and bitter struggle ensued between the Avars and the Byzantine Empire. During this period the bulk of Slavic migrations to the Balkans took place. This is a historical event of the first magnitude, which changed the ethnographical picture of the old Thraco-Illyrian territory. The Slavs took part in the sweeping incursions of the long Avarian campaigns, devastating the peninsula down to Salonica (Solun) and Constantinople. In 626 the combined force of Slavs and Avars laid siege to the Imperial Capital, and planned a concerted attack on the city with the forces of the Persians, who were stationed on the Asiatic side of the Bosporus. It was the task of the Slavs to ferry the Persian army across the bay, but in a naval engagement with the Im-

perial fleet their vessels were destroyed. Discouraged over this failure, the Slavic forces raised the siege of the capital and returned home. The Avars continued the siege, hoping to capture Constantinople with Persian aid, but their own forces were destroyed the same year before the walls of the city, while the Persians were defeated the next year (627) near Nineveh. Emperor Heraclius, the victor, followed up his success against the Avars with a policy of friendship toward the Slavs, in order to detach them from the Avarian alliance. He also encouraged uprisings of such Slavs as had been under Avarian domination. Moreover he invited the Croats from their northern homeland to settle south of the Danube and along the Adriatic as his allies against the Avars. Thus in a short time the Avarian power became confined to the territory of the central Danube, including present-day Hungary, Slavonia and Sirmium. It was further weakened by civil wars, and liquidated altogether by the armies of Charlemagne, a century later.

The next move of Emperor Heraclius (610-641) was to subjugate the Slavs. This plan never materialized because of the new dangers that beset the empire by the appearance of the Saracens, and their conquest of Palestine, Syria and Egypt, even before the death of Heraclius. Later the imperial throne was occupied by a succession of weak rulers who could hardly exert any authority over their distant subjects. Thus the Slavs knew of the Emperor only by hearsay.

At the same time the policy of the Slavs was not to defy the authority of the Emperor, nor to devastate his lands. They returned to their old tribal organization and devoted their time to peaceful occupations. This was of great importance for the empire because its Slavic subjects populated the devastated areas, cultivating the deserted lands and rebuilding the cities from ruins. The emperors finally realized the utility of the Slavic colonization, and were greatly reassured by their aversion to military organization. This peaceful and friendly relationship between the Emperor and the Slavic populations was sealed by Emperor Constantine (IV) Pogonate in 678 in an edict, in which he formally recognized Slavic possession of lands within the imperial territory, in exchange for their loyalty to the sovereign. Thus the Slavic occupation of the Roman territory was legalized by the authority of the Emperor himself. The

friendly relationship of the people and sovereign served as a basis for the gradual and peaceful reorganization of the old Slavic tribal system through consolidation of several tribes into a larger unit, and the ultimate formation of a national state.

Meanwhile the Croatian territory acquired definite contours and developed two organizing centers: one in Dalmatia, and one further north in the area comprised by the Danube, Sava and Drava. The first was called White Croatia, and the latter Pannonian Croatia. Another territory called "Red Croatia" extended from south of the Neretva river to Scutari Lake in Albania.

Chapter V

THE SLAVS

NOWADAYS the Slavs represent an exceedingly complicated racial mixture (there is no such thing as a "Slavic race" but merely Slavic 'people', which are, in point of their racial origins, of a multiple composition). To this mixture, in which the "eastern Baltic" elements prevail according to the region, other racial components have also been added, such as the plainly discernible "oriental," "pre-Slavic," "Nordic," and in part "western" racial strains. In the southeastern and northeastern areas Mongoloid (continental Asiatic) features are also conspicuous, being introduced chiefly through Tartars, Kalmuks, and in antiquity through Huns, Avars, etc."

To this definition of the Slavic race by an eminent German anthropologist, Otto Reche*, no valid objection can be made. In fact, it can be supplemented and amplified by reference to that racial promiscuity which is of ever increasing momentum in the historically active regions, or thoroughfares of the world, whereby each century has brought in new racial strains, and only the language remained the common denominator of the heterogeneous community. Such is the case in the Slavic countries of the Balkan peninsula where, through Turkish invasions, races of the Near East have left their imprint on the racial and psychological inheritance of the native populations. But where the other languages made inroads into Slavic areas, there the Slavic element was absorbed by alien populations, as it happened in the historical times in Thrace, Macedonia, Roumania, Greece, Albania, Julian Alps, Styria, Austria, Bavaria, Saxony, Elbe region, Baltic sea coast and Prussia, where the ancient Slavic landmarks were saved only by the geographical, tribal and personal names of the region.

Since most of these foreign elements were introduced through migrations and mixing with the local populations in the new settlements, it is reasonable to assume that the ancient Slavs in their original homeland represented a pure race, or as nearly pure as was at that time possible. Indeed, the graves of the old Slavs, from as recently as the 12th century, disclose en masse a vast preponderance of the dolichocephalic (long-headed) type over the brachycephalic (round-headed) individuals. The difference between them is easily made out, for dolichocephalic individuals have long, narrow skulls, with long and narrow faces, sharp and long nose bones, and round occiput (back of the skull). The round-headed individuals have short round skulls, with short faces, short broad nasal bones, and frequently prominent cheekbones. The Dinaric skull is round, short, with long face, and flat occiput ("planoccipital").*

On the whole, the ancestral Slavic race, on anthropological evidence, may be considered "Nordic" (homo europaeus), with some admixture of the Finnish and Turanian (Tartar) elements. The homeland of the Slavs was, on evidence from several quarters, the river area of present-day Poland, White Russia and the Ukraine, with possible extension into the region of the Carpathian tributaries of the Danube coinciding with the present-day Carpatho-Russia, and the major part of Slovakia. We should not think, however, that such a vast area was densely populated, or that in places other peoples or racial groups were not cohabiting with the Slavs. Thus through a long chain of generations the original racial type has been gradually changed, at first through admixture of the Mongolian blood (homo brachycephalus); later through mixing in Poland, Silesia and Bohemia, with the Sudetic race (homo sudeticus), and in the south with the Dinaric type (homo dinaricus).

The most interesting examples of racial mixture and change have been found in the Slavic provinces of former Austria-Hungary, where thorough anthropological investigations have been made. C. Toldt* reports that out of 118 old Slavic skulls which he measured, 39% were distinctly dolichocephalic, 52.5% mesocephalic and only 8.5% brachycephalic. He established the same ratio also in the old Slavic graves in Central and North Germany. Thus, Toldt arrives at the conclusion that within a thousand

* According to some modern anthropologists the brachycephalic skulls decompose more easily than the meso- or dolichocephalic skulls, hence the relative disparity of their numbers in necropoles of distant past.

* Die Schädelformen in den österreichischen Wohngebieten der Altslaven, einst und Jetzt, 1912.

* Rasse und Heimat der Indogermanen, p. 34ff.

years "the old long-headed Slavic race (in south-ern Slavic regions) *has been fully replaced by the brachycephalic type from among the old local population, or newcomers in this area.*" Thus the present-day Slavs would be the descendants, not of the original Slavs themselves, but of "Slavicized" aliens who adopted their language and culture.

This conclusion applies chiefly to the Slovenian area, but R. Munro* reports that the recent skull measurements of 2,000 individuals in Bosnia and Herzegovina revealed that 93% were brachycephalic (i.e. Dinaric) and only 7% dolichocephalic (long-headed). In Herzegovina proper, the long-headed type dropped to 6%. This is downright amazing since the Glasinac skulls reveal 76% long-headed and only 24% round-headed individuals.

Language

The present-day variety of Slavic languages differing in phonology (pronunciation), vocabulary (word supply) and morphology (inflection system), is in contrast to the old Slavic unity and uniformity in the ancient homeland. The two Slavic scholars, Cyril and Methodius, could translate the Holy Scriptures into their native Thessalian, and be understood in distant Moravia and far-off Russia. Such an experience nowadays is out of the question. Association with alien peoples contributed to the rapid tempo of change. In the middle of the 17th century Juraj Križanić, a Croatian Jesuit, attempted to construct an universal Slavic language through the combination of old Slavic, Croatian and Russian, with the result that no one understood him, although he wrote valuable books in this artificial language. Since the days of Križanić things have changed for the worse, and now without the support of a good dictionary and constant check on morphology and phonetics, no educated Slav can profitably read another Slavic language, unless he has made a special study of it. However, the study of an alien language within the Slavic family is not such a simple affair, because the word supply, in spite of some convenience in etymological derivation, shows overwhelmingly great semantic differences, so that similarity of form is not necessarily attended by affinity of meaning.

* O.C. 136/7.

Broadly speaking, the present-day Slavic languages fall into three groups:

1) the Eastern group, with Russian, Ukrainian (Little Russian) and White Russian;

2) the Western group with Polish, Czech, Slovak and Sorbian, and

3) the Southern group, with Slovene, Croat, Serb (probably Serbo-Croatian) and Bulgarian.

Through years of trade and cultural contacts with neighboring peoples, each of these groups, and even the individual languages, adopted loanwords from different sources. So Russian introduced both regionally and on a national scale words taken from Finnish, Tartar, Iranian, Dutch, German and French. The Polish and Czech languages borrowed mostly from German of all three periods. Slovenian borrowed chiefly from Italian and German, while a certain amount of Turkish loan-words came through Croatian. Croatian borrowed from Hungarian, Italian, German and Turkish, however, disproportionately from each, according to the area of the speakers. Serbian proper is replete with Turkish and Greek words, with a modern tendency to borrow from French. Bulgarians are also deeply in debt to Turks and Greeks for their vocabulary, with some local borrowing from Roumanian.

All these loan words are important and active elements of the vocabulary, being brought into existence by necessity or expedience in trade and crafts. Still more confused is the situation with scientific and professional terminology reproduced in each native language, for they follow entirely different principles of word formation, in best agreement with the local usage. So when it comes to word formation in two languages so close as Croatian and Serbian—considered in a broad application of the term, as one single language—one has to know both forms in order to make sure that they mean the same scientific term.

Thus in spite of their common origin, widespread use of the basic Slavic vocabulary, not too widely divergent phonology and fairly uniform inflections (except in Bulgarian), the Slavic languages of today differ so much from each other that their distant similarity is of little use for practical purpose, and is only of academic interest.

We could produce here a host of examples to show the difference in the use of loan-words, and

methods of word formation for the same ideas, but that would merely prove the well-known fact that no speaker of a Slavic language can make, without special study, proficient use of another Slavic tongue.

Aryans and Indo-European Languages

In spite of their present divergences, the modern Slavic languages can be reduced, with the aid of comparative grammar, to the common parent-forms of the primitive Slavic. For indeed there was once in the remote past a racial Slavic group, with a speech of its own, well-balanced and uniform so that every member of that community could understand it. We have already stated that this racial group was "Nordic," and inhabited the forest bedecked plains extending between the Baltic and the Black Seas. Now if we apply the comparative method to certain languages spoken east and west of this area, we shall be surprised by the similarities of word supply, sound-system and grammatical inflexions of the Common Slavic, with the ancestors of those languages.

Moreover, we shall find that the related Asiatic languages come closer to the original Slavic speech than the older dialects of certain western European languages. And from this group of reconstructed ancient languages we can conclude to parent-forms which will contain all the essential characteristics of each. The sum total of these forms is called by various authors Aryan, Indo-European or Indo-Germanic parent speech. Figuratively speaking, this is the trunk of a tree, with numerous branches and twigs in its crown. Or following another metaphor, this is the main impact on the water surface around which circular waves will form. Striking against some obstacle these waves will form new rings, and continue to spread other rings around the new centers. Neither of these two comparisons is flawless, but both are widely used in order to explain the apparent confusion prevailing among the present-day linguistic posterity, represented by the Latin, Greek, Germanic, Celtic, Illyrian, Tocharian and Hittite, on one side (centum languages), and the Slavic, Baltic (Lithuanian, etc.), Thracian (extinct), Armenian and Indo-Iranian (numerous languages of Persia and India), on the other (satem languages).

Slavs and the Aryan Race

Since the existence of a language postulates the existence of a race which created it and used it, the parent-language of Eurasia had also a parent-race, conventionally called Aryan. The original homeland of the Aryans has been widely discussed among linguists, archeologists and anthropologists and by consensus of the majority of them, it is placed also in the area between the Baltic and Black Seas. A more precise delimitation of this area finds the scholars divided into two groups: one of them (Prof. Kossina, etc.) arguing, on racial evidence, for the Baltic, and the other (Prof. Childe, etc.), on archeological evidence, for the Black Sea. This latter area would almost fully coincide with the homeland of the ancient Slavs, which makes many believe that the Slavs, together with the Lithuanians, never moved out of the homeland of the Aryan aborigines.

However, neither the place where they resided nor the time when they lived, can be ascertained from either anthropological or linguistic evidence. In all probability the Aryans, like many others, carried on in the post-glacial period in some steppe-land, where they domesticated the horse and used it both for draft and riding. Thus they formed fighting cavalry groups, as the conquest of Babylonia by the Hittites would indicate. Their swift and spectacular expansion over the vast plains of Eurasia also indicates a riding warrior race rather than immobile and land-tied peasants of the upper neolithic. Having conquered a peasant district, they may have settled down as a ruling class. In such case they either imposed their language upon the conquered, or were absorbed by the aborigines, leaving no trace behind them.

The Danubian Slavs in Historical Times. Croats and Serbs

The continuity of the widely scattered Slavic populations was disrupted by numerous intrusions. Such was in the first place the German colonizing of the eastern Alpic lands and the Danube valley. Likewise the conquest of Pannonia by the Magyars, the penetration of the Roumanians into Dacia, and further east, the invasions of nomadic tribes along the northern coast of the Black Sea into the lands of the Pontian plain, contributed to the scattering or elimination of Slavic elements along the Danube.

However, two Slavic tribes stood on their own throughout this period, maintaining their independence and defending their new homeland in the face of foreign attacks. These were the Croats and Serbs. Unlike the Slavs of Dobrudja on the western Black Sea coast, and those of the Balkan mountains who first submitted to the invading Utriguri and Kutriguri, and through coalescence with them later, formed the Bulgarian nation, the Serbs could successfully ward off the attacks of nomads. The Croats achieved more. They not only defeated and cleared from their country the powerful Avars, but expelled from the north-western Balkans the Merovingian Franks, after nearly a century of fierce fighting. In the meantime, they established, after the Frankish model, their national state, first under the dukes, and later under the kings of Croatia.

Since no other tribal names are known for the Balkan Slavs, it appears that both Croats and Serbs come from the north as two fully formed peoples, with their common and individual customs and institutions. Thus they were conscious of their tribal unity, in spite of the fact that locally, up to this day, they prefer to use their regional, geographical names.

This latter circumstance gives rise to the theory, accepted by Rachki, Yagich and others, that both Croat and Serb were at first only local names, designating no more than a few clans and then later, through historical process, were gradually applied to an ever wider area and increasing population. Naturally, historical examples of this kind are well known. But that both Croats and Serbs came from well organized countries in the north is indicated by the following facts, in addition to the tradition recorded by Emperor Constantinus VII, Porphyrogenete: 1) the still existing country of the Serbs (Lausitzer Sorben) in central Germany; 2) the recording of two tribes of Croats by the charter of the bishopric of Prague; 3) various place names in Germany derived from Croat settlers; 4) the place name "Harvati" near Athens in Greece; and 5) references from the Anglo-Saxon chronicle, from Nestor's Russian chronicle, and the writings of Arabic travelers.

Coming of Slavs to the Mediterranean

While in the north the Slavs proceeded straight west to the Atlantic, in the south they did not go to Italy, as did the Goths, Langobards, Vandals and other German tribes. The westernmost line of Slavic migrations was the river Tagliamento, Latin Tillamentus, (Slovene: Tilment), at the head of the Adriatic. In other words, the Slavs did not go into the western part of the Roman Empire, but remained in the eastern part controlled by Byzantium. Therefore, they directed their columns south toward the Aegean, Corinthian Bay, Ionian Sea and Adriatic. To use a broad analogy, the Slavs repeated the movement of the Achaean and Doric tribes of the Bronze Age.

The motives for their migration can only be guessed, but can be compared with the mass exodus of the European peasantry to the New World, where in the industrial civilization of America they expected and found an improvement of their lot. The migrating Slavic peasant mass advanced along the fertile river valleys, and thus naturally arrived on the seacoast. This bulk had no interest in the splendid Roman cities, but by-passed them, seeking out the best land for cultivation, and settled there.

Slavic Warriors

There was also another group of migrating Slavs, which had a different objective in mind and was moving toward the large and rich cities, notably Constantinople, Salonica, Sirmium and Salona. This group moved in company with the Avars, whose chief object was ransom, plunder and destruction. According to some writers, the Slavs served the warrior groups of Avars as food-producers, cattle-raisers, and engineering troops, expert in the building of bridges for the passage of the Avar forces. We see them in the battle for Constantinople in 626 A.D., fighting as sailors in their simple boats (monoxyla). Because of the powerful fortifications with which Constantinople was surrounded, the Avar-Slav raiders turned to the fertile lowlands of Salonica, the second largest city of the empire, which they attacked and plundered on many occasions (in 578, 579, 609, 623, 630 and 641 A.D.). In their monoxyles they raided the seacoast of Thessaly, the Cycladic islands, Achaia, Epirus, Asiatic ports and even the island of Crete in 623 A.D.

The Avaro-Slavic campaigns were not confined to the area of the Bosporus, Thrace and the Aegean. They were wide-spread and devastating also along the central Danube, where they captured and sacked the brilliant provincial capital

Sirmium in 582 A.D. Subsequently they invaded Bosnia and Dalmatia, where they captured the provincial capital Salona, Epidaurum (Ragusa), and many other coastal towns. Many of them settled down in the coastal area where later on, after years of stubborn fighting, they had to submit to the incoming Croats.

Such is in brief the story of the warrior Slavs and their Avar associates, who, after the manner of Huns, Goths, Alans, Langobards, Vandals and other barbarians invaded the Roman Empire for the purpose of plunder and conquest.

Slavic Peasantry.

The major and peaceful group of Slavic people moved continuously toward the seacoast and lined the coastal area from Constantinople to Sparta on the Peloponnese. Thence along the Corinthian Bay, up the Ionian coast and finally along the entire length of the Adriatic to the Bay of Trieste and the lagoons of Tagliamento.

Except for the abundance of Slavic place-names and geographic points, and the presence in Greek and Albanian of Slavic loan-words dealing with agriculture and handicrafts, there is nothing nowadays to indicate that the Slavs had ever lived in Greece or in Albania. On the other hand throughout the Croatian lands the Slavic blood maintained itself, and in time absorbed the old Greek, Illyrian, Roman and Venetian population .

The explanation of this peculiar phenomenon is very simple. It is another case of the scattering of forces and thinning of rank which reduces to impotence any originally strong group. Stretched along a seacoast-line of nearly two thousand miles from Constantinople to Albania, the Slavic newcomers were naturally assimilated by the neighboring populations. If armed force was applied against them, they had to succumb, for there was no ethnical background from which they could draw forces of resistance.

Throughout the Croatian coastland the situation was altogether different. There in the background was a solid Croatian population reaching far inland. South and east were Serbs, who at all times stood with the Croats until the last century, when conflicts arose from disposal of the post-Turkish situation. Furthermore, fresh masses of Slavic people came from the north, furnishing new vigor and lifeblood to the old settlers. Thus, neither Avars, Turks, Hungarians, nor Venetians could dislodge the Croatian population from its established seat along the Adriatic coast.

Aryan and Slavic Cultures

Through the agreement in the vocabulary of the historically recorded or still extant Aryan languages, we can reconstruct the word-supply of the parent-speech and go on from there to the foundation of its culture. Since words designate ideas, and ideas in turn reveal the contents of the human mind, with all its knowledge, experience and vision, its capacity for reflection, and power of reasoning, we can say with some accuracy what the original Aryan speakers were doing, thinking or believing. From the supply of words designating agricultural implements and pursuits, we can gather that the Aryans were engaged in farming. Hence, the word for "to plow" in Slavic *orati,* is in Lithuanian *aruoti,* Latin *arare,* and in Greek *aron.* In spite of the difference in ending the root of all these forms is the same (ar-). The Slavic *sĕme*—"seed", is in Latin *semen,* in German *same,* etc. The word for "field" in Latin is *ager,* in Greek *agros,* in German *acker,* etc., because all these forms came from the same Indo-European source. Similarly with the names of crops.

By the same process of comparison we find that Aryans were raising cattle, used dairy products, cultivated bees, hunted, fished, navigated, built frame houses, brewed beer from barley, made a special honey drink, lived a family life, and had a tribal system, with some evidence of rule by chieftains. This would place the time of the Aryan unity in the Neolithic Age, with their separation into tribes and migrations in the Copper or early Bronze Age. Such a conclusion is justified by the fact that in contrast to a uniform terminology for minerals, ores and metals, the terms of metal instruments and products differ in all the historical languages sprung from the Aryan stock.

The Social Organization in Slavic Antiquity

When the Croats settled in their present territory, they continued a social organization that was rooted in ancient Slavic tradition. This organization is what has guided the historical development of the Slavic peoples to the present day, and it explains both their strength nad weakness. It is in contrast to the organization of the Germanic and Roman society. It explains the lack of large military organizations, the absence

of the absolute state and the passive rôle of Slavic history in ancient times.

Contrary to the brilliant armed exploits of Goths, Langobards, Huns and Avars, the Slavs came to the new land more as settlers than conquerors, without any spectacular victories to their credit. But where the military conquerors of the post-Roman era spent their forces and disappeared, after a meteoric flash, from the stage of history, the Slavs have remained to this day. True, it took some time before they learned the art of political organization, yet they could defend and hold the occupied area, and reorganize at the same time. In other Slavic territories, where the native populations retained their ancestral seats, the organization of the state was completed by foreign invaders. Thus, the Russian monarchy was established by the Varengian conquerors of Russia.

Obviously, the ancient Slavs were not politically minded, and not equipped to establish a highly organized government. They were equally loath to submit to any member of their tribe, hence their distaste of monarchy. In case of emergency or war, they would assemble in council and select a leader. As soon as the campaign was over, the army would disband, and the leader (voyevoda) would resign his commission and return to normal life. Thus there was no higher authority over the separate tribes, all of which cherished their independence. Moreover, the authority of the tribal chief (župan) was limited to only a few functions, usually to arbitration and military affairs. Finally, he was subject to control by the council of elders from the brotherhoods of the tribe.

The mainstay of the Slavic society was the brotherhood, *"bratstvo,"* which was made up of several villages located in the same district. A brotherhood was identified by the common surname of its members representing the name of its founder. It had a common cemetery, a common shrine, grazing grounds and forest lands. A disgrace or injury caused to any member of the brotherhood was a challenge to the whole group, which retaliated in common. This gave rise to revenge *"osveta"** and blood feud, which was considered a sacred duty.

Besides husbandry and cultivation of land, the chief occupation was cattle raising and dairy farming. The chief of the brotherhood was called headman *"chelnik."* The brotherhood itself was made up of a number of clans *"rod,"* which lived on separate farms housing several families of the closest blood relations *"zadruga, zadruzhni dom."*

While this social organization made the ancient Slavs independent and prosperous, their military operations were confined to the defense of their farms and lands from the enemy. They did not equip large armies for the purpose of invading distant lands. Theirs was an organization fitted for peace, prosperity and survival, and not for military adventure. They seem to have craved no glory of military conquest, and thus were spared the dramatic exit of the conquerors from the stage of history.

Where the Slavs were conquered by the armed forces of a superior enemy they longed for freedom, and regained it by overthrow of the enemy through uprising or rebellion. Thus Russians regained their independence after three hundred years of the Tartar yoke; the Southern Slavs shook off the Turkish yoke after four centuries of submission. In combat the Slavs were noted for their bravery and tactics. Their weapons consisted of a spear, javelin, sword, dagger, bow and arrow. In battle they carried banners *"prapor"* after the manner of the symbols used by the Roman legions. They built their fortifications in marshes or on hill tops. The Slavic women were noted for their bravery, as they often accompanied their men in battle. The family life of the ancient Slavs was of a high ethical standard, and their hospitality, with the right of refuge, is common knowledge.

* *Osveta* actually means 'hallowing, sanctifying,' apparently a specific Serbo-Croatian word formation. In contrast, the Russian *mest* 'revenge' stands for 'pay-off, retribution.'

Chapter VI

FORMATION OF THE CROATIAN STATE

THE early history of the Croatian people cannot be fully understood if we fail to consider the ethnical grouping of Illyricum and Pannonia.

The Croatian nation and state were to develop among adverse influences and in conditions that were alien to its racial genius, and even in conflict with the traditions of its hoary past. Unifying of clans and tribal units was a slow process quickened now and then by distress or common danger. National unity was achieved gradually by formation of regional authorities which coalesced into larger organizations, and through fusion of provincial governments merged into one national state.

The internal strife and dissensions as well as rivalry of the tribal chieftains retarded the process of national unity, while attack from outside often threatened. Yet on the whole the course of events was favorable to Croatians through the first four centuries in their new home land. It permitted them to adapt their ancient tribal life and customs to the realities of the western world, with its higher civilization. And so they were able to survive as a branch of the Slavic race to the present day. The occasional raids, invasions and exactions from outside were not altogether without wholesome effect. They prompted the scattered Croatian tribes to band together and combine their forces for common defense.

Detached from their racial stock, the Croatians could not have survived as a member of the Slavic race in the center of the Greco-Roman world, but for the continuity of the Slavic tradition inherent in the mass of the neighboring Slavic populations, which settled down in the Balkan peninsula and adjacent territories. Thus they were well protected by the Slavic barrier in the Julian Alps, Noricum, Pannonia, Moesia, Praevalis and Macedonia. The eastern coast of the Adriatic offered a good protection by sea, and a still better one by the long island archipelago that runs parallel to the hilly coast. The deep inlets of the coast and narrow sounds separating the mainland from the adjacent islands discouraged the sea-raiders and even powerful navies from attacking the coast. This circumstance made the country invulnerable from the west, and yet assured it all the advantages of trade, seafaring and peaceful relations with Italy and other countries of the Mediterranean.

The large Dalmatian cities and many islands remained for a long time under the sovereignty of Byzantium and under the supervision of its officials and higher clergy. During this period the population of these cities underwent a great change through infiltration of the Slavic element from the countryside. So the change of allegiance from Byzantium to the State of Croatia took a natural course, hardly noticed and regretted by no one. In the spiritual domain the ever increasing rivalries between Greek Orthodoxy and Roman Catholicism made a deep impression in the life of the Croatian people. On one hand the schism divided the people between the Eastern and Western Church, but on the other it secured them an ever larger share of political and administrative autonomy. Thus the schism hastened the independence both of Dalmatia and the rest of the Croatian territory.

The inroads of the Franks under their Carolingian rulers, checked in part by Arab onslaught, helped further to create a sense of solidarity among the distant Croatian lands and to promote their political security by cooperation, common defense and political union. A brief review of the situation as established soon after their settlement will throw light on the general trend of events in a period where the separate facts and events are dimmed or obscured.

The long stream of Slavic migrations in the sixth and seventh centuries flooded the larger part of the Balkans from the western shore of the Black Sea to the eastern coast of the Adriatic. In the southern direction the Slavs reached the city of Thessalonica (Salonica), the birthplace of the two learned brothers Cyril and Methodius, known as the "Apostles to the Slavs."

Besides the generic names of Slavs or Antes, the tribal affiliations of these settlers remained unknown. Only after the arrival in their midst of the Touranian Utrigurs and Kutrigurs, did they become known as the Bulgarians or Macedonians.

On both banks of the lower and central Danube, the tribe of Branichi or Bodrichi settled to become later Roumanians, and on the right

bank the Timochani took roots and changed later into Bulgarians or Serbians. The left bank of the Drava and the western part of Pannonia were populated by the Slavs who would later form the empire of Kocelj and vanish from the stage of history after the coming of the Magyars. Following the upper course of the Drava and Mura the Slovenes settled down in Noricum, expanding west to the Isonzo and Piave rivers in the Julian Alps.

Under the successful leadership of Samo, they formed a federation of all the western Slavs to resist the pressure of the Franks. This confederacy reached far north into the present German territory, with Thuringia as a rallying center. In Liburnia as well as in inter-fluvial Pannonia and Sirmium (Srijem) the population was predominantly Slavic, yet for the most part under Avar, Frankish and Bulgarian domination.

In the Provincia Praevalis, along the course of Tara, Piva and Lim, affluents of the Drina, as well as on the banks of Rashka and Ibar, tributaries of the Morava, protected by high mountain ranges, lived the tribes that in due course of time were to lay the foundation of modern Serbia. The western part of Illyricum with Dalmatia and the territories extending between the Drina, Bosna, Vrbas, Una, Kupa, Tsetina, Neretva and Bosut, also became populated by Slavs.

There is no doubt that the Slavic tribes of Illyricum, Praevalis and Pannonia came from their northern homeland with about the same language, ancestral customs and worship of the gods. Within the limits of dialect variations they speak nearly the same language to this day, but this unity has not been preserved in religion and political organization. Separation came under the pressure of political and religious differences which intensified the antagonism between the eastern and western half of the Roman empire in their struggle for supremacy. The division line between the two rival powers passed through the Balkans, so that east of that line the Slavic tribes became used to the Byzantine political administration and were attached to the orthodoxy of the Eastern Church, while those west of this line managed to emancipate themselves from the early Byzantine influence, and became identified with the Catholic Church and the culture of Western Europe. Thus the kindred racial elements of Pannonia, Moesia, Praevalis, Macedonia and Dalmatia could not develop into one single nation with a unified state bearing the same name.

Against such a background the destinies of the Croatian people have developed to this day.

Adjustment to New Conditions

From the time of Heraclius (610-641) until about the coronation of Charlemagne (800) as emperor of the Western Roman Empire, very little is known about the life of the Croatian people in their new homeland. This very absence of information indirectly confirms the assumption that the Slavs lived in their respective districts peacefully and free from outside interference. On devoting their efforts to reconstruction of the devastated areas, they continued their traditional ways by tilling the soil and plying a variety of crafts and occupations. In many respects they carried on a life similar to that of the ancient Illyrians before the coming of Romans.

Although lacking dramatic climaxes and devoid of spectacular engagements on the battlefields, this period is of utmost importance for the racial composition and cultural development of the Croatian people, and still more so for the evolution and structure of the early Croatian state. The great political achievement of this period is the shaking off of the Avar yoke and liberation from foreign tutelage. Apparently the Avar ruling class was not expelled from the country, but was assimilated by the bulk of the population. Besides other things, thus we can explain the tradition of the *"banate"* (banovina) and elevation of Ban (from the Avar *Bayan*) to the rank of viceroy, to survive in this capacity until recently. Just as the early Roman monarchy followed Etruscan models, so the Croatians took over this Avar institution as a basis for their new social organization. Somewhat later they adopted the Frankish model, with the name of Charlemagne (kralj "king," literally "Carl") to designate the new institution.*

Remnants of the Gothic, Illyrian and Latin populations were also assimilated. Not only the survival of loan words taken from these languages, but also the persistence of racial traits

---

* The form *kral* "king" comes from the Frankish 'Carl' by way of metathesis or transposition of the liquids (*r* and *l*), common to all the Slavic languages except the Modern Russian. So S.-Cr. *grad* 'town,' Czech *hrad*, Polish *gród*, but Russian *gorod;* related to English *garden*, German *Garten*, etc.

among the present day Croatians, is a sure indication of such a process of absorption. Since peaceful contacts, cooperation and community of interests are the best means to this end, we may safely assume that the Croatians lived for nearly two hundred years in relative peace and prosperity in their respective sections of Illyricum and Pannonia. When the storms of history later broke upon their heads, they were fairly well prepared to defend their territory and independence. They could also adjust their social organization to the new situations while tackling the tasks that confronted them.

Decline of Byzantium

This long period of lull and respite enjoyed by the Croatian people was not accidental. It came at a time when peaceful development was necessary both for conservation of their race and consolidation of their holdings. A series of events of world-wide significance assured the Croatian people peace and tranquility throughout the seventh and eighth centuries. The most potent single factor promoting their security was the gradual decline and military weakening of the Byzantine Empire. With the exception of a few capable rulers, the throne at Constantinople was occupied by weaklings or adventurers who rose to power through military coups or assassinations. The ever increasing stream of powerful barbarian hordes pounding at the frontiers of the vast empire demanded costly military expeditions against the invaders, or heavy ransoms to keep them at peace. In either case the resources of the emperor became depleted, while the revenue was derived from heavy taxes levied on the loyal population.

Even the great Justinian barely escaped assassination in the Nika revolt (532) that would have deprived the world of its most noted lawgiver. Ruin, misery and disorder was common in every part of the empire. Religious strife added to the general bitterness and suffering. Preoccupied with their internal troubles and spending their armed forces on the distant borders of the empire, the rulers of Byzatium were in no position to restore order in their nearest provinces, or rid them of the undesirable barbarians who spread in mass to the very gates of Constantinople. There is no doubt that they were tempted. The prospect was alluring for such a task in the reign of Heraclius, a great military leader. A war of annihilation was spared the Slavs at this crucial moment only by a long series of wars imposed upon Byzantium by two powers of Asia: Persians and Arabs.

War-like Peoples

From the ruins of the Parthian kingdom arose in the third century the powerful state of Persia. The Sassanidan Empire was established over a vast stretch of Central Asia and Iranian territory and with the passing of time its frontiers moved westward at the expense of the Byzantine provinces. Iraq or Mesopotamia, with parts of Armenia and Syria, passed under the sovereignty of the Shah. Further advance of his troups was halted by the heavy tribute paid him by Byzantium. When the ransom money stopped flowing, the Persians resumed their raids in the rich provinces of Asia Minor. Their attacks became especially violent after Justinian's death, when his impoverished successors could no longer meet the Shah's demands for tribute.

The struggle came to a head after the assassination of both Mauricius and his usurper Phocas, when the young and brilliant Heraclius ascended the throne. In rapid succession the Persian armies took Antioch, Damascus and Jerusalem. By 619 they began the invasion of Egypt, while another army reached Chalcedon, a suburb on the Asiatic side of Constantinople. Heraclius did not despair, but at the head of a small army he invaded Armenia in 622, and struck at the Persians from the rear. After five years of successful campaigning he defeated Chosroes, king of Persia, in a decisive battle near Niniveh (627). He pursued the routed enemy to Mesopotamia, where Chosroes took refuge in the stronghold of Ctesiphon. Heraclius then returned to his base in Armenia, where he heard soon that Chosroes had been assassinated in a palace rebellion. His successor signed a peace treaty with Heraclius and agreed to withdraw all his troops from Byzantine territory. On his return to Constantinople Heraclius was received with triumph as a savior of the empire (629). His victory was all the more portentous, as the capital itself was delivered from a long siege by the combined forces of Avars, Slavs and Persians.

The day of reckoning with the barbarians to the north of the capital was approaching. But in the next few years a new storm burst in Asia which prevented retaliation in the Balkans.

This was the Arab drive against the imperial armies stationed in Syria, Egypt and Africa, an attack which opened a new chapter in the world's history.[20]

The Caliphate and World Conquest

At the time of Mohamed's death in 632, Islam's supremacy extended hardly beyond the borders of the Hadjaz, the prophet's native land. Within a year, central Arabia had been brought under the sovereignty of the first Caliph, Abu Bekr, and the Holy War was being carried into Syria and Mesopotamia in defiance both of the Byzatine emperor and the Shah of Persia. The moment was propitious, for these two rival powers were exhausted from their long and bloody wars. Khalid's invasion of Mesopotamia and his victory at Hira (634) added momentum to the drive. Soon all Syria, too, had been overrun. Meanwhile Omar became caliph (634) and the systematic conquest of the old Roman provinces began.

In retaliation Heraclius organized a large and well-equipped army against the daring enemy and early in 636 attacked Khalid's army with great force. The elusive Bedouin troops retreated for over a hundred miles and rapidly withdrew in the valley of the Yarmuk, a tributary of the Jordan. The Byzantine army followed and fell into a trap at the mouth of the Yarmuk where the entire imperial army was annihilated in August 636. After the victory at Yarmuk, where the entire imperial army was annihilated, the conquest of the former Roman proinces soon followed. Palestine was overrun, and with the capture of Jerusalem in 638, and Caesarea in 640, the conquest of the Roman territory north of Egypt was completed. Still more spectacular was the conquest of Egypt. Under the command of Amr-ibn al-Ras, the Bedouin army fell upon the imperial troops in 640, and in 641 took Alexandria and founded the city which later became Cairo. In 643 the adjoining province of Barca (also known as Lybia) submitted to Amr.

Rolling from the Indus and Himalys, the tide of Moslem conquest reached southern Europe. Beginning with a heavy raid on Sicily in 655, the Saracen* campaigns in the Mediterranean continued for a long time unabated. The conquest of Spain was achieved in the

---

* Saracens—literally "orientals."

eighth century, and the second conquest of Sicily, followed by occupation, in the ninth century. Then from bases in Sicily, Corsica, Sardinia and Balearic Islands, the Arabs raided the coasts of Provence and Italy. In 846 they laid siege to Rome. From Sicily the Saracens extended their territory over southern Italy, including Tarento and Bari.

In 841 they sent under the command of Sahib Kalfoun a fleet to raid the ports of the Adriatic, on which occasion they sacked and burned Osor, Ancona, Budua, Cattaro and other cities along both coasts. As allies of the emperor Louis the German, the Croatians, with strong naval forces under the command of Prince Domagoy, attacked the Saracens near Bari, and materially helped the Franks to deliver this city from under the Arab domination (871). The Arab raids in the Adriatic were directed chiefly against the Venetians, who suffered defeat in several naval engagements. However, the Arab raiders did not venture to enter the numerous inlets and bights formed by the coastal archipelago in Dalmatia, and the Croatian lands were spared for the time being.

The Croatians and Islam

Croatian history is interlocked with the destinies of Islam for more than a thousand years. At first Islam appeared as an accidental ally which by his very growth and expansion saved the Croatian people in critical moments of its existence from certain doom. Eight centuries later, when the Moslem hosts appeared on the borders of the Croatian lands, this friendly power changed into an overwhelming destructive force that shook the very foundations of the civilization on which the Croatian people had built up their national existence.

On the other hand, Islam won over a good part of the Croatian population in the occupied territory, and especially in Bosnia and Herzegovina. Mohammedan converts came mostly from the Bogumil (Patarene) sect,* which in the Middle Ages grew into a ruling power in these two provinces. In the course of time the Bosnian Croats became the "bulwark of Islam," as the Croats of the unoccupied territory became famed as the "bulwark of Christianity." Islam brought the oriental culture to Bosnia, and the first monumental buildings ever erected in that country were Mohammedan. It introduced in

---

* Also called the "Bosnian Church."

Bosnia its literature, art, world outlook and ways of life. It attracted the zeal and ambitions of youthful converts. Among them we find many capable scholars, statesmen (e.g. Grand Vizier Sokolovich) and generals (e.g. Omer pasha Latas) of the Ottoman Empire. At present the Mohammedan literature in Bosnia shows sound realism, with a modern and liberal trend of thought.

The epic struggle of the Croatian Christians with the striking forces of Islam will be presented as a major part of this account in chronological order. However, as a savior and guardian of the Croatian people at the very beginning of its historical existence, the rôle of Islam is hardly known, fully misunderstood or unwisely interpreted. Indeed, few will concede that the survival of the Croatian people hinged for centuries on the triumphs of Moslem arms and rapid advance of the Mohammedan civilization. Moreover, after a careful consideration of all the pertinent facts we shall feel justified in saying that the Croatian political and social history begins roughly with the Hegira (hijra), or Mohammed's voluntary exile in 622 from his native city of Mecca. Thus the Moslem calendar records almost with annalistic accuracy the long series of events forming the chronological shaft of Croatian history. The connections are all but obvious.

From a geographical point of view the Croats and Arabs lived on opposite borders of the vast and powerful Byzantine empire. Before the coming of Mohammed there was no other power in the world comparable with the might of the emperors of Byzatium. No single people could defy that power and survive. The examples of the Ostrogoths, Vandals and in part Visigoths are eloquent in testimony of this fact. While the Arabs were living in their own territory and, therefore relatively safe, the Croatians, Avars and other Southern Slavs came as intruders within the boundaries of the Empire. They overran nearly all the Balkans and settled down at the very gates of Constantinople, Salonica and Athens. Without knowing it, they drove a thorn into the flesh of a lion, who had to extricate himself from his fetters before he could destroy the intruder. Without hope of ever winning his clemency the Slavic settlers placed themselves at the mercy of the emperor, who could strike at an opportune moment to expel or annihilate the barbarians.

A generation after the ambitious conquests of Justinian, who assembled the lands of the western Roman Empire, came the impetuous and warlike Heraclius, who restored with his brilliant generalship the prestige and striking power of the imperial armies. He was determined to destroy the military power of Persia, in order to assure the peace and safety of his possessions in Asia Minor and Africa, and after years of strenuous campaigning he succeeded, crushing the armies of Chosroes, the mighty emperor of Persia. A few years of respite and gathering of new forces was all that was required for a campaign in which he would have cleared the Balkans and all Pannonia of the Avars and their Slavic allies. Its military success would have been much easier than the victories of Justinian over the successors of Theodoric, the Ostrogoth.

Who at this point, in the sixth year of Hegira, would have ventured to forecast that both the Croatian and Bedouin tribes were to survive while the Byzantine colossus, with all his power, glory and wealth would go down to his doom as did the western half of the Roman Empire? Yet such was to be the course of history. Like the western Empire in moments of distress, Byzatium was not capable of mustering up enough power to resist synchronous pressure or attacks on all frontiers of the empire. It took eight centuries of continuous struggle to destroy Byzantium, but in the meantime the successors of Constantine and Justinian could never marshall forces large enough to start a successful counteroffensive and recover, except locally, the lost ground. In this process of slow, but unceasing attrition of the Byzantine imperial power, the beneficiaries were the Croatians and other Slavs of the peninsula, who could peacefully go about their daily tasks for centuries, unmindful of the Byzantine menace which made their very names a symbol of bondage and slavery (Byzantine: *Slavenoi* or *Sklavenoi*— "slaves, servants, Slavs").* The arm that broke these chains of bondage and slavery wielded the sword in the name of Islam.

Even if one should doubt that the Croatian people and other Slavs of the Balkan peninsula owe their survival to the Arab campaigns in Syria and Egypt, one cannot deny the synchronous character of the two events: settlement of Croats and other Slavs, with a long period of

---

* The French *l'esclave* and Italian *lo schiavo* 'slave' reflect the same etymology.

peaceful development in their new homeland, coincident with the furious attacks and spectacular victories of the Arabs over Byzantium. Heavily engaged in a desperate struggle to save its vast and rich dominions in Asia Minor and Africa, Byzantium had no energies to spare for a showdown with the unwelcome intruders from the north.

The combined forces of the Avars and Slavs would have been no match for the well-trained armies of the empire, but the auxiliary troops alone could not cope with the invasions from across the Danube. Flanked in its most vulnerable spot, the Empire had finally to succumb, a victim of Justinian's daring policy to conquer the West, while leaving the approaches to his capital unprotected. This set of circumstances so fatal for the destinies of the Byzantine Empire, made possible both the coming of the Slavs to the Balkans, and their undisturbed development within striking distance of the imperial armies.

Equally valuable was the assistance given by the Saracens in the Mediterranean and Adriatic to the peaceful development of the Croatian people and their state. Through their occupation of Sicily and the southern part of Italy the Saracens prevented the formation of a strong Roman-Italian state, which might have coveted the old province of Illyricum across the Adriatic. Similarly, through their control of the Ionian bottleneck and their frequent raids in the upper Adriatic, the Saracens prevented the growth of the Venetian power, for many centuries a deadly foe of Croatian independence. Thus the unwitting hand of Islam gave its protection to the Croatian people both from east and west, assuring them a period of undisturbed peace and growth when they needed it most. It came at a time when the Croatians were changing their ancestral traditions to the western standards of life, and before they had learned how to organize an efficient government and state. Therefore, we venture to say that in the early history of the Croatian people the fortuitous aid coming from the warriors of Islam, was the most important single factor in the survival and strengthening of the young Croatian nation.

Other Ethnical and Cultural Influences

The above digression in our chronological narrative has been made so that we may clearly understand the determinative forces of Croatian history, and the factors behind the specific ethnical grouping and political formations in the northwestern part of the Balkan peninsula. Besides the fact of their coming to Illyricum, there is hardly any other historical event during the lifetime of the Byzantine Empire, so important for the security and peaceful development of the Croatian people as the rise of Mohammedanism and the triumphs of the Caliphate.

In addition to Mohammedanism some other forces worked toward the same end, although not without a measure of hindrance and damage. So the Avars and Bulgarians contributed to the weakening of the Byzantine Empire, yet their expansion brought them into conflict with Croats, both before and after the formation of the national state. Similarly, the Frankish campaigns against the Avars eliminated this element from Pannonia, but the troops of Charlemagne and his successors occupied a large part of the Croatian territory. This in turn brought about the epic struggle of Ludevit Posavski against the Frankish invaders. With the appearance of Hungarians in Pannonia the vestiges of Frankish authority were wiped out both in Illyricum and Dalmatia, but the warlike Magyars who settled down along the Croatian borderlands made themselves a serious menace for the future peace and security of the Croatian people.

The inroads of Vikings or Norse conquerors in various parts of the Carolingian Empire aided materially in checking the Frankish expansion over the Croatian area, and in suppressing that power east of the Adriatic. Not unlike the Arabs, the Normans assisted the Croatian people by attacking the common foe. Finally, the growing wealth and power of Venice was also to affect the destinies of the Croatian State. At its height the Venetian power became as destructive for Croatian independence as the invasion of the Ottoman Turks.

However, the most important social and cultural influence of Croatian history was the introduction of Christianity, chiefly through the missionary activities of the Church of Rome.

Chapter VII

THE FIRST CROATIAN RULERS

THE historical drama of the Croatian people unfolds more rapidly with the expansion of the Frankish power east of the Adriatic under Charlemagne. At the death of his father Pepin in 768, the kingdom of the Franks consisted mainly of the territories of present day France, Belgium and western Germany. This was Charlemagne's inheritance which he shared for a few years with his younger brother Carloman, until the death of the latter in 771. During his lifetime Charles extended the Frankish authority far to the north, east and southeast, until it included the territory of the Lombards, Frisians, Thuringians, Saxons, Bavarians, Avars and Slavs on a wide front extending from the Baltic to the Adriatic Sea. So he became the successor of the Caesars, the restorer of power and vitality in the west, the founder of the first Holy Roman Empire.

Following the example of Pepin, who had conducted two successful campaigns against Aistulf of Lombardy, Charles himself invaded Lombardy in 773, and upon deposing Desiderius, successor of Aistulf, proclaimed himself king of the Lombards in 774. He also confirmed the Charter of 756, by which his father Pepin had Aistulf cede the exarchate of Ravenna and the area of Pentapolis (Ancona) into the permanent possession of the Vatican. This territory hence became known as the Papal State. Thus Lombardy together with Tuscany and the Friulian province came immediately under the Frankish sovereignty, while the duchies of Spoleto and Benevento in central and lower Italy recognized of their own accord the authority of Charles. By establishing a march in Friulia, Charles made it a springboard for subsequent campaigns against the Slovenes and Croats.

Conquests of Charlemagne

Having completed his campaign in Italy, Charles once more turned his attention to the north, determined to bring under Frankish dominion all the Germanic tribes living hitherto independently. He had already made one campaign against the Saxons, in 772, and after tightening his hold on the Alamans, Thuringians and Frisians, he made the subjection of Saxons his main objective. Year after year he returned to the campaign until in 785 he had annexed all of Saxony as far as the Elbe, while the Saxon chieftain Widukind submitted to Charles' authority and accepted the Christian faith. Charles then was free to move against Bavaria, which he occupied in less than two years, 787-88, practically without bloodshed. With Bavaria, Charles acquired also Carinthia, a Slavic country, which was at that time a Bavarian dependency. From this region the authority of the king spread rapidly southeast along the coast, probably after the example of the duchies of Spoleto and Benevento. Byzantine Istria also became Frankish.

In possession of many new lands, Charlemagne had to think of their security and protection. They lay open to attacks from the east, and the Avars were a powerful neighbor, known for their many raids in Italy, Bavaria and adjacent lands. In the days of Charles they were no longer so formidable as they had been in the sixth and seventh centuries, yet their power had to be reckoned with. They still held a strategic position along the central and lower Danube, where they inhabited the lowlands of Pannonia and Dacia. They lived in fortified camps of circular shape, and were ready for action on short notice. After a preliminary raid in 791, Charles sent another army from Carinthia against the Avars. After two years of strenuous warfare (795-96) the Frankish forces crushed the Avar resistance. The campaign ended with the capture of the Avar strongholds and seizure of the fabulous wealth massed by the Avars through centuries of looting and plunder. With this defeat the Avars vanished from the scene of history, without leaving a trace of their language and culture behind them. The Avar disaster relieved the Croats and other Slavs in the Balkans of the continuous harassment and overlordship of Bayans successors.*

As a result of the Frankish victory over the Avars two great events took place: the conversion of the Pannonian Croats to Christianity and the establishment of Frankish rule in the

---

* Even though their political power became extinct, racially the Avars, through a long series of generations, maintain themselves to this day. The name *Bavaria* and *Bavarians,* assumed a contraction of "Bayu-Avar," together with distinct phenological characteristics of its people indicate their survival.

territory between the Sava and Drava extending to their confluence with the Danube.

Voynimir, duke of Pannonian Croatia, had taken part in the campaign against the Avars and contributed to its success. He now became a vassal of Charlemagne's, expected to pay tribute and to supply troops when called upon. Reflecting the new situation, the Croatians took the name of Charlemagne (*Karl*) to denote the office of the king. Most other Slavs took over this word with the same meaning, since Frankish authority was extended also over the Slovenes, Slovaks, Czechs, Serbs and Vilts, from the Adriatic to the Baltic Sea.

From among the many marches which Charles established in his extensive borderlands for the defense of the frontiers of the kingdom, the most important for Croatian history was that of Friulia. The power of the king was exercised in this region through the authority of the Friulian margrave, and all Frankish inroads in Croatian territory were directed by this official. So in 799 margrave Erich of Friulia attempted to overrun Dalmatian Croatia, but was defeated near Tersat (above Fiume and Sushak) and slain in the battle. However, a new force of the Franks soon conquered the territory. This acquisition was ratified in a peace treaty, concluded in 803 between Nicephorus, emperor of Byzantium and Charlemagne. In exchange for his renuciation of Dalmatian Croatia, Nicephorus retained the coast towns and islands along the coast. Soon another war broke out between the two emperors, and after a naval defeat of the Franks, a new peace was concluded in Aachen (812), confirming the former treaty. Thus Dalmatian Croatia remained under Frankish domination, and the Frankish missionaries soon converted the Dalmatian Croats to Christianity. A special Croatian bishopric was founded in Aenona (Nin) under the direct jurisdiction of the Pope. The Croatian duke, who was elected by the people, submitted to the authority of the Friulian margrave. The first known Dalmatian duke is Visheslav, a Christian, who also resided in Nin between 800 and 810. The first Croatian cathedral erected in Nin, was named after Asel, a Frankish saint.

Wars of Lyudevit Posavski against the Franks

After the death of Charlemagne the imperial throne passed to his son, Louis the Pious (814-840), a well-intentioned, but ineffective ruler.

During his reign the high officials of the empire abused the power of their rank, in promotion of their selfish ends and for personal aggrandizement. Through their exactions the lot of the people became difficult and there was considerable disaffection. The conditions in the Friulian march were no better and the oppressive rule of violence and depredations by margrave Kadallo brought the Croatian people of Pannonia into a rebellious frame of mind.

The duke of Croatian Pannonia Ludevit (literally: man-healer), called Posavski, took to heart the grievances of the common people and aroused by the injustice wrought on his folk by the imperial officials, sought to remedy the situation. After several protests sent to margrave Kadallo remained ineffective, Ludevit sent special envoys to the imperial court in Heristal (818), complaining to the emperor about the oppressive rule of Kadallo. Unable to obtain redress from the emperor, Ludevit and his council decided to call the people to arms. Apprised of the insurrection, Kadallo advanced at the head of the army (819) against the rebellious prince. However, Ludevit defeated the imperial army and Kadallo returned to Friulia, where he died not long after.

In spite of his victory over the Friulian margrave, the Croatian duke sued for peace and offered to the emperor the terms under which he could submit to his sovereignty. The emperor rejected Ludevit's plea, yet expressed willingness to consider other terms. At this turn Ludevit decided to overthrow the Frankish rule and restore full independence of the Croatian people. Realizing the magnitude of the task, Ludevit sought alliance among the neighboring Slavic peoples, smarting under the Frankish rule. The Slovenes, Dacian Slavs and Serbs agreed to join him, but the Dalmatian Croats, influenced by the ambitious and scheming duke Borna (810-821), refused to join the alliance. Borna preferred to remain a vassal of the emperor, and took his position with the margrave against Ludevit.

Loyal to their pledge, the Slovenes soon took up arms against the Franks, and Ludevit hastened with his own troops to their aid. In the meantime a Friulian army, headed by margrave Balderic invaded the Slovenian lands. The two armies had several clashes, without coming to a decisive battle. Apparently the forces of Ludevit had been ambushed without serious injury

and he decided to retreat. However, his retreat was attended by a series of spectacular victories, the echo of which rang far and wide. While he was absent from Pannonia, the Dalmatian duke Borna as an ally of the Franks, invaded his land. The army of Ludevit fell upon the invaders and in a battle on the banks of Colapis (Kupa) near Sisak annihilated the Dalmatian army. Borna himself barely escaped death. In retaliation, Ludevit invaded Dalmatia, smashing the remainder of Borna's forces. Borna took refuge in a fortification, but did not attempt to meet the invaders in the open. After some lingering in Dalmatia, Ludevit returned with his army to Sisak, his capital.

As the news of Ludevit's victories spread, the rest of the Slovenian population joined in the campaign, and the general disaffection reached as far as the river Socha (Isonzo) in the west. The matter was brought up in the imperial diet early in 820, and the emperor decided to send three armies to the land of the rebellious duke. Borna was present at court and helped to work out a plan for the campaign against Ludevit. So in the spring of the same year three large Frankish armies advanced against the Slovenes and Pannonian Croats. Resistance was stiff, but both territories were overrun. Retreating before the overwhelming force of the imperial troops, Ludevit took refuge with his army in an impregnable fort and watched the movements of the enemy. After plundering and devastating the country, the Frankish army returned home without having destroyed the power of Ludevit, now free to prepare his country for further struggle and resistance.

The Franks were back in the summer of 821 with three new armies, plundering the towns and laying waste the fields, but they could not defeat the army of Ludevit, nor force him into submission. Again they retired from Pannonia. This new failure caused the emperor to order a campaign with overwhelming forces. It was incidentally the tenth army to be sent against Ludevit. At the news of the impending invasion Ludevit withdrew his troops to Serbia, obviously with the intention of staging a comeback with the united forces of the neighboring Slavs.

Meantime the traitorous Borna died, and Vladislav (821-835) was placed in charge of the government in Dalmatia. Believing that he could win the new duke over to his cause, Ludevit went to Dalmatia. He made the fatal error of accepting the hospitality* of Lyudemisl, an uncle of Borna. Probably at the instigation of the Franks, Lyudemisl assassinated the great leader. Although death cut short his plans, Ludevit Posavski stands out as the greatest national figure of the early Croatian history. He had the courage to defy the power of a giant, and vision enough to unite all the oppressed Slavs against the common foe. From his struggles we may conclude that he had planned a large Slavic state along the course of the Danube, which would have succeeded the Avar power.

Bulgarian Raids in Pannonia

After their conquest of Ludevit's land the Franks were not left undisturbed to consolidate their holdings. Under the pressure of a Bulgarian invasion in 827 they had to retire from the country, while the Bulgarians overran most of the territory and left their own chiefs in place of the Frankish counts. In the following year the Friulian march was abolished, its territory reapportioned and its defense reorganized. Friulia, Istria and Croatian Dalmatia were formed into one unit and transferred to the kingdom of Italy, while Carinthia and Pannonia on both sides of the river Drava were subordinated to Louis the German, king of Bavaria. Louis resumed the war with the Bulgars, rather ineffectually. In 829 the Bulgars made a successful drive against the Franks but both being vitally interested in other theaters of war, the situation remained largely stationary, and a peace treaty was concluded in Paderborn (845). Before this treaty, the Bulgars controlled the eastern half of Slavonia, Sirmium, Belgrad and the northern part of present-day Serbia, while west of that area duke Ratimir (829-838) asserted his power with Bulgar aid.

After the treaty of Paderborn the Bulgars retained only Sirmium; the rest of Pannonian Croatia seems to have fallen then or a little later under the authority of the Bavarian king. The administration of the territory during this period is somewhat uncertain, since the sources speak only of a Croatian Pannonian duke,

---

* Hospitality or guest-friendship was sacred among the Slavs. It offered the right of refuge to those suing for it. The guest, in Slavic tradition, was a privileg person, always welcome to a Slavic home.

named Braslav (880-896), who was a loyal vassal of the emperor. Upon the election of Charles the Fat as emperor (884-887), Braslav came to render homage to his chief.

During the reign of Arnulf (877-899) Braslav assisted the emperor with advice and troops in his war against Svatopluk, duke of Moravia. During this campaign the Magyars appeared on the Danube, joining the forces of Arnulf against Svatopluk. At the same time Arnulf appointed Braslav duke of northwestern Pannonia (north of Drava), assigning to him protection of this region from the Magyars. However, during the reign of Arnulf's son, Louis the Child (889-911), the Magyars overran Bavaria, and since that time no trace is left of the Frankish rule in Croatian Pannonia. Instead we find soon the Croatian Pannonia in close cooperation with the Dalmatian Croatia, both of which will form a united Croatian kingdom.

Frankish Rule in Dalmatian Croatia

The first three Dalmatian rulers, Visheslav, Borna and Ladislav, are known to have been little more than loyal vassals to the Frankish king. However, the Frankish overlordship over the Adriatic coast ended sooner than it did in Pannonia. This change came about in part through the resistance of the Dalmatians to foreign domination, and in part through the mutual antagonism of Venice, Byzantium and Carolingian emperors. The internal strife in the Western Empire and gradual weakening of the Byzantine power aided the cause of emancipation materially. At the same time the Saracen domination of the sea and their naval victories over Venice kept this maritime power in check for a long time and helped to encourage the trade centers that were forming along the eastern coast of the Adriatic.

Torn by three years of internal warfare, Byzantium lost the island of Crete in 826 and Sicily in 827 to the Saracens. This was a signal for the Balkan Slavs to rise and overthrow the authority of the emperor. Thus the balance that had been established for two centuries between Constantinople and the vast Slavic territory north and west of the imperial city was definitely upset. The Narentian Slavs inhabiting the seacoast and its hinterland between the rivers of Tsetina (Tilurus) and Neretva (Narenta), were also drawn into the stream of general unrest. Having the advantage of numbers and good naval

forces, the Narentians (Neretvlyani) isolated the Dalmatian cities and occupied the nearby islands, including Mlyet, Korchula (Corcyra), Hvar (Pharos) and Brach (Brattia). In order to save them from fusion with the Slavic population, and from merger with the hinterland, Emperor Michael II made a treaty with Louis the Pious, son of Charlemagne, which guaranteed the independence of the imperial territory in Dalmatia.

Struggles with Venice—Mislav (835-845).

The loss of imperial authority along the eastern Adriatic coast expedited the emancipation of Venice from Byzantium. But in attempting to seize control of the Adriatic and exercise the policing function on that sea, hitherto an imperial privilege, Venice met with the stubborn resistance of both Narentians and Croatians. Her first attacks were directed against the Narentians, who as pagans did not enjoy the protection either of the Byzantine or Western emperors. The Croatians of Dalmatia were protected by the authority of Lothair (840-855), who was both emperor of the West and king of Italy. Thus the Venetians at first avoided conflict with the Croatians.

On the other hand, the growing sea power and daring raids of the Narentians who cruised all over the Adriatic, and raided both the Italian and Istrian coasts made them close rivals of the Venetians. Soon war broke out between the two rivals. Under the reign of duke Mislav (835-45) the Croatians joined the Narentians in their struggle against Venice.

The course and outcome of this war is not known, except that the Venetian doge,* Peter Tradonicus, came personally to the court of Mislav and signed a treaty. Having made peace with the Croatians, Tradonicus approached the Narentian duke Druzhak with the same mission. However, the peace with the Narentians was not of long duration, because the next year (840) saw the Narentians win a great naval victory over the Venetians on the high seas. The Venetian sea power was at this time on an ebb. Between 820 and 842, Venice suffered three naval disasters in close succession at the hands of the Arabs. The Narentians took over the ascendancy in the Adriatic, and in 846 they even raided the town of Caorle, a suburb of Venice.

* Latin *dux*, Italian *duce* 'leader, duke.'

Chapter VIII

THE FIRST NATIONAL DYNASTY

THE reign of duke Mislav was followed by that of Terpimir (845-864), founder of a dynasty that was to rule over two hundred years. Like his predecessors, Terpimir was a vassal of the king of the Franks and emperor of the West. After the suppression of the Friulian March in 828, Dalmatia, together with the other Friulian dependencies, came under the immediate authority of the king of Italy. During the civil wars caused by the division of the empire among the sons of Louis the Pious, the Italian authority in Dalmatia became nominal, and both Mislav and Terpimir took advantage of the dynastic wars to strengthen their own power. During this period the capital of Dalmatia was transferred from Nin (Aenona) to Klis.

The weakening of the central power tended to exalt the authority of the local prince. Both Mislav and Terpimir exercised nearly sovereign power over extensive areas. Their principal function was to ccommand the armed forces, administer justice and protect the Church. Each held a court (curtis) after the fashion of the Frankish kings. The household of Terpimir was distinguished by wealth and glamor. In his palace in Klis he was surrounded by important tribesmen (Zhupani) who helped him with their counsel in the affairs of government. The clergy formed a special chapel under the authority of the archchaplain who administered the Holy Sacraments to the family of the duke, and who was also in charge of the chancellery and legal affairs of the prince.

As in the court of Charlemagne, here, too, the affairs of the sovereign's household were not strictly separated from the affairs of the State. Both services were rendered at the same time by a retinue of high court officials. Chief among them was the chamberlain acting as a treasurer of the State and governor of the palace. The court larder and the estates supplying it, were in charge of the seneschal.. The butler supervised the cellar, while the constable or marshal had authority over the stable of the court. This office carried with it the high command of the army.

Justice was administered by the common law of the native tribes, and in part probably after the Salian Law of the Franks. The cities, on the contrary, were following the Roman tradition as codified in the edicts and Pandects of Justinian. Terpimir assumed the title: "By grace of God the duke of the Croatians" (dux Chroatorum iuvatus munere divino).[21]

Two important events fall in the reign of Terpimir. A Bulgarian invasion of the Dalmatian territory led to war. In a battle fought in 855 Terpimir defeated the Bulgarian army and forced the Bulgarian Khan Boris to sue for peace. This episode is significant, because it shows that Bulgaria and Dalmatia had a common frontier, probably somewhere in the northeastern part of Bosnia, or on Machvan territory (present-day Serbia). Toward the end of Terpimir's reign a momentous struggle broke out in Constantinople, which had for its immediate effect the schism or separation of the Greek and Latin churches (857-868).

The schism created a great confusion among the Balkan Slavs and advanced problems which still await their solution. Due to the growing estrangement between the two churches and the ever widening chasm between the two political dominions, a lasting union between the Croats and Serbs, in spite of the propitious outlook at the beginning, never could be effected. The Bulgars were divided between the two churches, by assuming first the Byzantine ritual (865-866), then changing the allegiance to the Church of Rome (866-870), and finally returning to the Greek Orthodoxy during the eighth ecumenical council in Constantinople (870).

As a result of some dynastic quarrels at home, and following intervention by Rome, Photius, the patriarch of Constantinople, denounced as anathema some teachings of the Western Curch, and in 867 excommunicated the pope Nicholas I. This move had a stunning effect both on the clergy and laity throughout the Christian world. The clergy living under Byzantine sovereignty rallied around Photius and severed their ties with Rome. The separation of the eastern clergy created grave problems in Dalmatia, because the cities were still under the Byzantine rule, while the countryside was administered by the native clergy of Roman-Frankish allegiance.

The two factions were soon at cross purposes, and friction in the ranks of clergy continued through many generations in the future.

Domagoy (864-867)

Terpimir was succeeded by Domagoy (864-867). His reign was momentous in early Croatian history, because it brought about the struggle for independence from the Frankish overlordship. A number of outside factors precipitated this struggle. Upon Domagoy's accession to the throne Dalmatia was suddenly attacked by the naval forces of Orso Particiaco, the doge of Venice (865). In view of the peace treaty of 839 binding both Venice and Croatia to mutual peace and friendship, the attack of Particiaco came as a surprise, which Domagoy was not prepared to meet. Therefore he sued for peace and gave hostages for fulfilment of the terms of the treaty.

In the next year (866) a strong Arab fleet appeared before Dubrovnik (Ragusa), and laid siege to the city. Exhausted by the strain of a 15 months siege the Ragusans appealed for aid to Basil I, emperor of Byzantium. Basil, who was eager for military glory, sent a strong imperial navy under the command of Admiral Nicetas Oriphos to relieve the Ragusans in their distress. On appearance of the fleet the Arabs raised the siege and fled.

The fame of the exploit at Dubrovnik restored the emperor's prestige throughout the Balkans and along the Adriatic coast. The Slavic tribes of southern Dalmatia renewed their allegiance. Only the proud Narentians refused to give up their independence by submitting to Constantinople. This favorable turn of affairs encouraged the emperor to form some ambitious plans. If he could eliminate the Arabs from the Adriatic and southern Italy, he would considerably strengthen his position in the Mediterranean. Yet the episode of Dubrovnik showed clearly that this could not be achieved without the supporting action of sizable land forces. Obviously the Frankish emperor alone could supply the necessary land troops.

Siege and Capture of Bari (871)

Spurred by the Arab defeat at Dubrovnik, Louis II, son of Lothair, who combined both the title of the Frankish emperor and king of Italy (855-875), came similarly upon the idea that the Arabs could be expelled from Italy by armed force. He coveted possession of southern Italy and Sicily no less than his imperial colleague, Basil. To Byzantium the claim of Louis was as much of a violation of its legal rights as the Arab occupation of this territory. It was a three-cornered fight, in which Byzantium and the Saracens were to lose, while the Croatians and other Adriatic Slavs had to fight in both imperial camps, in order finally to rid themselves of the authority of both.

The momentous events developed as follows. In 867 Louis sent an army against Bari, the chief Saracen stronghold in southern Italy. The slow progress of the campaign soon convinced the emperor that the city could not be taken without an effective blockade of the seacoast by a strong fleet. At this turn Basil, who was eagerly watching the Bari episode, thought that his opportunity had come and he offered an alliance, with naval aid, to Louis. The Frankish emperor accepted the proposal, and Basil took immediate steps to organize a large sea force. He ordered his new subjects from across the Adriatic, including Travunyani (Trebonians), Konavlyani (Canalese), Dubrovchani (Ragusans), the Dalmatian cities and islands to send all their naval forces to the siege of Bari. In charge of the operations was the veteran admiral Niceta Oriphos. In the summer of 869 Oriphos appeared with a fleet of four hundred vessels before Bari, in order to supplement the land action of the Frankish army. On his arrival, however, he found only scanty troops stationed before the beleaguered city, instead of the large Frankish army that had been agreed upon between the two emperors. Oriphos was deeply disappointed, and suspecting bad faith on the part of the Frankish emperor, raised the siege and left for Constantinople.

Struggle for Independence and National Unity

On the other hand, Louis II, seeing the vast naval power of the Adriatic Slavs, did not object to Oriphos' withdrawal. He also had Slavic subjects along the northern coast of the Adriatic, and made up his mind to use the naval resources of Dalmatian Croatia. So he summoned Domagoy and the Dalmatian Croats to appear with all their naval forces before Bari and assist him in capturing the city. Domagoy collected an impressive fleet, with considerable

land forces, and hastened to the aid of the emperor. With the combined land and sea operation of the Croats and Franks, Bari was taken on the second of February 871. This event raised the prestige of Domagoy—the Pope called him *dux gloriosus*—glorious duke—and his Croatian warriors. At the same time Louis took possession of southern Italy, while Basil I turned his vengeance on Domagoy and devastated the Croatian islands.

The fact was that the antagonism between the two emperors had begun to show. Seizing upon a minor incident caused by some Narentian pirates, Basil sent Admiral Oriphos to raid the Narentian territory and harass its inhabitants. Apparently as an extension of this operation the imperial forces landed all along the Croatian coast, destroying the cities and dragging their residents into slavery. There is little doubt that with this attack Basil aimed at forcing Domagoy and his host to abandon the emperor's camp at Bari, and rush to the defense of their native land. However, Domagoy refused to play Basil's game, and continued the siege of Bari until its fall.

Meanwhile, the troops of Oriphos had conquered the Narentian area and all the lands from the mouth of Tsetina (Tilurus) to that of Drim, imposing the emperor's authority upon the land of Hum and Praevalis as well. Thus for the loss of southern Italy Basil was compensated with the gain of an extensive area on the eastern Adriatic coast and its hinterland. The Frankish emperor protested this action, demanding the return of the Croatian prisoners and reparations for all damage done by Byzantine troops in the Croatian coast land. Thus ended the friendship of the two emperors, while the Balkan peninsula became divided between the Bulgarian, Byzantine and Frankish power.

After their victorious return from Bari, Domagoy and his warriors were confronted with serious tasks at home. The country had been laid waste by the Byzantine marauders. Moreover, a new war broke out (873) with Venice. The Narentians joined the forces of Domagoy in a long and bitter struggle against the Venetians. By the abuse and maledictions heaped upon Domagoy in various Venitian documents we may judge that the course of this war favored the Croatian and Narentian arms. In the midst of the conflict, Emperor Basil through some of his adherents, undertook to stir up dis-

sension in order to create a favorable opportunity for the assassination of Domagoy. This was a familiar business to Basil, who had ascended the imperial throne after assassinating his predecessor Michael III (842-867), and his uncle Bardas. The plot against Domagoy failed, and one of the conspirators was put to death.

The Last War with Franks

In 875 emperor Louis II died and left Italy to his nephew Carloman (876-880), son of Louis the German. As a dependency of Lombardian Italy Croatian Dalmatia also fell under the German sovereignty. This change of allegiance was repugnant to the Dalmatians and they rose against the Frankish rule. After years of struggle both on land and sea the Croats of Dalmatia overthrew the Frankish rule forever. In 876 they defeated the Frankish army headed by Kotsel of Pannonia, a Slavic leader in the employ of the German king. Kotsel himself fell in the battle.

On sea the Croats had to engage the Veneians, who were supporting the Franks in this war. According to the chronicle of Emperor Constantine Porphyrogennete. this war lasted seven years and was extremely brutal. For example he states that the Franks killed Croatian infants and threw their bodies to the dogs. In the midst of the struggle, death overtook Domagoy, a resolute man of great courage, ability and vision. There can be no doubt that he was the greatest ruler in the early history of Dalmatian Croatia.

Ilyko (876-878)

While the war of liberation was still raging, Domagoy's son Ilyko (876-878) succeeded to the ducal throne. In order to concentrate on his struggle with the Franks, the new duke made a treaty of peace and friendship with Venice. However, the Narentians did not join in the treaty and continued their naval war with the Venetians. Neither the course nor the outcome of this war between the Narentians and the Venetians is known. In the meantime the authority of Ilyko was overthrown by Zdeslav (878-879), a son of Terpimir.

Zdeslav (878-879)

During the short reign of Zdeslav (878-879) important politcal changes took place in Damatian Croatia. For reasons of his own Zdeslav

recognized the sovereignty of the emperor Basil, and thus took his country from under the Frankish rule to that of Byzantium. Furthermore, Zdeslav invited Greek missionaries who converted the Narentians and the residents of Praevalis to Christianity, attaching them to the Eastern Church. This brought the new duke into open conflict with the Croatian bishopric of Nin (Aeona). The people at large watched with misgiving the moves of Zdeslav, and became alarmed at the prospect of Greek overlordship in the wake of the bitter struggle to shake off the Frankish yoke. Amid a general disaffection Branimir, a prominent tribesman, rose against the duke and slew him. With the consent of Theodosius, bishop of Nin, and supported by his friends, Branimir seized the power. His reign (879-892), became a turning point of early Croatian history for he established the political independence of the new Croatian State.

Branimir Establishes the Independent Croatian State

In keeping with his anti-Byzantine course, Branimir sought to establish friendly relations with the Holy See. For this reason he sent bishop Theodosius to Rome, affirming his loyalty to the pope and the Western Church. Gratified over this act of friendship, Pope John VIII, bestowed his apostolic benediction upon the duke, the people and the land of Croatia in a solemn mass celebrated on Ascension day (May 21, 879) over the tomb of St. Peter. Thus a tie was formed between the Croatian people and the Church of Rome that has not dissolved to this day. After this event Pope John VIII made a strenuous effort to attach the Dalmatian cities also to his authority.

In the midst of the strife created by the activity of patriarch Photius, this policy failed, but after prolonged negotiations the Pope induced the emperor and patriarch of Constantinople to waive their claim to the diocese of Nin, and to renounce all sovereignty over the Croatian lands. Thus Dalmatian Croatia became in 880 politically independent, with no secular sovereignty over the power of the duke as the chief of state. Theodosius returned the next year (881) to Rome and was consecrated by the Pope among solemn rites as the first "Croatian bishop of Nin." In a special bull John VIII confirmed this important act, and promised the blessing and protection of the Holy See in return for loyalty on the part of the Croatian people. He also invited the Croatians to send their representatives to the Holy See, and promised to send his own legates to apprise him of the needs and wishes of the Croatian people.

Through a sequence of fortunate events the power and prestige of Branimir rose to a point where even Emperor Basil deemed it best to cultivate the friendship of the Duke of Croatia. Toward the end of his reign Basil instructed the population of the Dalmatian cities and islands to pay annual tribute to the Croatian ruler as a rent for the use of the lands outside the city walls, and as a token of good will for the continuation of friendly and peaceful relations with the Croatian authorities. The amount of this tribute would be deducted from the taxes paid by the towns and islands to the emperor. This decree is significant of the future assimilation of the cities and their populations within the body of the Croatian nation.

After the death of Basil I a new attempt was made to reconcile the ecclesiastic organizations of the imperial cities to the Croatian bishopric of Nin. With the death of Marinus, archbishop of Spalato (Split), in 887, sponsors of the religious unity of Dalmatia were given an opportunity to advance their plans. The residents of Split elected Theodosius, bishop of Nin, as their archbishop, thus giving proof of their friendship both for Rome and the Croatian people. Theodosius accepted the high office, but retained also his Croatian diocese of Nin. Branimir favored the action of Theodosius and gave him his support. Although protests came from Rome, Theodosius retained his dual office until his death. Concerned over attacks of the Arabs, Stephen V, the new Pope, had to rely on the friendship and armed support of Leo VI, the Wise (886-912), successor of Basil I on the throne of Byzantium. In such circumstances the Pope was unwilling to sacrifice the good will of the emperor for administrative friction, and discouraged further cementing of ties between the municipal dioceses and the Croatian bishopric of Nin. Thus this temporary union was dissolved and the imperial Dalmatian Church continued under the authority of the patriarch of Constantinople.

Submission of Venice

Some foreign political developments also contributed to the enhancement of Branimir's power and prestige. In 887 Peter Candiano, the doge of Venice, landed at the head of large naval and land forces on the Narentian coast, meaning to conquer the country and subjugate its warlike population. However, the Venetian armies suffered a crushing defeat at the hands of the Narentians, and Candiano himself fell in the battle fought near the town of Makarska. This disaster forced Venice into a humiliating peace, by the terms of which the doge agreed to pay an annual tribute to the Duke of Croatia as the sovereign ruler of the Narentians. Following the example of the Byzantine emperor, the Venetians preferred to pay a price for peace and contribute in kind toward friendly relations with their southeastern neighbors. Through this sacrifice Venice gained much in good will and prosperity by assuring herself unchecked navigation and full freedom of commerce on the Adriatic seaboard. After the conclusion of this treaty there is no record of conflict or struggle between the Croatians and Venice for more than a century.

Dynastic Struggles in Serbia

During the reign of Branimir a quarrel began in neighboring Serbia that lasted for a full generation. Upon the death of Duke Vlastimir Prosigoyevich in 850 the throne was occupied jointly by his three sons: Mutimir, Stroyimir and Goynik. This division of power soon found the brothers in arms against one another. Mutimir finally overpowered his brothers and sent them into exile and captivity in Bulgaria. He kept as a hostage at his court his nephew Peter, the son of Goynik. Unwilling to stay with his uncle, Peter Goynikivoch fled to Croatia and took refuge at the court of Branimir. Mutimir died in 890 leaving the Serbian throne to his three sons: Pervoslav, Bran and Stevan. Just before the death of Branimir, Peter Goynikovich invaded his native Serbia at the head of Croatian troops, and defeated the forces of his three cousins. Recovering the throne of his father, Peter ruled for twenty-five years (892-917) over Serbia cultivating friendship and good neighborly relations with Duke Mutimir of Croatia, and his successor king Tomislav.

During the reign of Branimir, and partly under his auspices, two careers of the first magnitude began, with an immediate bearing upon the political destinies and religious life of the Balkan Slavs, and of the greatest consequence for the cultural development and political division of all Slavic peoples throughout Europe. We refer to the missionary activity of the two learned brothers, Constantine and Methodius, sons of drungaros (admiral) Leo of Salonica.

Chapter IX
CYRIL AND METHODIUS

THERE is little doubt that the historical destiny of the Slavic race, and in a measure the fate of Europe is closely connected with the work of the two learned Macedonian brothers. Fortunately for western civilization, this activity came at a time when there was a temporary ebb in the missionary zeal of Islam, the waves of which were rolling toward the heathen territory of the eastern Slavs. The effort could therefore have its maximum effect. Had it been otherwise Europe might well have worked out its destiny within the pattern of an oriental civilization. For had the vast masses of the Slavic race embraced Mohammedanism instead of Christianity, at a time when Spain, Sicily and southern Italy were already under Moslem domination, the striking forces of Islam supported by the crusading zeal of the Slavic masses, might have overwhelmed the rest of Europe. Conditions were ripe for precisely such a course of development. For example the Pontian Khazars, who lived south of the Slavic territory along the northern coast of the Black Sea were already Moslems in part. Through the successful work of the two Slavic Apostles and their disciples this trend was reversed, and the Slavs became champions of Christianity who stemmed the Mohammedan tide, and after centuries of gigantic struggle brought about the downfall of the Turkish empire. Such was the main historical significance of the Slavic apostolate of Saints Cyril and Methodius.[22]

Slavic Settlements in the Aegean

Linguistic evidence alone encourages us to assume that Cyril and Methodius were of Slavic origin and spoke as their native tongue the language of the Macedonian Slavs who settled along the Aegean coast and established residence in the lively port and commercial center of Salonica. Other evidence will tend to confirm this assumption.

In the southeastern part of the Balkans the skill and daring of the Slavic navigators had attracted the attention of the Byzantine chronicle writers as far back as the seventh century. The participation of a Slavic fleet in the siege of Constantinople in 626 has already been mentioned.*

Along the Thracian and Thessalian or Macedonian coast of the Aegean sea there were numerous Slavic sttlements engaged in fishing and navigation. From such a sturdy stock came forth men like admiral (drungaros) Leo, who rose to a commanding position in the imperial navy. In such households the native Slavic language was spoken in alternation with the Greek.

Supported by the racial background of the surrounding countryside, Slavic became the current language of Salonica, most of whose residents were known to have spoken it. At the same time Salonica was an important educational center, in which many ambitious Slavic youths obtained their education and a good command of the Greek language. Rather than to assume a perfunctory and artificial interest on the part of two highly educated Greek aristocrats in the unpolished language of uncouth foreigners,* we shall give a better account of the racial genius present in the literary work of the two brothers by recognizing their Slavic origin.

The elder of the two brothers was Methodius (820-885). In his early life Methodius entered upon a public career and served as the imperial governor of a Slavic district in the Balkan peninsula. After several years of service he retired from secular life and entered a monastery in Asia Minor. There he spent his time in study and religious devotion. The younger brother Constantine (827-869) had a studious disposition from his early youth and devoted his time to study and education. In pursuit of higher education Constantine went to Constantinople, where he joined the classes of Photius, a leading philosopher of the time and later patriarch of Constantinople. After being ordained to priesthood he was appointed librarian of the cathedral of St. Sophia, and later became a teacher of philosophy. However, he resigned his honors,

---

* On purely linguistic grounds the writer believes (see: Language, 1930; pp. 279-296) that the Greek word *karabos* "ship, vessel," with its Romanic variation *caravel* 'a kind of vessel,' is of Slavic origin and reflects the Early Slavic form *korab'* (modern *korablja*) 'ship, vessel.'

* Cyril could not overcome the difficulties of the Khazar language, why should he fare better in Slavic?

and retired to the Bithynian monastery where his brother Methodius was living. After a brief retreat in monastic life, he was called upon by Emperor Michael III to go to the country of the Khazars for missionary work. His short stay in the Don region of the Black Sea was not successful, and he returned in 860 to Constantinople.

Ministry in Moravia

Upon the invitation of the Moravian duke Rastislav the two brothers set out in 864 on a missionary journey to Moravia. Enjoying the support of Rastislav, and his nephew Svatopluk, Constantine and Methodius spent nearly four years in their missionary work. They baptized many and gave instruction to the young by teaching them useful arts and the ecclesiastic chant in their native language. Furthermore they taught the art of writing and reading in the glagolitic script. which was an invention of Constantine himself.

As an ordained priest, Constantine celebrated the Mass and performed other divine services in the language of the people using in all probability the Macedonian dialect of his native Salonica. There is no doubt that in this period both brothers were engaged in literary activity, translating the Gospels and other sacred texts into the Moravian dialect.

They attracted a group of young men who became their disciples, and who continued the work of the great masters, organizing cultural groups and centers throughout all Slavic lands, including those of the eastern Slavs. From such centers came the original encouragement to use the Slavic liturgy in the Croatian Church of Dalmatia and Pannonia (Posavina). This innovation gave a new impetus to the religious and cultural life of the Croatian people.

The Glagolitic Script—Its Purpose and Merits

The Glagolitic script as well as its later off-shoot known as the Cyrillic, (according to some Cyrillic was the original script) are a combination of two types of sound-recording: the alphabetical and syllabary. Constantine saw that neither of these two systems alone was suited to cope with the phonetic problems of the Slavic language, known to him from his personal experience and observation. He probably found that for the alphabetical notation of the Slavic sounds there was not a sufficient supply of Latin or Greek characters. Hence the idea of a synthesis, capable of expressing the single sounds: the consonants, vowels and semi-vowels, as well as the more imporatnt sound-groups, by individual graphic symbols. Thus the disparity between the visual and acoustic, between the letter and sound will be avoided.

As a scholar of great erudition and a practical linguist of wide experience, Constantine devised a system in which all the advantages of the syllabary were assured without its handicaps, while the precision of the alphabetical writing was enhanced by the graphic delineation of some specific Slavic sounds, the symbols for which existed neither in Latin, nor in Greek. Minute fluctuations of sound were expressed with sure hand and accurate notation. Thus the glagolitic script has to be regarded as the product of a great scholarly mind endowed with fine musical feeling. Except for the time-value and tone variation of single phonemes, it represents the phonetic notation of the Slavic language of the ninth century with the precision of the notes of modern music. Unfortunately, Constantine failed to include in his system symbols of tone-inflections and to mark down the position of the accent as observed in the language of his experience.[23]

Activities in Moravia

The enthusiastic acclaim of the missionary zeal of the two brothers by the people of Moravia, attracted wide attention and caused some alarm among the Frankish clergy, which was also engaged in missionary work among the Moravians. Accordingly, some of these clerics raised objections to the use of Slavic as the language of liturgy, and accused the two brothers of heresy. Eager to clear themselves of the unjust accusation, the two brothers set out on a journey to Rome, in the course of which they passed through Western Pannonia (the present-day Hungarian *Dunántúl*), the country of Kotsel and Pannonian Croatia. On their journey people acclaimed them and gave support to their mission. In Rome they were received with high honors by Pope Hadrian II who approved their translations and authorized the use of Slavic as a language of divine service in the Slav territories. Methodius was ordained a secular priest, while Constantine, stricken by a disease, retired into a monastery where he assumed the name of Cyril and died in 869.

After Cyril's death Methodius and his disciples left Rome intending to return to Moravia. At this time, however, Rastislav was at war with Germany, and engaged in a bitter struggle with the emperor. Because of this complication, Methodius remained in Western Pannonia, the country of Kotsel. His missionary activities continued here with their customary success. Kotsel took great interest in Methodius' work and hit upon the idea of reviving the old Sirmian archbishopric (srijemska nadbiskupija). After some negotiations in Rome, Pope Hadrian II approved of this plan, and Methodius was made archbishop of Sirmium with jurisdiction over Pannonia as well. Later also the Moravian archdiocese was placed under Methodius' authority. However, this act aroused the German clergy, because Moravia was, according to tradition, under the jurisdiction of the archbishop of Salzburg. In the meantime, Methodius went to Moravia, but the fortunes of war and internal treachery turned the tide against Rastislav, who was captured and later put to death by the Germans. Methodius, too, was seized and imprisoned in a monastery, where he spent nearly three years. On the accession to the Holy See of Pope John VIII, and at his vigorous insistence, Methodius was released from prison and returned to Moravia as archbishop. At this time, the ruler of Moravia was Svatopluk, a powerful prince, who made his country an independent and leading State in central Europe.. However the opposition of the German clergy to the work of Methodius continued unabated, and under strong pressure from Germany, the pope now forbade the Moravian archbishop to use the Slavic language in the sacred texts and divine services. At the same time he detached Western Pannonia from Methodius' jurisdiction. This ruling was left unopposed, because Kotsel, the originator of the plan, soon lost his life (876) in a battle fought against Domagoy, duke of Croatia.

Struggle with the Frankish Clergy

In Moravia proper the papal interdiction had no effect and Methodius continued to use the Slavic language in church. The policy of Svatopluk was not consistent in the matter of church affairs. He appears to have been in sympathy with the work of Methodius, but was unwilling to antagonize the German clergy for political reasons. Through such a conciliatory attitude to both opponents, Svatopluk was forced into a position of ecclesiastic dualism, a policy later adopted by the Croatian rulers. Instead of establishing one single Slavic church in these countries, the sovereign permitted the rivalry of the German and Latin clergy to continue. This naturally split the people into two opposing camps, with much friction and antagonism in the country at large.

In the meantime, Methodius' disregard of the papal decree enjoining the use of the Slavic language in church was used by his German opponents as a pretext to accuse him of heresy before the Holy See. Summoned by the pope, Methodius went back to Rome in 879 to clear himself of the charges and prove his orthodoxy. Defending his case before a papal synod, Methodius again rejected the unfounded charges, proved his own orthodoxy, and the propriety of the use of the Slavic language in church. The synod promptly approved of the work of Methodius, and endorsed the use of Slavic as a language of liturgy. It also reaffirmed Methodius in his rank of archbishop. This was a great victory for the cause of the Slavic liturgy in the Catholic church and a vindication of the methods of Cyril and Methodius. It came also as a bitter disappointment to the German clergy. In order to relieve a tense situation John VIII made also some concession to the opposing party, and in a letter dispatched in 880 to Svatopluk he ruled that the Gospels during the Mass should be read first in Latin, and that the members of the sovereign's household could at will hear the Mass in Latin. The most important concession, however, was the elevation of Wiching, the bitter foe of Methodius, to the rank of a bishop presiding over the diocese of Nitra.

The compromise reached through this settlement failed to compose the differences or to restore tolerance and harmony. Bishop Wiching forbade the use of the Slavic language in the diocese of Nitra, and again accused Methodius of heretic leanings toward Photius, the patriarch of Constantinople, who at that time was in open conflict with Rome. Confronted with a growing antagonism to his teachings, Methodius sent a protest to Rome, and announced his intention of going to Constantinople. In 881-882 Methodius made his memorable trip to Byzantium, on which occasion he saw both the emperor and patriarch Photius. In all probability he

discussed with these men the all important problem of the Slavic liturgy, and obtained their permission and approval. This is an act of vast importance, because the missionary activities of the Byzantine clergy were henceforth conducted in Slavic, and contributed a great deal to the rapid spread of Christianity among the Eastern Slavs. Blending with other influences from Constantinople, the Greek Orthodox church thus became the foundation and organizing center of the Slavic-Byzantine culture.

Methodius' journey took him through Croatia and Dalmatia, where he spread the use of the Slavic liturgy and glagolitic writing. He was probably received at the court of Branimir. Together with later developments these contacts may be regarded as the foundation of the Croatian national church, which for many generations to come was able to maintain itself without the official approval of the king, and in the face of a stiff opposition on the part of the Latin clergy.

On his return to Moravia the archbishop now devoted much of his time to literary work. Assisted by his disciples he translated into Slavic the remainder of the sacred texts, initiated in cooperation with his brother Cyril. He reaffirmed his faith in the success of his work by expanding his missionary activities in Slavic through a host of trusted disciples and followers. In 884, together with Svatopluk, he was received with high honors at the court of Emperor Charles III in Tulln near Vienna. However, his old enemy Wiching did not cease to work against him. Indignant over the continuous intrigue, Methodius excommunicated Wiching, but it came to nothing, for in the end he was not supported by the Roman curia. This was the last important act in his life. He died in April 885. The site of his grave is unknown, although the claims of several cities in his diocese have been advanced in conjecture.

Disciples of Methodius

Shortly before his death Methodius recommended Gorazd, one of his Moravian disciples to succeed him. This appointment was frustrated through the untiring intrigue of Wiching. With the support of the German clergy Wiching again took his case to Rome, as a result of which Pope Stephen V prohibited the use of the Slavic language in the churches of Moravia, thus reversing the decision of the Synod of 879. As to the appointment of Gorazd to the archbishopric of Moravia, Stephen made it dependent on the outcome of a trial which Gorazd would have to stand in Rome. Rather than to give up the right to use the Slavic liturgy, and see the lifework of Methodius destroyed, Gorazd left Moravia with a band of his friends and followers to settle down in Croatia and Bulgaria.

There, through his own work and that of his missionary friends, an example was set and a tradition was established which in due course of time introduced Christianity and the Slavic liturgy among the Bulgarians, Roumanians, Serbs and Russians. The Croatians, too, accepted it with delight, although after a prolonged and bitter struggle, they had to abandon it because of the opposition of the Latin clergy which held the upper hand in Croatia. However, its historical importance and beneficial effect can be felt to this day, for national sentiment crystallized in the struggle around the Slavic liturgy in the Croatian Church. In critical moments this sentiment grew in pitch and volume to the point where it saved Croatian Dalmatia from becoming latinized and helped it to retain its Slavic character. From this angle we can appreciate best the vast importance of the lifework of Saints Cyril and Methodius to the destinies of the Croatian people.

In the lifetime of the two Macedonian teachers, the Croatian state rose rapidly to power. Freed from the Frankish yoke, Dalmatian Croatia moved through a short period of prosperity toward the status of kingdom. The last of the dukes was Mutimir (892-910), the youngest son of Terpimir. His reign was outwardly uneventful, but contributed much to internal consolidation. The long standing differences and friction between the bishopric of Nin and the archbishopric of Split came to a head at this time. In a contention over land grants made by his father, Mutimir decided in favor of the archbishop of Split. The end of Mutimir's reign marks the rise of Croatia to a new level of prosperity and power, under the leadership of her first and glorious king Tomislav.

Chapter X

KINGS OF CROATIAN BLOOD

THE first Croatian ruler to bear the title of king was Tomislav (910-28), the son of Mutimir. During his reign the early Croatian state rose to the peak of its power, and went a long way toward unifying all the Croatian lands. Both external and internal developments contributed to this progress. The most important single event of lasting effect was the extension of Tomislav's power over Pannonian Croatia. The first condition for this development was the delivery of Pannonia from Frankish rule, and second, the occurrence of events momentous enough to make the chiefs and princes of Pannonia seek support or protection from the common enemy in the well-organized and powerful State of Dalmatian Croatia. Both these conditions were provided by the coming of the Magyars or Hungarians, who in the closing years of the ninth century occupied the plain extending from the Carpathians to the central Danube (896-900). Next to the Christianization of the Slavs, the advance of the Magyars is probably the most important event which took place in central Europe following the collapse of the Avarian empire.

Magyar Invasions

The origin and early history of the Magyar or Hungarian race is still a moot question, subject to much discussion and controversy.[24]

Besides some scanty reports on the early invasions, the chief evidence of the origin and distant past of this people is in its language. From such evidence it appears that on a Finn-Ugrian foundation there is an important Turkish-Tartar superstructure in the early Hungarian. However, many elements of the vocabulary dealing with cultural concepts are drawn from Iranian (Persian) dialects. Such a linguistic synthesis can be explained only by racial mixture, achieved by conquest or by a long period of neighborly contacts and friendly relations.

The original homelands of the Magyars can be traced along the upper courses of the Volga, and its tributary Kama, west of the Ural mountains (the so-called Zyranian territory).* As in the case of many other peoples, the cause which impelled them to leave their homeland is unknown, and can be merely conjectured. In the eighth and ninth centuries they moved south toward the Caucasus mountains, and then turning west proceeded over the rich grasslands of the Dnieper, and the mouth of the Danube.

Having settled for some time between the Don and Dnieper, they were pressed from the east by a powerful kindred people, the Petchenegs. So the Magyars moved further west reaching the mouth of the Danube toward the middle of the ninth century. From here they raided the adjacent territories. At the invitation of Arnulf, emperor of Germany, they invaded Moravia, the country of Svatopluk in 882. Subsequently they repeated their raids in this territory, until both Moravia and Western Pannonia, the countries of Svatopluk and Kotsel, were crushed under the hoofs of their horsemen in 907.

The Magyar invasion of Pannonia was not altogether a voluntary affair. It came under the continuous attacks of the Petchenegs who raided the Magyar settlements along the lower Danube while the Magyar armies were absent in the field, and put to the sword both young and old. Under the leadership of Arpad, son of Álmos,* and other chiefs of their seven tribes, the Magyars settled down in the lowlands of the central Danube and its tributaries, an area which they hold to this day. With the coming of the Magyars into this region, the Frankish influence in central Europe vanished altogether. At the same time the age-old tie between the Slavs of the north and south was broken, the Magyar wedge now separating them into two large and distant groupings.

On settling down along the Danube, the Magyars did not turn to farming, but continued to raid and plunder the neighboring lands for more than half a century. Weakened by Norman attacks in the west, the Frankish emperors could not effectively resist the Magyars on the opposite front. Using the old Roman highways as their

---

* Through personal contacts in Russia with individuals of Zyranian blood, this writer found them to be people of high culture and of phenological characteristics, not distinct from those of Slavs or Germans.

* Etymology of *Árpád and Álmos* (almosh); perhaps from the original *almás*, points to the Turkish origin of both, for both in Turkish and Hungarian *árpa* means 'barley,' and *alma* is 'apple.' So probably: barley cultivator' and 'apple cultivator.'

avenues, the Magyar cavalry overran Carinthia, Italy, Bavaria, and penetrated even into Thuringia and the distant Rhineland. As a result of their inroads by 900 the once flourishing land of Western Pannonia lay in ruins. This caused the population to leave their ancestral homes and pour in large streams into Pannonian Croatia.

Fortunately Tomislav of Dalmatia had a powerful army, and came willingly to the asstistance of his Croatian brothers. In a series of engagements Tomislav defeated the Hungarians and was able to establish a boundary along the southern bank of Drava. Thus, with the exception of Syrmium, still held by the Bulgarians, Tomislav became the master of nearly all Croatian territory. In accordance with this change of political power, the diocese of Sisak (Siscia), heretofore a province of the patriarchate of Aquileia, an exponent of the Frankish power, came under the jurisdiction of the archbishop of Split, the supreme ecclesiastic authority of the new Croatian kingdom. The earliest evidence of such transfer of authority goes back to 925.

The Bulgarian Wars

More serious than the Hungarian menace in the north was a situation created along the southern and southeastern boundaries of Dalmatian Croatia. The rivalry of Byzantium with the Bulgarian empire over the domination of Serbia precipitated a period of struggle which imperiled most of the Balkans. Torn by internal dissensions and dynastic feuds, the duchy of Serbia became so weak that it was an easy mark for the ambitious plans of her powerful neighbors: Bulgaria and Byzantium. Restored in 892 by the armed support of Branimir, duke of Croatia, to the throne of Vlastimir, his grandfather, Peter Goynikovich ruled over Serbia for 25 years. He restored peace at home and made his native state so strong that he was encouraged to think of armed conquests in his own name. So he invaded the Narentian territory and occupied the coastal strip, thus arousing the jealousy of Michael Vishevich (910-930), duke of Hum, and sovereign of Travunia (Trebinjska oblast) and Doclea (Montenegro and northern Albania). In order to check the advance of his rival, Michael concluded an alliance with Simeon, emperor of Bulgaria, who at that time

was waging war against Byzantium. Since Peter was a vassal of Constantinople, Simeon invaded Serbia, crushed her army and captured the ruler himself. In place of the dethroned Peter Goynikovich, Simeon installed Paul Branovich (917-929), another Serbian prince who had been held prisoner in Bulgaria. At the same time Michael Vishevich recovered the Narentian territory and formed a powerful state in the southwestern part of the Balkans.

While this struggle went on Zachary Pervosavlyevich, a cousin of Paul Branovich, sued for aid in Constaninople, and broke into Serbia at the head of an imperial army in a vain attempt to dethrone and expel his cousin Paul. Instead, he was defeated and captured by the Bulgarians. This failure did not deter Roman Lecapinus, the Greek emperor, from still a new attempt to undermine the power of Bulgaria, and he made overtures to Paul Branovich for an alliance against Simeon. Paul was flattered; in a moment of vanity he forsook the man who had established him in Serbia and became a vassal of the Greek. On the news of this treason Simeon sent a new army to Serbia, deposed Paul, and enthroned that same Zachary Pervosavlyevich whom he had been holding prisoner from the earlier campaign. Thus freed from further entanglements in the west, Simeon could devote his attention to a major campaign, and threw all the armed forces of Bulgaria into attack against Constatinople.

Pressed hard by the victorious armies of Simeon, Emperor Lecapinus sought the mediation of Rome to obtain an alliance with Tomislav of Croatia. The price he paid included concessions to the church which had the effect of ending the long period of schism and restoring the cclesiastic unity of Christendom. Equally important concessions were made to the king of Croatia. In the first place the patriarch of Constantinople renounced fully his authority over the churches and dioceses of the Dalmatian cities and islands, all of which came under the immediate authority of the Holy See. At the same time the emperor gave up his sovereign rights and political power over the same cities and islands in favor of Tomislav, king of Croatia. In addition, he bestowed on Tomislav the rank of proconsul, a rare distinction given to the allies of the emperor.

Through this significant act the cities and islands of Dalmatia came into a lasting union

with the Roman Catholic Church, and gradually became integral parts of the Croatian state, upon whose political destinies their own future depended. From the magnitude of the imperial sacrifices it may be inferred that they were made for cause, and that the services expected in return were to match the grants. Indeed, the risks assumed by Tomislav were great, and in case of an adverse outcome, the gains would have been nullified by the destruction of the Croatian state. However, the power of Tomislav was equal to the task. Indeed, according to the chronicle of Emperor Constantine VII Porphyrogenetus, Tomislav had a land force of 60,000 horsemen, and 100,000 foot soldiers. On the sea he commanded a fleet of 80 large vessels (sagenae), manned with a crew of 40 each, and 100 small vessels (condurae), manned with a crew of 20.

Following up his success in Croatia, Lecapinus made an alliance with Michael Vishevich, duke of Hum, whom he distinguished with the title of proconsul and entrusted with administration of the cities Kotor and Dubrovnik. Unfortunately for the cause of Serbia, her ruler Zachary Pervosavljevich also joined the alliance. Incensed over this new treason by an underling whom he had fostered, Simeon suddenly abandoned the siege of Constantinople and invaded Serbia with overwhelming forces. The year was 924. He conquered the land, laid waste the country and decimated the population. Hosts of terror-stricken people sought refuge in Croatia, while Simeon destroyed the Serbian state and incorporated it as a province into his vast Bulgarian empire. This brought the Bulgarian dominion to the borders of the lands of Tomislav and Michael Vishevich. After some minor engagements the two armies met in a decisive battle, and the Bulgarian forces suffered a crushing defeat. Tomislav was now at the height of his power, the strongest ruler in the Balkans. However, he did not long survive the crowning achievement of his reign for he died in 928.

Simeon of Bulgaria died in 927 and left the throne to his son Peter (927-969) under whose long and inefficient reign the power of the Bulgarian empire ebbed until it was destroyed altogether by John Tzimisces, Emperor of Constantinople, in 972, three years after the death of Peter.

Internal Consolidation

The power of the Croatian king had been greatly enhanced by the imperial grant of the cities and islands of Dalmatia. His country became united politically and in theory was no longer divided between the two Churches. Subordinated directly to the authority of the Holy See, the new ecclesiastic territory had the same status in the kingdom as the Croatian bishopric of Nin. This raised the question of supremacy and jurisdiction. Based on a local tradition, the authority of the archbishop of Split was accepted all over the country. However, the Croatian bishopric of Nin was by far the most important as to territory and population. In addition, its bishop Gregory (Grgur Ninski) was a staunch advocate of the Croatian National Church and sponsor of the Slavic liturgy. Gregory resisted, therefore, the advance of the Latin clergy, and friction grew ever more intense. Tomislav was greatly concerned over the situation, for he desired to meet the Latin clergy on friendly terms, in order to strengthen his friendship with both the Pope and emperor. He therefore acceded to the desires of the Latin bishops to hold a church council in Split, at which all the points at issue should be debated and settled. In the presence of the papal legates the council met in 925 in the cathedral of Split.

This significant assembly saw a brilliant gathering of notables consisting of all the bishops and abbots of Dalmatia, the court of the king Tomislav and the Croatian nobility, Serbian noblemen and the duke Michael Vishevich, with the higher clergy of his realm. By the consent of the assembly the authority of the archbishop of Split was recognized over the whole Adriatic coast down to the city of Kotor. A powerful move was made to outlaw the Slavic liturgy and divine texts, but Grgur Ninski succeeded in modifying this proposal so as to permit the use of the Slavic liturgy by the lower clergy.

After the victory of Tomislav over the Bulgarian army another council was convoked in Split in 928. The Latin clergy renewed their attack on the native language and Slavic liturgy, but Gregory again fought back, and the attempts failed. However, his opponents succeeded in suspending the bishopric of Nin, the magnificent fort of Gregory, and he was made bishop of Skradin. Otherwise the enact-

ments of the second council of Split did not reach beyond the decisions of the first.

Thus through the political submission of the cities and islands, and through at least the semblance of ecclesiastic unity in his realm, Tomislav stood at the head of a wealthy and powerful state as no other Croatian ruler ever had in the past.

Since Pope John, in a message dated 925, addressed Tomislav as "King of Croatia, etc." it is assumed that the coronation of Tomislav took place prior to the sending of this message. Full description of the elaborate ceremonies of the coronation is given in the "Annals" of the priest of Doclea and confirmed by collateral evidence. The coronation followed the Frankish and not the Byzantine ceremonial, hence the reluctance of the Byzantine writers to give Tomislav a royal status.

Successors of Tomislav. Terpimir (928-935) and Kreshimir (935-945)

Tomislav was succeeded on the throne by his younger brother Terpimir, whose reign was short and uneventful (928-935). Terpimir's son, Kreshimir I (935-945), inherited the throne. During his reign the internal consolidation of the state was further advanced, and the royal power more fully developed. In this period some important changes took place in the Balkans. Taking advantage of the weakness of Simeon's empire, the Hungarians invaded Sirmium and drove out the Bulgarians, Thus Sirmium and eastern Slavonia came for the first time under Hungarian rule. At the same time the Serbian Duke Cheslav Klonimirovich restored the independence of Serbia through a successful uprising assisted by Byzantium. Also the Narentians regained their freedom by overthrowing the Duke of Hum.

Dynastic Wars

After the death of Kreshimir the throne was left to his two sons: Miroslav (945-949) and Mihaylo Kreshimir II (949-969). During the reign of Miroslav a rebellion broke out headed by banus Pribina. It degenerated into a long and bloody civil war, in which the king himself was assassinated by the rebel banus. Mihaylo Kreshimir succeeded to the throne of the war-torn country and was almost immediately faced

with the loss of considerable territory. The islands of Brach, Hvar and Vis returned to their Narentian motherland, Bosnia broke away, while the Dalmatian cities and islands again submitted to the authority of the Byzantine emperor. Red Croatia asserted her independence, and later joined Serbia. The military power of the king was considerably reduced, while his navy counted only 30 sagenae, instead of 80 as during the reign of Tomislav.

Little is known about the reign of Mihaylo Kreshimir, except that it fell in an era of confusion and strife. Pannonian Croatia remained attached to him throughout the worst trials and toward the end of his life he regained the western part of Bosnia. His wife Yelena is credited with construction of two churches, one of which, Sv. Styepan pod Klisom,* became the burial place of the Croatian kings. The annals of Porphyrogenete fall in this period of civil war, and the writer paints a dark picture of Croatia, greatly underestimating her power.

The Kreshimir Dynasty. Styepan Derzhislav (969-995)

Kreshimir became the head of a dynasty called Kreshimirovichi, a line that reigned continuously for over a hundred years. The first in this line is the son of Mihaylo Kreshimir, Styepan Derzhislav (969-995). On the accession of Styepan to the throne important developments took place in the Balkans. After the death of Duke Cheslav Klonimirovich in 960. Serbia had become once more the scene of internal strife and disorder. This brought the intervention of Byzantium and in 971 Serbia was again deprived of her independence, and incorporated into the empire. The imperial throne in Constantinople was occupied at this time by John Tzimisces, an Armenian adventurer, who proved to be an able ruler and great commander. He revived the power of Byzantium through many victories and conquests. In 972 Tzimisces invaded Bulgaria and conquered its territory all along the Danube.

However, the vitality of the Bulgarian nation was not sapped by this defeat, and a new state was organized in Macedonia, with its capital in Ohrid. Happily the Bulgarians found an able leader in the person of Samuel (980-1014), a

* The full meaning of this name is: Church of St. Stephen located at the foot of this stronghold. See the picture of this on plate.

man of military genius and commanding personality, who within a few years conquered Serbia, Bosnia, Herzegovina, Doclea and the Narentian territory. In addition, he launched a vigorous campaign against the Hungarians and forced them out of Sirmium and eastern Slavonia. In short, Samuel not only restored the old empire of Simeon, but enlarged it through the addition of the dominion of Michael Vishevich. Unfortunately for him, Samuel did not rest at this, but nursed Simeon's old ambition to conquer Croatia. So he invaded Dalmatia, ravaged the country and reached the outskirts of Zadar (Zara). Here his forces met the same crushing blow which the army of Simeon had suffered in 926. The decisive victory of Styepan Derzhislav over the troops of the Macedonian conqueror proves the degree of recovery the Croatian state had achieved in a short time after the disasters of the civil war.

The fame of the new Croatian victory traveled far and wide. The emperor hastened to renew the alliance of Lecapinus with the king of Croatia. The emperor returned again the cities and islands of Dalmatia. In token of his friendship and esteem, the emperor sent his new ally badges of royalty: a crown, scepter, purple robe and a golden apple. With these regalia Styepan Derzhislav was crowned king of Croatia and Dalmatia in 988. This coronation is not in contradiction with that of Tomislav (925) as assumed by some writers. It was simply achieved by the Byzantine ceremonials, the Croatian king thus obtaining the recognition of his royal title also by the court of Byzantium.

The king established friendly relations with all the neighboring states and especially with Venice, which had been paying taxes to Croatia since the times of Branimir. Even the warlike Magyars left his territory unmolested. Toward the end of his life Styepan Derzhislav reigned over a country that had regained most of its ancient power and prestige.

Civil Wars and Decline of Power. Svetoslav (995-1000)

On his deathbed, Styepan Derzhislav left the throne to the care of his three sons: Svetoslav, Kreshimir Suronja and Gojslav, under the primacy of Svetoslav (995-1000), the oldest of the three brothers. This arrangement called for a joint administration of the affairs of the kingdom.

Such provisions were known both in the Slavic and Germanic law. Dissatisfied with the will of his father, and longing for personal rule, Svetoslav attempted to exclude his younger brothers from the exercise of power. This soon resulted in an open civil war. The leader of the struggle was Kreshimir Suronya, a man of sanguine temperament and exceedingly embittered over the plot of Svetoslav to deprive him of his patrimony.

At that time the chief of the Venetian state was the doge Peter II Orseolo (991-1009).* This ambitious ruler seized upon the disorders plaguing the Croatian State to establish the supremacy of Venice in the Adriatic Sea. His first move was to refuse to pay the customary tribute to the Croatian king. Svetoslav answered this challenge by persecuting the Venetian merchants, whereupon the doge sent a fleet of six war vessels which seized the island of Vis (Lissa). The city of Zadar (Zara) placed herself under the protection of Venice and other Dalmatian cities soon did the same. Svetoslav was not discouraged at this defection, but sent another demand for payment of tribute to Venice, in accordance with the old custom.

In reply Orseolo prepared for war. Taking advantage of the difficult situation in Constantinople, the doge induced the Byzantine emperor to assign to him the administration of the Dalmatian cities and islands, alleging that the latter were endangered by the Croatian civil wars. In addition Orseolo made an alliance with Svetoslav's brother, Kreshimir Suronja. Then in May of the year 1000 the doge invaded Dalmatia and defeated the Croatian navy near Zadar. Besides occupying several islands by armed force (Kerk, Osor and Rab), the doge extended his power over Zadar, Trogir, Split and, according to some, Dubrovnik.

All these cities placed themselves under the authority of Venice, and Orseolo made a triumphal entry within their walls. The crowning success of his campaign was the submission of Kreshimir Suronja to his power. They met in Trogir for a treaty of friendship and alliance. As a guarantee of his good faith in carrying out the terms of the treaty, Kreshimir delivered his

---

* The term *doge* used frequently in this passage denotes the title of the head of the Venetian State. In the Venetian dialect *doge* meant 'leader' and is the local variation of the Latin *ducem*, (from dux) and the modern Italian *duce* 'leader.' In Croatian it presents the familiar form: *duž* or *dužd* 'idem'.

son Styepan to Peter Orseolo as a hostage. King Svetoslav lost his throne, and probobly fell victim to the hand of an assassin. There is no trace of his whereabouts after the year 1000.

Goyslav (1000-1019) and Kreshmir III (1000-1030)

Following the collapse of the opposition, Kreshimir Suronja ascended the throne and his brother Goyslav reigned jointly with him in accordance with the wishes of their father, Styepan Derzhislav. By the terms of his treaty with Peter Orseolo, Kreshimir III renounced the tribute that had been collected yearly by the king of Croatia from Venice. He also permitted Orseolo to assume the title of Duke of Dalmatia. In this period of civil war and foreign invasion grave damage was caused to the prestige of the Croatian State, which never again recovered its lost supremacy in the Adriatic Sea. Instead, the strength of the state was frittered away in a long and bitter feud with Venice over the possession of Dalmatia itself.

At the beginning of his reign Kreshimir entertained friendly relations with both Venice and Constantinople. His son Styepan not only received a good education at the court of the doge, but was given the hand of Hicela, daughter of Peter Orseolo in 1008. Through this union close dynastic ties were established with Hungary, whose king, Saint Stephan (Szent István),* gave his sister in marriage to Otto, son of Peter Orseolo. This was the first contact of a Croatian dynasty with the members of the house of Árpád, an incident that was to lead up to eight centuries of political union between Croatia and Hungary. Later in his reign Kreshimir changed his policy toward Venice and seized the Dalmatian cities and islands. The doge, Otto, answered the challenge by invading the seacoast, and capturing the cities. About this time Basil II, emperor of Byzantium, was successfully winding up his long struggle with Bulgaria. After forty years of warfare heroic Macedonian Bulgaria was exhausted and fell before the overwhelming might of Constantinople. The country was subdued, and, together with Serbia and Sirmium, became a simple province of the Byzantine empire. With this handwriting

on the wall, Kreshimir and Goyslav sent their submission to the emperor, recognizing his sovereignty over their kingdom.

In a spirit of conciliation Basil II respected their authority and left full independence to their kingdom. He also sent them bountiful presents and distinguished the two kings with the title of "patricians" (1019). Shortly after this event Goyslav passed away, while Kreshimir reigned on for another decade. Somewhat offsetting the many disasters that fell upon the Croatian State in the reign of Kreshimir III, was one fortunate event. Before the death of Goyslav the Narentian territory (Neretvlyanska oblast) effected its union with the Croatian kingdom. Ever since the Narentians have appeared in history under the name of Croatians.

Soon after the death of Goyslav a rebellion broke out in Venice, and the rule of the Orseolo family was overthrown. Otto himself was forced to flee the country. As the father-in-law of Hicela, Otto's sister, Kreshimir III intervened in the Venetian quarrel and once more occupied the Dalmatian cities and islands (1024). However, the Byzantine general Buzianus defeated his army in battle and forced him to surrender the cities. Moreover, Kreshimir's queen and his younger son were captured by the imperial invaders and taken to Constantinople.

The immediate result of these reverses and troubled events was reestablishment of the Byzantine authority and power over Dalmatia. The imperial administration of the territory was headed by the prior of Zadar, who in token of his exalted rank bore the title of proconsul. Two years later (1026) the family of Orseolo was sent into exile, and Styepan, the husband of Hicela, returned to the court of his father. The last years of Kreshimir's reign were devoted to a policy of restoration and recovery after the ravages of civil wars and defeat in battles with foreign invaders. Through negotiations with the emperor in Constantinople, he attempted to restore his possessions, including the return of the Dalmatian cities. The new emperor, Romanus III Argyrus (1029-1034), was at first willing to listen to Kreshimir's overtures, but later these negotiations were broken off, and the Croatian envoy was thrown into a Constantinople prison, where he soon died.

The reign of Kreshimir III is marked by the familiar phenomenon of the sudden decline of the Croatian state, following an era of great

* Before his conversion to Christianity, his name was, allegedly, *Vajk*, a meaningless word in Hungarian and in conflict with the Hungarian sound-system.

prosperity and power. As ever, this decline originated from disaffection and civil wars occasioned by the problem of succession or joint exercise of the sovereign power. The idea of sovereign rule and strong monarchy still had to work its way through the old Slavic tribal tradition. Thus whenever contention arose among those who exercised power, the unity and strength of the state were sacrificed to personal interests.

protection. By his title Togrul Beg became "the right hand" of the caliph; in fact, he was his head. Through his capture of Bagdad (1055), Togrul Beg, grandson of a barbarian chieftain, became the actual ruler of the Moslem world.

After his death, Togrul Beg was succeeded in power by his son Alp Arslan (1063-1072), who extended his father's dominion with the zeal and success of the early caliphs. After completing the conquest of the territories on both banks of the Oxus river, he turned west in the direction of the Byzantine empire. Soon he had entered Armenia, massacred the population and devastated the country, for a long time the eastern outpost of Byzantium and Christianity. The Armenian refugees established new homes in Cilicia, while the Turks conquered Cappadocia, the native country of Nicephorus Phocas. At that time, Romanus IV was enthroned as emperor in Constantinople, and he decided to crush the Turkish invaders. A soldier of great personal courage, Romanus had shortcomings as a general. He started with a brilliant campaign, and elated over his initial success he drove the Turks far back into mountainous Armenia. In so doing he overextended his supply lines, and at a critical moment, the Turks swooped down on his disjointed forces, and annihilated them near Manzikert (1071).

The consequences of this victory were momentous and reversed the history of the world. Its effect can be compared with the echoes of the victory at Yarmuk, won over the armies of Heraclius by the generals of the first caliphs in the seventh century. A new tide of Mohammedan invasion followed, and the course of history was changed. The whole territory of Asia Minor was overrun, and even Anatolia, the heart of the Byzantine realm, was occupied by the Turks. Attracted by the glamor and wealth of this country, the kin of the conquerors migrated from central Asia to Anatolia in large numbers, and changed its ethnical composition permanently and altogether. The population of Anatolia remains Turkish to the present day. However, the coastal towns were Greek until the First World War, when Greece and Turkey exchanged their alien populations.

Moslem Expansion under the Turks

Under the blows of the Turkish victories the military power of Constantinople was perma-

nently crippled. There was no further prospect for a Byzantine revival in Asia Minor, all of which now came under the sovereignty of the victorious Alp Arslan and his son Malik Shah (1072-92). Although Alp Arslan did not live long enough to develop his ringing victories, the completion of his task was laid in the able hands of Malik Shah, in whose reign the Seljuk power reached its zenith. Under Malik's overlordship his cousin Suleyman established in Anatolia and surrounding territory the sultanate of Roum, with its capital in Nicaea, a suburb of Constantinople on the Asiatic side of the Bosporus. In Syria and districts farther south the armies of Malik overcame the resistance of the local Arabic emirs in a series of decisive victories. Thus by 1080 the Turks became the sole masters of Jerusalem, Damascus, Aleppo and Antioch By the death of Malik Shah the world-power of Islam had been reconstituted under the guidance and leadership of the Seljuk Turks.

The echo of the Turkish victories in Asia Minor reverberated far and wide in Europe. Their immediate repercussions, however, came in the Balkans, where the Byzantine power was in ascendancy once again. Through armed conquest the emperors of Constantinople had acquired wide areas south of the Danube. Thus Bulgaria, Macedonia, parts of Serbia and eastern Slavonia, with Sirmium, came under the Byzantine authority as provincial possessions of the emperor. During the period of the civil wars in Croatia and subsequent weakness of the state, the emperors restored their strict rule over the islands and cities of Dalmatia, including the city of Zadar (1050). Under Catapan Leo the imperial administration in Dalmatia reached the height of its unity and effectiveness in 1067, with every prospect in store to enhance this power, and extend the political dominion of the emperor over the Croatian territory.

Full Sovereignty over Dalmatian Cities

On Peter's accession to the throne, therefore, the Dalmatian cities were again under the rule of Byzantium. Toward 1050, as we have said, even Zadar freed itself from the overlordship of Venice, and renewed its allegiance to Constantinople. Thus all of municipal Dalmatia and its archipelagos were united again under the rule

nacular. This created a wide gap between the Latin clergy and the ministers of the national church.

Alliance with Latin Clergy

Having control over the cities and high ecclesiastic offices, the Latin clergy was in a position to influence the higher nobility and court. At the same time, the representatives of this group championed the reform of Cluny, one of the main objectives of which was the suppression of clerical marriage. The friction between the two opposing groups grew in intensity, and before long it broke out into open conflict. The social disturbances were profound. As a result of the king's support, the success of the moment was on the side of the reformist Latin clergy, and the very existence of the national church came into jeopardy. Yet this success did not outlast the reign of Peter Kreshimir, and as soon as the throne became vacant, the suppressed will of the people broke out with elementary force, causing grave disorders throughout the kingdom.

The king's aversion to the ancient cult introduced by the disciples of St. Methodius may be explained in part by his foreign education and Venetian family ties, but the chief clue lies undoubtedly in his desire to win the support of the Latin clergy and the approval of the Holy See for his move to bring the Dalmatian cities under his immediate authority. The scheme worked, for his pro-Latin policy, coming at a most opportune time, brought him the good will and submission of the municipalities of Dalmatia. Their change of heart was long overdue, and came at the end of a long period of development.

Through frequent changes of allegiance the urban population had lost its sense of security, and faced the future with a painful uncertainty and growing misgivings. This was in contrast to their prosperous past, when the cities and islands of Dalmatia had been the mainstay of Byzantine power along the eastern coast of the Adriatic. With the passing of time the Slavic population of the country slowly filtered through the city walls, yet never in numbers large enough to change their racial composition. The example of Trieste at the head of the Adriatic, with its Slavic background, yet preponderantly Latin character, should serve as an illustration of the ethnical condition prevailing in the Dalmatian cities throughout the Middle Ages.* In addition, medieval Dalmatia had no lack of purely Croatian urban centers and cities, built by the Slavic settlers without the assistance of the native Latin population. One of such Croatian municipalities was Biograd, capital of Peter Kreshimir IV.

In such a motley setting of racial, linguistic, cultural and religious mixtures, the Croatian people had to meet their destiny. Therefore any method that would help create a semblance of national unity even on a non-Slavic foundation, must have been welcome to the king and his advisors. His attempts to win the support of the universal Latin Church and achieve the absorption of the Latin cities, was prompted by his vision of a strong and united Croatian state. Under his guidance and in the favorable circumstances of his reign, the Croatian state reached the climax of its might and significance as the leading power of the northwestern part of the Balkan peninsula.

The Seljuk Turks

Toward the end of Peter Kreshimir's reign important developments took place in the neighboring countries. They came as a result of momentous events in Asia Minor, which shook the very foundation of the Byzantine empire. Early in the 11th century a band of Turkish mercenaries descended from the regions of the river Oxus in Central Asia to place their services at the disposal of some local governors who ruled in the name of the caliph of Bagdad. In their military adventures they achieved spectacular success. From the name of their chief and leader, this tribe is known in history as the Seljuk Turks.

Moving westward in the manner of his ancestors, Togrul Beg, grandson of Seljuk, established himself in the city of Nishapur as a sultan of Khorassan, the mountainous country located in the northeast of Persia. From this capital Togrul Beg extended his dominion over the neighboring provinces and awaited an opportunity to interfere in the affairs of the caliph. Taking advantage of a palace rebellion, he intervened in favor of an Abbasid caliph, destroyed the latter's enemies, and placed the "Commander of the Faith" himself under his tutelage and

---

* Their purely Croatian character in modern times is the result of a long evolutionary process.

(Spalato), with instructions to hold a church council there. On this occasion John made a thorough investigation of the life and morals of the local clergy. He found their deportment offensive and removed from office the archbishop Dobral, who himself had a legal wife and a large family. Dobral defended the legitimacy of his position, which was fully in harmony with the customs of the Eastern Church. Nothing further is known about the cardinal's reforms, which must have been numerous and drastic since the lower clergy, and especially that of the Slavic liturgy, practiced marriage as a general rule.

The Great Schism

Another important event affecting the history of the Croatian people is connected with the pontificate of Leo IX. That is the Great Schism or final separation of the two Churches, which took place in 1054. An unfortunate combination of political developments, together with the untimely revival of the Photian spirit in Constantinople, precipitated the final break. At the outset a close cooperation between Leo and the Byzantine emperor promised a tightening of political ties and eventual ecclesiastic union. For a time they were in military alliance against the Normans of southern Italy. However, the Normans routed their combined armies and the alliance was disrupted amid the mutual recriminations of the losers.

At about this time, Michael Cerularius, the impetuous patriarch of Constantinople, took a vigorous stand in religious matters. He condemned certain teachings and practices of the Church of Rome and soon closed all the churches in Constantinople which followed the western ritual. The pope retaliated, and excommunicated the patriarch. Shortly thereafter Leo IX died. Taking advantage of the vacancy created on the papal throne, Cerularius induced the emperor to reverse his friendly policy toward Rome. At the same time he called a synod in Constantinople, at which he secured the formal condemnation of the Western Church. The synod also condemned all who submitted to the authority of the pope and followed the western "heresy." Thus after intermittent conflicts and periods of appeasement between these two champions of Christianity, the final breach was made. This event sorely affected the destinies of the Croatian and Serbian people, who could not bridge the gap separating them even in the face of the Turkish invasion, nor during the centuries of Mohammedan rule and oppression in their lands.

The last years of Styepan's eventful reign are shrouded in darkness, and nothing is known with certainty about the closing period of his life beyond the date of his death. His remains were laid at rest in the Church of St. Stephen at Klis. The king was succeeded in power by his son Peter Kreshimir IV, the greatest of all the Croatian rulers.

At the Height of Power.
Peter Kreshimir IV, the Great

The reign of Peter Kreshimir IV (1058-1074) is marked by a sequence of events which raised the power of the Croatian State to a height never reached before, or since. This was largely a result of the sagacious and farsighted policies of the king. A Venetian from his mother's side, Peter Kreshimir possessed the intelligence and shrewdness of his two grandfathers: Doge Peter Orseolo and King Kreshimir III. At the Venetian court the young prince had obtained a thorough western education, and had been in a position to learn much from the masters of political intrigue. He was a mature man when he ascended the throne. The fact of his crowning can hardly be doubted, and he chose for his residence the capital of the kingdom, Biograd-on-the-sea. The king's attachment to this city is reflected by the fact that he built there a Benedictine monastery, with the Church of St. John.

The extent of his political success contrasts with his failure to solve the religious problems which pressed for solution in his day. Probably he never realized that by sacrificing the fond dreams of the Croatian people for an independent church of their own, he shook the foundation upon which the peace and tranquility of his kingdom rested. The political advantage of the moment was too alluring to permit an adamant stand in defense of the Slavic liturgy. Thus he sided with the Latin faction and reformist clergy who were bent on eradicating the Eastern canon and all vestiges of the Greek orthodoxy in the Croatian Church. Like the clergy of Orthodox faith, the Croatian priests were married, wore long hair and went about unshaven. Worst of all, they had no knowledge of Latin, and officiated at all times in the Croatian ver-

Chapter XI

PERIOD OF RECOVERY AND ASCENDANCY

AFTER the long period of internal disorders and military disasters during his father's reign, the ambition of Styepan I (1030-1058) became to restore his realm to the position of power and grandeur it had enjoyed during the lifetime of his grandfather, Styepan Derzhislav. He strove to repair the damage caused by the continuous struggle, and to regain the lost territory. This course was favored by external developments, and in a moment of confusion and friction in the Byzantine empire, he seized the opportunity to occupy all the Dalmatian cities and islands. A long war followed this action, and there was fighting both on land and sea.

The imperial forces failed to achieve their usual success, however, and a peace treaty was concluded by the provisions of which all the titles of the Croatian king over the Byzantine possessions in Dalmatia were restored. The only exception was that of the city of Zadar, which placed itself in 1050 under the protection of Dominic Contarino, doge of Venice.

During the reign of Styepan (Stephen) I important events took place abroad, which had a bearing upon the situation at home. As a result of internal clashes in Germany, the authority of the Croatian king was extended north toward Carinthia, while Pannonia became firmly cemented with Dalmatian Croatia. The ecclesiastic jurisdiction over this area was transferred to the newly-formed bishopric of Knin. Mark was the first bishop of this diocese (1042), the northern boundary of which ran along the river Drava. Its military and civil administration was assigned to a governor (banus). This extension of Styepan's sovereignty to the north came as a reward for his alliance with Adalbert, duke of Carinthia, who controlled the vast stretch of frontier territory extending from Bavaria down to the head of the Adriatic. In a moment of general disaffection over the imperial policies, Adalbert in 1035 took to arms against Conrad II, emperor of Germany, and a long struggle ensued. The Croatian troops fought on the side of the rebel duke. The details of this struggle are not known, but the favorable outcome of the uprising can be concluded from the fact that the authority of the Croatian king was extended northward, and firmly established in an area which heretofore had been but loosely attached to his State.

The Cluny Reforms in the Church

The reign of Styepan I coincided with the pontificate of Leo IX (1049-1054), considered by many the greatest pope in the history of the Catholic Church. As a champion of the Cluniac Congregation he used all the powers of his office to purge the Church of the worldly abuses which blighted the ecclesiastic institutions of the ninth and tenth centuries. In parts of the Carolingian empire the influence of the secular princes in the affairs of the Church became so thorough and pervading that some bishops and abbots hardly differed from the feudal landlords or governmental officials. Preoccupied with secular affairs they neglected their spiritual offices. They lived in concubinage, and attached the estates of the Church to their own children, thus laying claim to property which clearly belonged to the parish, abbey or diocese. High positions in the Church could be purchased and dispensation of the sacraments was made a source of income.*

Upon his election to the See of St. Peter, Leo IX assumed leadership in the moral regeneration of the Church with the zeal of a crusader. He was a man of dynamic personality and in his brief pontificate he carried the message of the Cluniac reform and spiritual rebirth of the Church throughout Europe. Traveling all over France, Germany and Italy, he held regional councils, in which he weeded out the unholy element and imposed severe punishment for simony and clerical marriage. At the same time he sought to extend effectively the authority of the pope over the high prelates and secular princes of the western Europe.

Leo IX did not travel in person to Croatia, but the conditions prevailing there attracted his attention, and in the second year of his pontificate (1050) he sent Cardinal John to Split

* The abnormal situation can be summed up best with the following excerpt from a competent source (Carl Stephenson, Medieval History, p. 305, lines 23-29) : "In most religious houses, particularly in those given to lay abbots, the ancient discipline had utterly collapsed and the brethren lived as they pleased from the proceeds of the monastic endowments. Most bishops were entirely submerged in secular activities and were frequently as vicious as their non-clerical associates."

nacular. This created a wide gap between the Latin clergy and the ministers of the national church.

Alliance with Latin Clergy

Having control over the cities and high ecclesiastic offices, the Latin clergy was in a position to influence the higher nobility and court. At the same time, the representatives of this group championed the reform of Cluny, one of the main objectives of which was the suppression of clerical marriage. The friction between the two opposing groups grew in intensity, and before long it broke out into open conflict. The social disturbances were profound. As a result of the king's support, the success of the moment was on the side of the reformist Latin clergy, and the very existence of the national church came into jeopardy. Yet this success did not outlast the reign of Peter Kreshimir, and as soon as the throne became vacant, the suppressed will of the people broke out with elementary force, causing grave disorders throughout the kingdom.

The king's aversion to the ancient cult introduced by the disciples of St. Methodius may be explained in part by his foreign education and Venetian family ties, but the chief clue lies undoubtedly in his desire to win the support of the Latin clergy and the approval of the Holy See for his move to bring the Dalmatian cities under his immediate authority. The scheme worked, for his pro-Latin policy, coming at a most opportune time, brought him the good will and submission of the municipalities of Dalmatia. Their change of heart was long overdue, and came at the end of a long period of development.

Through frequent changes of allegiance the urban population had lost its sense of security, and faced the future with a painful uncertainty and growing misgivings. This was in contrast to their prosperous past, when the cities and islands of Dalmatia had been the mainstay of Byzantine power along the eastern coast of the Adriatic. With the passing of time the Slavic population of the country slowly filtered through the city walls, yet never in numbers large enough to change their racial composition. The example of Trieste at the head of the Adriatic, with its Slavic background, yet preponderantly Latin character, should serve as an illustration of the ethnical condition prevailing in the Dalmatian cities throughout the Middle Ages.* In addition, medieval Dalmatia had no lack of purely Croatian urban centers and cities, built by the Slavic settlers without the assistance of the native Latin population. One of such Croatian municipalities was Biograd, capital of Peter Kreshimir IV.

In such a motley setting of racial, linguistic, cultural and religious mixtures, the Croatian people had to meet their destiny. Therefore any method that would help create a semblance of national unity even on a non-Slavic foundation, must have been welcome to the king and his advisors. His attempts to win the support of the universal Latin Church and achieve the absorption of the Latin cities, was prompted by his vision of a strong and united Croatian state. Under his guidance and in the favorable circumstances of his reign, the Croatian state reached the climax of its might and significance as the leading power of the northwestern part of the Balkan peninsula.

The Seljuk Turks

Toward the end of Peter Kreshimir's reign important developments took place in the neighboring countries. They came as a result of momentous events in Asia Minor, which shook the very foundation of the Byzantine empire. Early in the 11th century a band of Turkish mercenaries descended from the regions of the river Oxus in Central Asia to place their services at the disposal of some local governors who ruled in the name of the caliph of Bagdad. In their military adventures they achieved spectacular success. From the name of their chief and leader, this tribe is known in history as the Seljuk Turks.

Moving westward in the manner of his ancestors, Togrul Beg, grandson of Seljuk, established himself in the city of Nishapur as a sultan of Khorassan, the mountainous country located in the northeast of Persia. From this capital Togrul Beg extended his dominion over the neighboring provinces and awaited an opportunity to interfere in the affairs of the caliph. Taking advantage of a palace rebellion, he intervened in favor of an Abbasid caliph, destroyed the latter's enemies, and placed the "Commander of the Faith" himself under his tutelage and

---

* Their purely Croatian character in modern times is the result of a long evolutionary process.

protection. By his title Togrul Beg became "the right hand" of the caliph; in fact, he was his head. Through his capture of Bagdad (1055), Togrul Beg, grandson of a barbarian chieftain, became the actual ruler of the Moslem world.

After his death, Togrul Beg was succeeded in power by his son Alp Arslan (1063-1072), who extended his father's dominion with the zeal and success of the early caliphs. After completing the conquest of the territories on both banks of the Oxus river, he turned west in the direction of the Byzantine empire. Soon he had entered Armenia, massacred the population and devastated the country, for a long time the eastern outpost of Byzantium and Christianity. The Armenian refugees established new homes in Cilicia, while the Turks conquered Cappadocia, the native country of Nicephorus Phocas. At that time, Romanus IV was enthroned as emperor in Constantinople, and he decided to crush the Turkish invaders. A soldier of great personal courage, Romanus had shortcomings as a general. He started with a brilliant campaign, and elated over his initial success he drove the Turks far back into mountainous Armenia. In so doing he overextended his supply lines, and at a critical moment, the Turks swooped down on his disjointed forces, and annihilated them near Manzikert (1071).

The consequences of this victory were momentous and reversed the history of the world. Its effect can be compared with the echoes of the victory at Yarmuk, won over the armies of Heraclius by the generals of the first caliphs in the seventh century. A new tide of Mohammedan invasion followed, and the course of history was changed. The whole territory of Asia Minor was overrun, and even Anatolia, the heart of the Byzantine realm, was occupied by the Turks. Attracted by the glamor and wealth of this country, the kin of the conquerors migrated from central Asia to Anatolia in large numbers, and changed its ethnical composition permanently and altogether. The population of Anatolia remains Turkish to the present day. However, the coastal towns were Greek until the First World War, when Greece and Turkey exchanged their alien populations.

Moslem Expansion under the Turks

Under the blows of the Turkish victories the military power of Constantinople was perma-

nently crippled. There was no further prospect for a Byzantine revival in Asia Minor, all of which now came under the sovereignty of the victorious Alp Arslan and his son Malik Shah (1072-92). Although Alp Arslan did not live long enough to develop his ringing victories, the completion of his task was laid in the able hands of Malik Shah, in whose reign the Seljuk power reached its zenith. Under Malik's overlordship his cousin Suleyman established in Anatolia and surrounding territory the sultanate of Roum, with its capital in Nicaea, a suburb of Constantinople on the Asiatic side of the Bosporus. In Syria and districts farther south the armies of Malik overcame the resistance of the local Arabic emirs in a series of decisive victories. Thus by 1080 the Turks became the sole masters of Jerusalem, Damascus, Aleppo and Antioch By the death of Malik Shah the world-power of Islam had been reconstituted under the guidance and leadership of the Seljuk Turks.

The echo of the Turkish victories in Asia Minor reverberated far and wide in Europe. Their immediate repercussions, however, came in the Balkans, where the Byzantine power was in ascendancy once again. Through armed conquest the emperors of Constantinople had acquired wide areas south of the Danube. Thus Bulgaria, Macedonia, parts of Serbia and eastern Slavonia, with Sirmium, came under the Byzantine authority as provincial possessions of the emperor. During the period of the civil wars in Croatia and subsequent weakness of the state, the emperors restored their strict rule over the islands and cities of Dalmatia, including the city of Zadar (1050). Under Catapan Leo the imperial administration in Dalmatia reached the height of its unity and effectiveness in 1067, with every prospect in store to enhance this power, and extend the political dominion of the emperor over the Croatian territory.

Full Sovereignty over Dalmatian Cities

On Peter's accession to the throne, therefore, the Dalmatian cities were again under the rule of Byzantium. Toward 1050, as we have said, even Zadar freed itself from the overlordship of Venice, and renewed its allegiance to Constantinople. Thus all of municipal Dalmatia and its archipelagos were united again under the rule

of the emperor and his representative the imperial "Catapan" or governor. The supremacy of Byzantium, so well established at this time, seemed to have become perpetual. Then came the stroke which removed this territory from Byzantine control and in less than two years made it subject to the authority of the king of Croatia. Peter Kreshimir IV chose the moment when the military power of Constantinople was fully occupied with the advance of the Seljuk Turks into Asia Minor to demand from the emperor full authority of the Croatian State over the imperial possessions in Dalmatia (1069). The emperor granted his request, and the cities themselves approved of this arrangement under the guarantee of their municipal privileges. Catapan Leo, governor of this territory, remained in office, but now as a subject of the king.

It will be recalled that the Dalmatian cities and islands had several times previously been under the authority of the Croatian king. Tomislav (924) and Styepan Derzhislav (990) had also ruled over this area. However, their rule was in the nature of a protectorate dependent on the title of proconsul or imperial eparch granted to them by the emperor for considerations of friendship or services rendered. In the case of Peter Kreshimir the Croatian sovereignty was recognized in its own name. The authority of the king was no longer dependent on any imperial title or rank, and Peter Kreshimir carefully avoided taking any. In this way he was no longer a ' protector" of the old imperial territory, but its supreme ruler, without limitation of power or lease by any foreign authority.

The shift of the imperial territory into the political orbit of the Croatian State was an event of first magnitude. Its cultural significance was paramount, because the cities of Dalmatia had been centers of trade, culture and refinement ever since the days of Diocletian and St. Jerome. Likewise, the islands represented the Roman tradition. The continuous contact of this territory with the Romanic culture of Byzantium and the practices of the Eastern Church, gave the Dalmatian cities the colorful background of both the Latin and Greek civilizations.* Both Latin and Greek were spoken in the Dalmatian cities, although the Croatian

*Similar were the conditions in Southern Italy and Sicily, where Arabs and Normans stood in place of the Slavic populations of Dalmatia.

speech was gradually filtering in from the countryside. It is precisely this rural language that was to complete the racial unity of the cosmopolitan population, after the artificial barriers between the city and countryside had fallen through the achievement of political unity. By knitting ties of friendship with the Latin cities, Peter Kreshimir established a tradition which hastened the process of ethnical fusion and the national consolidation of Croatia. On the other hand, he exposed the Croatian masses to the danger of complete romanization as had happened in Roumania.

The Royal Power and Court

It should be understood that even in the agreement of 1069 the emperor of Constantinople retained his "historical sovereignty" over the Dalmatian eparchate. In terms of practical experience this meant no more than would a claim of some of the present descendants of the last Byzantine dynasty to the same territory. The validity of the "historical rights" of Byzantium over Dalmatia from then on became dependent upon the military power of the emperor and his ability to enforce them; or upon some political deal which he could amicably consummate with the sovereign of Croatia. Attempts of this kind we shall see later after the downfall of the national dynasty. For every practical purpose therefore Peter Kreshimir became the sole ruler of the eparchate. In this way besides the traditional "friendship tax" he collected other taxes and dues to the extent of one-third of the cities' revenue. In turn, the king guaranteed the cities their communal independence and old municipal rights such as free trade, independent judicial system and ecclesiastic privileges.

The power of Peter Kreshimir was extended also in other directions. Historical documents refer to several bani or provincial governors among other dignitaries residing at his court. So we are informed of the presence of ban Gycho, governor of a "maritime" province, probably the Narentian territory. The banus of Pannonian Croatia was Zvonimir, son-in-law of the Hungarian king Béla I. (1061-1063). Finally, the banus of Bosnia is mentioned, without indication of name. From this we see that Peter Kreshimir assembled nearly all the Croatian lands under the aegis of the Croatian crown.

The king was at the height of his power in his declining days. One of his greatest concerns was his lack of children who could assume succession to the throne. At first he appointed his nephew Styepan as heir presumptive, but later Zvonimir of Pannonia appears as a regent during the lifetime of the king. By 1070 Styepan seems removed from the picture. The young banus Zvonimir was a glamorous person adding to the prestige of the court through his blood ties with a foreign power. Such a tradition had been introduced by the coming of the Venetian Hicela, the mother of Peter Kreshimir, to share the Croatian throne. Zvonimir's wife was the "beautiful" Helena, sister of the princes Géza and László, both of whom became kings of Hungary. With their aid Zvonimir repulsed the attacks of the Carinthians who invaded his territory in 1065. In his reign the Croatian territory reached along the Danube to the Bulgarian town of Vidin, and south to the city of Nish (Naissa).

Chapter XII
POLITICAL CONSOLIDATION AND STRUGGLE FOR THE EMANCIPATION OF THE CROATIAN CHURCH

IN the stunned and dreadful moments which followed the Turkish victories the opponents of Constantinople took advantage of the situation to wipe out the Byzantine power in the Balkans. Peter Kreshimir was not the only ruler who showed a firm hand in the situation, and capitalized on the difficulties of the empire. The Petchenegs of Roumania invaded the territory south of Danube, and laid waste Thrace and Macedonia. On their return from the Aegean, the Petchenegs raided also northern Serbia and Sirmium, captured Belgrad (Alba Bulgarica) and broke into Hungary. Incensed over this intrusion, king Salomon (1063-1074) of Hungary charged laxity and negligence on the part of the imperial governor of Belgrad, and in retaliation broke into Sirmium. The Hungarian troops took the city of Sirmium (Mitrovitsa) in 1071, and on heels of this victory captured Belgrad. After this conquest the Hungarians kept Sirmium in their possession for almost 500 years until the battle of Mohács (1526) when their own state was destroyed by the forces of Sultan Suleiman II, the Magnificent (1520-1566).*

In the midst of general pressure brought to bear on Constantinople, the Bulgarians and Macedonians staged an uprising of heroic proportions. The drama of this incident unfolds some of the most beautiful pages in Bulgarian history. Under the able leadership of the Boyar Georg Voytekh the Bulgarians shook off the Byzantine yoke and reestablished their independent state for the first time since 1018. Unwilling to assume the responsibilities of the crown, George Voytekh offered the title to Constantine Bodinus, the youngest son of Michael, Duke of Serbia, who held sway also over Doclea (Zeta), Herzegovina, and the imperial city of Cattaro (Kotor). Michael accepted the offer and sent Constantine at the head of an army to Bulgaria. Having thus consolidated their victory with the military aid of the Serbs, the Bulgarians proclaimed Constantine their emperor in the city of Prizren.

The new Bulgarian state also obtained the friendship and armed assistance of the king of Croatia. However, the foreign alliances and the

* He was also called *El Kanuni* 'the law giver.'

new brave posture at home were not sufficent to cope with the imperial menace, once the emperor made up his mind to deal seriously with the situation. Byzantium still possessed vast reserves of power, and in a desparate struggle with their rebellious subjects, the imperial governors crushed the Bulgarian forces. Thus ended the brief chapter of Bulgarian independence, and the Bulgars were forced once again into Byzantine bondage.

Passing of a Great King

Such was the world outlook and situation abroad in the last year of Peter Kreshimir's reign. The revival of Moslem power in the East and its victorious advance toward the Balkans was to have momentous consequences for the Croatian people. In the immediate future it would bring about the downfall of the national dynasty. Centuries later its effects would be felt in the Mohammedan invasion of the Croatian lands.

With the death of Peter Kreshimir, the greatest ruler in Croatian history goes off the stage. He was a man of natural wisdom, a shrewd diplomat who had taken advantage of every turn of events to benefit the Croatian State. His western education inclined him to prefer the enlightment and brilliancy of the West to the rugged tradition and religious practices of his Slavic kinfolk. This attitude of the sovereign could not help but promote the cultural progress of Croatia, regardless of its political consequences.

However, Peter had underestimated the attachment of the common people to the simple and convincing word of the native faith. The Slavic liturgy of Methodius had taken deep root among the Croatian people of his time, and the foreign speech of the Latin clergy caused a great deal of irritation. Thus the pro-Latin policy of the king brought in its wake a wide-spread disaffection which was to break out after his death all over the kingdom. A brief survey of the religious developments that took place during his reign will assist in placing a more adequate appraisal upon the course of subsequent events.

Religious Problems in the Reign of Peter Kreshimir

The greatest ecclesiastic event of Peter Kreshimir's reign is the episcopal synod convened in the Cathedral of Split in 1060 under the auspices of the papal delegate, the abbot Maynard. This council followed by ten years the first attempt to introduce the Cluniac reform in the religious life of Croatia. The papacy at this time was occupied by Nicholas II (1058-61) who continued the reform activities of Leo IX with zeal and devotion. In his determination to purge the church of worldly abuses, Nicholas II took some severe measures against simony and clerical marriage. He sought also to increase the authority of the Holy See, and make it independent of the encroachments of the emperor. For this purpose he convoked in 1059 a council in the Lateran, which was destined to reform religious life throughout the Catholic Europe. Essential changes in the canon law made at this synod furnished the foundation for the religious revival and spiritual rebirth of the Church.

In the following year Nicholas II promulgated the decrees of the synod throughout his ecclesiastic dominion, and sent apostolic delegates into some countries to enforce the new laws. Abbot Maynard was one of these. He went first to Biograd, where he participated in the celebrations occasioned by the grant of property rights and royal privileges (regia libertas) to the new Benedictine monastery of St. John the Evangelist. After these festivities the nuncio went to Split in order to preside over the synod of the Dalmatian bishops and abbots assembled in the presence of the local clergy, high nobility and other influential laity.

The Third Council at Split

On opening the council, Abbot Maynard made public the decrees passed by the Lateran synod, and recommended enactment of a series of special canons to meet the situation in Dalmatian Croatia. He was apprised of the special conditions existing in this area, strongly influenced as it was by the Eastern Church, which by tradition was antagonistic to the western reform movement. In the first place the marriage of priests was considered in all Croatia legitimate and above social censure. Secondly, the dress and appearance of the long-haired and bearded Croatian clergy was identical with that of the Greek Orthodox faith. Again, the high ecclesiastic positions were under the rather effective control of the king. Thus, had Peter Kreshimir sided with the national clergy, the reformist cause would have been lost, and the Croatian Church would have carried on as a separate organization or eventually effected its union with the Eastern Church.

The matter that most disturbed Maynard was the use of the Slavic language in divine services and sacred texts. Irritation over this point was so wide-spread among the reformist clergy that the orthodox character of the Slavic liturgy was misinterpreted, and the Slavic cult by some zealots accused of Arian heresy and Gothic origin. St. Methodius himself was decried as an Arian heretic, probably through confusion with bishop Ulfilas, translator of the Gothic Bible. Similarly the Croatian glagolitic writing, owing to its angular design, was taken for Gothic and held up in full view as something of Arian origin.

There is no reason to believe that the grotesque charges were made as deliberate falsehoods; rather they reveal the passionate nature of the controversy in an age when the memory of both St. Methodius and Pope John VII had nearly faded out. Even in the absence of malice the consequences of such confusion were devastating; Abbot Maynard himself was swayed into this view, and he in turn succeeded in convincing the Pontiff. Thus the controversy about the Slavic liturgy in Croatia was no longer a matter of administrative expediency or disciplinary character, but was shifted into the dogmatic field.

In such a tense atmosphere, charged with prejudice and animosities, the proceedings of the council took a decidedly anti-Slavic course. We may assume that the deliberations were frequently interrupted with the vehement protests of the Croatian abbots and bishops, yet the reformist majority, supported by the authority of the papal delegate, carried a full course of reform, intended to assure the administrative, linguistic and doctrinal unity of all the Catholic churches in Dalmatian Croatia. The canons enacted at the episcopal synod in Split leave no room for doubt that the reformist movement scored a great victory in Croatia.

Anti-Croatian Decrees of the Council

A brief review of a few pertinent canons will best reveal the state of mind and sentiment prevailing at the synod of Split. Concerning clerical marriage we read the following: *"If any ordained person, whether a bishop, priest or deacon contracts marriage, or retains, in defiance of this decree, a wife formerly wedded, he thereby is dismissed from the orders; is excluded from any group of persons officiating before the altar, and is barred from the source of revenue of any church."*

The personal appearance of the Croatian priests is reproved in unequivocal terms: *"If any priest should in the future grow long hair and beard, he shall not be admitted to church, nor permitted to perform divine services; he will be also subjected to punishment provided for by the canon law, in accordance with his rank."*

Another important decree directed against the native clergy reads as follows: *"Under the threat of excommunication it is prohibited to ordain any person of Slavic birth who is not experienced in the use of the Latin speech and letters. It is equally unlawful to subject a clergyman of whatever rank to secular authority, or to collect from him any kind of tax."* Finally, it was decreed that mass could be celebrated only in Latin or Greek, therefore to the exclusion of the Slavic language.

Such enactments were obviously aimed at the suppression of the Glagolitic script and elimination of the Slavic speech as a language of divine services. The drastic action reflected in these canons is the best single proof of the popularity of the Slavic liturgy. It shows how deeply rooted were the rites introduced less than two centuries past by the enthusiastic disciples of Saints Cyril and Methodius. The enforcement of these canons, with other reformist decrees, was assigned to Laurentius (Lovro), bishop of Absorus (Osor), a young Dalmatian of Latin blood. For this purpose he was now elected archbishop of Split.

Upon receiving the report of Abbot Maynard, Nicholas II confirmed both the canons and the election of the new prelate. They were also approved and confirmed by another Lateran council which was then in session for the consecration of Laurentius as archbishop of Split. Tseudo, bishop of Orvisto, was sent to Dalmatia as a special delegate of the Pontiff. After the ceremonies of induction were over, Tseudo took time to study the conditions in the country and did not fail to take notice of the many complaints and the bitter feeling of the population against the enactments of the synod.

Therefore he deferred their enforcement long enough to post the pontiff on the true state of affairs prevailing in the country. Before anything could be done, Nicholas II died and was succeeded by Alexander II (1061-1073). The new pontiff was confronted with a rising tide of opposition to the canons of 1059 in many countries, especially in Italy and Germany. For the time being therefore, decrees of Split were left in abeyance until the situation became settled and further moves could be made. A new Lateran council was held in 1063, at which all the canons of 1059 were reaffirmed, and the synodal decrees of Split definitely approved. Soon after this decision had been taken, the pope conveyed the final decrees to the king, Peter Kreshimir, and to all the bishops and abbots of Croatia for compliance and execution. This order of the pontiff marks one of the turning points in the religious life and ecclesiastic history of Croatia. It is also the point of departure for the establishment of a separate church of Bosnia.

Opposition to the Latin Church

After papal decree had been promulgated throughout the dioceses and parishes of Croatia, it became necessary to enforce its provisions. Concentrating on ideals and objectives, the authors of the disputed canon had lost sight of the practical angles of the cause they championed. They were so remote from reality that without the active support or complicity of the political authority, they would have been shattered against the rock of national life and its institutions. Under the constant threat of excommunication, branded with heresy and cruel punishment meted out on heretics, the national church broke down, but under its ruins it buried the social harmony and political independence of the Croatian state.

The opposing forces met at too sharp an angle to permit an adjustment of their differences. In the first place, the vast majority of the Croatian clergy did not speak Latin, nor could they make any intelligent use of it in the performance of their official duties. Secondly, practically all of the Croatian clergy led family life,

and no one saw anything objectionable in it. On the contrary, this patriarchal mode of life had an archaic charm and elevation about it, hallowed by the tradition of the Eastern Church, whose influence continued to be felt all along the Adriatic coast in spite of the administrative divisions between Constantinople and Rome. An order to abandon one's family for disciplinary reasons seemed cruel and wanton. Hence the general refusal to obey the order.

The common people stood by their ministers, and begrudged the introduction of Latin into the church services. Their attachment to the meaning as well as form of the divine services, repudiated the mere form and spectacle. To the Slav *"Gospodi pomiluj!"* (Lord, have mercy on us!) meant everything, and its equivalent: "Kyrie eleison!" was an unintelligible alien substitute. The first he would repeat indefinitely; through an endless variety of modulation of tone, rhythm, inflection, volume and coloring in the pronunciation of these two pathetic words, he scattered his soul through a prism of intense feeling and ecstasy.

Unfortunately the protagonists of the reform in those days lacked tact and circumspection. They failed to see in Croatia a situation utterly distinct from that in Western Europe, where clerical marriage was usually a mark of simony creeping into the high ecclesiastic ranks through the induction of feudal lords or others whose interests and occupations were worldly and self-centered. The Cluniac reform was the need of the moment in the west, while in the east it disturbed unnecessarily a hoary and dignified patriarchal institution. Upon refusal of the clergy to submit, sanctions were applied with undue haste and rigor. The Slavic churches were closed, Slavic services prohibited, and the priests unfrocked or removed from their parishes. Through the partisan policy of the king, the political authorities remained either neutral, or assisted in the ousting of priests and other measures of repression.

Vuk,* the Champion of the National Church

The energy and speed with which the canons of the synod were enforced, caused widespread

---

* *Vuk* 'wolf' is a common name in Croatian and Serbian, not unlike the German *Wolfgang*. A number of patronymics derived from this name survived as family names Vučić, Vukelić, Vučetić, Vučković, etc. However, the original form was 'volk' as in Russian *volk*, Polish *wilk*, Czech *vlk*, etc.

resentment and unrest throughout Croatia. Two antagonistic camps formed in the country, the more numerous national party joining the forces of the common people, lower nobility and Croatian clergy. The second was the more influential reformist party which lacked the support of masses, but was made up of the higher nobility, Latin clergy and the court. Even though the conflict between these two camps was more violent than in other similar clashes throughout Europe it should be born in mind that it came with a tide of general opposition to the reorganization of the Catholic Church along the principles of Cluny.

The chief organizer of resistance in Croatia was Vuk, a high-minded Glagolitic priest residing on the island of Kerk (Corcyra, Veglia). This spot had long been a stronghold of the national Church and Slavic liturgy. A man of strong will and keen intelligence, Vuk succeeded in organizing a powerful movement against the Latin clergy and Roman reforms. His goal was the re-establishment of the autocephalic Croatian bishopric which had existed until the second council of Split in 928. As an autocephalic diocese, it had come under the immediate authority of the Holy See, and was therefore independent of the archdiocese of Split.

The people rallied to Vuk's support. The idea of a national Church with Glagolitic traditions and full independence from the Latin authorities was widely acclaimed, and the movement grew in force and volume. On a wave of optimism Vuk was sent to Rome, there to assure the pontiff of the loyalty of the Croatian clergy and people to the Catholic Church and the Holy See, and to refute the charges of heresy preferred against them by the Latin clergy. He also was authorized to demand the restoration of the Slavic liturgy as well as the respect for the family life of the Croatian clergy.

The pope took a sympathetic view of the Croatian grievances and demands, but declined to grant concessions, which were in excess of his own power and authority. However, he encouraged Vuk to initiate an action for approval by the synod of Split, composed of all the bishops and abbots of Dalmatian Croatia. Obviously the success of the national cause hinged on a new show of popular strength and unanimity. On his return home, Vuk reported the decision of the Holy See.

Chapter XIII

BREAKDOWN OF THE CROATIAN CHURCH.—REIGN
OF THE LAST THREE KINGS

THE encouragement given by the pope to Vuk was received with great relief in Croatia. From the attitude of the pontiff the people gained the impression that the Holy See was not adverse to their demands, and believed that by reopening the case in Rome, and through a more forceful presentation of their grievances, the solution of their problems could be promptly effected. For this reason a new delegation was sent to Rome. Vuk was again head of the delegation, and was accompanied by two prominent clerics: Abbot Potepa and the aged Zdeda. By the consent of the people Zdeda was to be made the head of the Croatian Church, and consecrated by the pope as a bishop of the old autocephalic diocese. In this way he would rank with the archbishop of Split, and be made independent of his authority. That would make the Croatian Church an independent national institution as it was in the times of Bishop Theodosius and Pope John VIII (881).

But once again the delegates failed in their mission to the Holy See. The patriarchal appearance of Zdeda and his lack of familiarity with Latin had an adverse effect. His long beard and eastern garb estranged the pope and his council from the idea of Slavic liturgy and ecclesiastic independence. After long deliberation Alexander II rejected the Croatian demands and pointed out that the Slavic liturgy was of Arian origin. He further demanded that the Croatians submit to the synodal canons of 1060. However, he took care to explain that he would soon send apostolic delegates to their country to restore peace and contentment. Vastly disappointed over the papal decision, the three men returned to Croatia and decided on an open break with Rome.

Open Rebellion

The conditions in which the rebellion broke out, do not seem clear. One thing only seems certain and beyond dispute, and that is that there was considerable violence on the island of Kerk between the parties of enforcement and resistance. The Latin bishop George was ex-pelled from the island and Zdeda elevated to his office. In defiance of the papal decree, Zdeda acted as an autocephalic head of the Croatian Church, and performed all the functions attached to such rank. He consecrated Croatian priests for Slavic liturgy, reinstated the use of the Glagolitic books and Slavic language in the churches, and reopened all the churches which had been forcibly closed. With his encouragement, the priests who under the papal decree had severed their family ties were again united with their families.

Reaction to this assertion of national spirit and independence in matters of faith, was prompt and intense in both camps. The whole country was in turmoil, and there were many bloody clashes. In Rome Zdeda's seizure of episcopal authority was branded as simonistic heresy. Not only Zdeda, but all his followers were struck with anathema, and as heretics became subject to severe persecution. Cardinal John was sent to Croatia as apostolic delegate. With the assistance of the king, John had the three leaders of the rebellion seized and hailed before the authorities. The fate of the Abbot Potepa is not known, but pressure was brought upon the aged Zdeda to have him renounce his episcopal authority and rank. Zdeda refused to yield, and soon died in prison. The proud Vuk, champion of the national church, was brought before the synod in Split for trial. After a thorough investigation of his case the vindictive Latin bishops deprived him of priestly rank, had him shorn, and after much humiliation threw him in prison, where he remained for twelve years. By 1064 the rebellion was crushed, and upon his return to Rome Cardinal John could report to the pope that order had been restored in the troubled land. Indeed the country was outwardly calm, but this was merely a lull before the storm.[25]

Slavats and the Norman Invasion

The death of King Peter Kreshimir was a signal for the rebellion of all those who had suffered defeat at the hands of the Latin party. Both the national clergy and people, reduced

to voiceless submission, were embittered over the growing influence of the Latin clergy, which gave a foreign appearance to the Croatian Church. When discipline broke up, the Slavic liturgy was restored and the national spirit revived all over the kingdom. The center of the revolutionary movement was now in the Narentian territory, which was ruled by the powerful tribe of Kachich. The prince regent of this territory, Rusin, died shortly before the death of Peter Kreshimir, and the authority passed to his brother Slavats as regent for the son of Rusin, who was still in his minority. Dissatisfied with the conditions prevailing in the country, Slavats mustered up forces large enough to prevent Duke Stephen, Peter Kreshimir's nephew and the last living member of the dynasty of Terpimirovichi, from succeeding to the throne. Stephen was forced into retirement in a monastery, and Slavats, with his supporters assumed the reins of government. Slavats was proclaimed king, but there was much opposition to his personal rule. The Latin party, together with the Dalmatian municipalities and higher Croatian nobility refused him allegiance, and sought aid abroad to overthrow him. The Duke Zvonimir, banus of Pannonian Croatia, joined them. The opposition sent a delegation to Rome and complained to the Pope against the usurpation of the power by a "heretic" and his band. The Pontiff and his council listened to these grievances all the more intently as their own prestige and power in Croatia were at stake.

The pope at that time was Gregory VII, who as the archdeacon Hildebrand had been adviser and chief assistant to the former two popes: Nicholas II and Alexander II. He made the name of Gregory VII one of the most illustrious in papal history. As a grand figure of the Cluniac reform, he strove to subordinate the power of the worldy princes to his own. He was well versed in the ecclesiastic affairs of Croatia, since he himself had participated in the settlement of disputes arising from the enactments of the synod of Split. The occasion for intervention in the affairs of Croatia seemed propitious to Gregory, for he could place upon the Croatian throne a man of his choice, and eradicate finally the "Arian heresy" of the Glagolitic Church. He decided, therefore, to act with speed and firmness.

Early in 1075 he sent messengers to the court of Denmark for military aid, offering to place a prince of the royal blood on the throne of Croatia. When Denmark refused, he turned to Amico, the Norman duke of Appulia, with the request to invade Croatia, and overthrow the king. The domestic enemies of Slavats also sent envoys to Appulia suing for military aid. Toward the end of 1075, the Norman leader equipped an armed expedition to Croatia, and landed with his forces on the Dalmatian coast. Slavats was captured and made prisoner. Since there is no record of any military engagements, it may be assumed that Slavats fell victim to treachery, and was seized by his enemies at a parley. The lot of Slavats after his capture is unknown, and it stands to reason that he was either slain, or kept by Amico abroad. At any rate the Normans now established their control over a number of Dalmatian cities, including Split, Trogir (Trau), Biograd, Zadar and Nin. The cause of the Slavic liturgy in the Croatian Church suffered another setback, but was far from extinction. The Norman occupation of the Dalmatian cities led to another complication: intervention by the doge Dominico Silvio, and new struggles with Venice.

The Reign of Demetrius Zvonimir

After the fate of King Slavats had been sealed, several important developments took place in the Croatian lands. Early in 1076 a new synod was held in Split, at which the archbishop Gerard presided in his capacity of apostolic delegate. The purpose of this synod was to consolidate the earlier gains and pacify the Croatian clergy which had sided with the rebel king. The early canons of Split were reaffirmed, and clerical discipline restored. As a further concession to the national spirit, the bishopric of Nin, which had been abolished at the council of 928, was reestablished. The venerable Vuk, who had already spent twelve years in prison, was released under promise to leave the country and never return.

The most important event of this troublesome era of turmoil and upheaval was the invasion of the Dalmatian coast by the forces of Dominico Silvio, doge of Venice. The Venetians could not brook the Norman conquest of the eastern Adriatic, and decided to expel the forces of duke Amico from their Dalmatian strongholds. After a brief but stiff fight the Normans were defeated, and doge Silvio made a triumphal entry into the main coastal towns. In the

city of Split he summoned all the high nobility and notables, and had them take the oath of loyalty to Venice with the solemn promise not to invite the Normans or other foreigners to their country again. Dominico Silvio now took the title of Duke of Dalmatia.

Another important event of this troublesome period was the election of the banus Zvonimir as king of Croatia and Dalmatia. This union of the two provinces under one ruler checked the tendency of the time toward disintegration and dismemberment of the national territory. Through the trials of the revolutionary period all the factions had come to realize that in their disunion there was far more at stake than mere ecclesiastic questions and administrative advantages. The glamorous duke Zvonimir was not without shortcomings as a candidate for the throne. He did not belong to the family of Peter Kreshimir, and the dynasty of Terpimirovichi. However, he was somewhat compensated in prestige by the fact of being a brother-in-law to Géza I, king of Hungary, and after the downfall of Slavats he was the only commanding figure available to fill the vacant throne. He was therefore the logical choice of the high nobility, the Latin party, and all the other elements who had opposed Slavats.

Partly from fear of Venetian intervention, and in part owing to uncertainty of the attitude the Holy See would take toward a king who lacked dynastic legitimacy, the coronation of Zvonimir was postponed. Complications from the pope's position in the matter were avoided by a fortunate set of circumstances favoring the new king. Pope Gregory VII was then in the midst of his struggle with Henry IV, emperor of Germany. It was the climatic year between the council at Worms (January, 1076), and Canossa (January, 1077). On the first occasion Gregory VII was deposed at behest of the emperor by the bishops of Germany and labelled a "usurper" and "false monk." He was declared to have secured the papal throne through violence, and to be "accused through all the ages." The pope retaliated by excommunicating Henry, depriving him of his imperial title, and encouraging his subjects to elect a new sovereign. It was less than a year (October, 1076) before the princes met at Tribur and declared Henry IV deposed, unless he should come within three months to terms with the Apostolic See. At the same time, the military campaigns of the emperor met with reverses,

and to save the situation Henry swallowed his pride and decided upon reconciliation. On foot and in the coarse garb of a penitent he crossed the Alps and appeared bare-footed and stripped of all badges of his imperial authority before the pope at Canossa. This was the greatest moral victory of the Church over the political power, short of the proud gesture of bishop Ambrose of Milan, who had passed the mighty emperor Theodosius of Constantinople through a humiliating course of penitence.

In the interim between these two events, the council of Worms and penitence in Canossa, the cause of the pope looked at times hopeless. Most of Lombardy was against him, together with Venice and the southern provinces of Germany, including Carinthia. It was therefore of the utmost importance to check the spread of the imperial influence in the disaffected area along the Adriatic coast. This made Gregory very cautious in his attitude to the problem of succession in Croatia, and prompted him to waive the customary objections of legitimacy, which plainly would have been in order here since duke Styepan, the nephew of Peter Kreshimir was still alive, and available to occupy the throne.

Gregory VII had another weighty reason for the approval of Zvonimir. He had established friendly relations with the emperor of Byzantium, who still claimed political rights over Dalmatia. Since the friendly Normans had been forced out of Dalmatia by the Venetians, the pope saw in a combination of Byzantine influence with a strong national monarchy a way to check or counteract the Venetian overlordship in Dalmatia. Thus Zvonimir, who had the support of the high nobility, the Latin party and other national elements, was the logical person to champion the cause of the Roman Church in Croatia.   ,

Elevation to the Throne

It was, therefore, necessary to attach Zvonimir more closely to the policies of Gregory VII, and fit him into the papal conception of a perfect Christian ruler. For this reason Gregory sent two apostolic delegates to Croatia in the persons of Abbot Gepison and Bishop Fulcoin. The papal envoys summoned a council in the Cathedral of St. Peter in Solin (Salona) and announced the terms under which the Holy See could approve of the election of the new king.

When Zvonimir accepted the papal terms, he was forthwith acclaimed by the assembly, and in the presence of the notables and common people proclaimed king. On the 9th of October, 1076, the crown was placed on his head by Abbott Gepison, the papal delegate, in the Cathedral of St. Peter in Salona. Zvonimir took an oath of loyalty to Gregory VII, and promised to discharge certain duties to the Holy See. In recognition of the spiritual supremacy of the See of St. Peter over temporal powers, he took from the hands of Gepison the papal flag. He made donations of property to churches and promised a yearly gift to the Pope of two hundred ducats.

The reign of Demetrius Zvonimir, which began under high auspices, is replete with dramatic episodes. It is marked by important foreign developments, which were attended by armed clashes with his powerful neighbors. Military successes both on land and sea were constant companions of his armed forces, and Zvonimir started out on a career which promised the feats of a crusader or conqueror. His premature death arrested both and prevented him from vying for the honors of Godfrey of Lorraine, Bohemund Guiscard and Robert of Toulouse as deliverers of Jerusalem and defenders of the Holy Sepulcher. Zvonimir is the most spectacular and dramatic of the Croatian rulers, whose tragic end revealed a heroic character.

In the year of Canossa (1077) the world situation was such that it was nigh impossible for any country in Europe to stay aloof from the swift stream of events in the East and West. So much more difficult was the position of those countries, which, like Croatia, were close to the center of powerful conflicts. On one hand the pressure of the Seljuk Turks, by this time already in possession of Jerusalem, and on the other the weakness of Byzantium, created a situation which was to affect the destinies of the whole Christian world. Furthermore, the gigantic struggle between the papacy and the emperors of Germany upset the foreign alignments of the neighboring countries. In the Croatian State both these situations affected deeply the alliances and struggles of the new king.

Alliance of Normans and Croats

For siding with Pope Gregory VII in his struggle with Henry IV, emperor of Germany, Zvonimir was attacked by Vetselinus, duke of Istria,

a vassal of the emperor. Although the details of this struggle are not known, the length of the campaign would indicate a serious conflict. It was ended through the intervention of Gregory VII in 1079. The most important campaign of Zvonimir is one he undertook in alliance with Robert Guiscard, the Norman duke of Sicily, against Venice and Alexius Comnenus, emporor of Constantinople. A number of matters may have inspired this cause, but the most obvious is that traditional conflict with Byzantium through which Croatia asserted her longing for independence, and resistance to the increasing aggressiveness of Venetian raids and encroachments. In command of strong naval forces, and supported by the fleets of Dubrovnik (Ragusa) and other Dalmatian cities, Zvonimir joined the Norman duke in the attack and siege of the imperial city of Durazzo (Drach). The city was stormed and captured in 1083 after the Croatian-Norman navy won a decisive victory on the sea over the combined fleets of Constantinople and Venice.

In the next year the allied forces of the Croatians and Normans scored another victory over the Venetian navy near the island of Corfou. Soon after this event Robert Guiscard died, and this ended the Croatian-Norman alliance which had made such a powerful bid for domination of both Adriatic coasts. In compensation for the losses of his Venetian ally, Emperor Alexius rewarded the doge* with the title "Ruler of Croatia and Dalmatia," thereby renouncing all his own political titles and claims to this territory in favor of Venice. It was a completely hollow gesture at the time, but with the growth of Venetian power along the eastern Adriatic coast, it came to serve as a source of Venetian claims and sanctions in the future. After the death of Robert Guiscard, Zvonimir soon lost another powerful friend and ally with the passing of Gregory VII (May 25, 1085). The death of these two famous historical figures dealt a blow to the ascendancy of Zvonimir's power and ambitions from which he never recovered. A new set of political circumstances was soon to arise which reversed the favorable course of his policies, and paved the way to his own tragic end.

Estrangement of the People from Zvonimir

Even during the period of his ringing victories, the war-like policies of Demetrius Zvonimir

* Then Vitelo Faliero.

did not meet with the unanimous approval of the Croatian people. The burden of his military expeditions and sacrifices, imposed upon them through continuous warfare, caused much dissatisfaction. In addition, the oppressed national party and supporters of the Croatian Church were set stubbornly against the rising power of the Latin faction. In fact they considered the king a puppet in the hands of the Latin magnates and churchmen. They were also opposed to the new trends in the civil administration of the state.

Following the models of western feudalism, the king replaced the old tribal chieftans (zhupani) and their leaders (bani) with a group of counts (comites) and high royal officials or lieutenants (vicarius regis) both in his court and the general administration of the country. Thus the court became a place of assembly for the Latin dignitaries, where Archbishop Laurentius, the chief opponent of the Croatian Church, was very influential. Foreign influence was further accentuated by the entourage of Queen Helen, surnamed "the beautiful" (Yelena Liyepa), daughter of one Hungarian king and sister of another. Under such auspices the Croatian people gradually became estranged from their king, and an undercurrent of sentiment was formed that was to doom the Croatian State. Finally, a dynastic problem arose with the death of Radovan, son of Zvonimir and Helen.

Dramatic developments that now took place in the Orient and the Balkans had disastrous consequences for the brilliant reign of Demetrius Zvonimir. Under the blows of the Petchenegs south of the Danube, and the Seljuk Turks in Asia Minor, Byzantium began to crumble. Emperor Alexius made a frantic appeal to the Christian West which found a sympathetic echo throughout western Christendom. The chief supporter of Alexius' plea was Pope Urban II (1088-1099), who was inspired by the emperor's request for a strong force of mercenaries to form a grandiose scheme for the military revival of western Christianity under the leadership of the Holy See. This magnificent enterprise grew in scope and momentum as its details were revealed and discussed. It called for the conquest and colonization of the heathen lands by the excess populations of the West and provided opportunity for atonement through the risks and sacrifices of the hazardous campaign. The missionary fervor of Urban led to the Council of Clermont (1095), which may be called one of the dramatic climaxes of European history. For there he preached the First Crusade, unfading symbol of the militant spirit of Christian Europe, which was to establish the most cherished of all traditions of Western man, the memory of those moments in the Middle Ages when he appeared at his selfless and generous and dedicated best.[26]

Croats Reprove the Foreign Policy of Zvonimir

With the approval of Urban II, Emperor Alexius sued for the military assistance of his former enemy Demetrius Zvonimir. This took place at the beginning of the emperor's quest for armed support in the West, and before the crusading activity of Urban had taken root in the minds of the faithful. In spite of the best intentions of Urban, his plea in favor of Alexius, their traditional enemy, must have caused consternation in the minds of many in Croatia. Even the inducement of delivering the Holy Sepulchre was taken largely with indifference. In the eyes of many Croatian warriors, Alexius was an enemy whose destruction by a foreign power was not an altogether unwelcome prospect. Thus the efforts of Demetrius Zvonimir to induce his people to render assistance to hard pressed Byzantium fell on deaf ears. Zvonimir summoned an assembly of his warriors and noblemen in a field near Knin (1089) to deliberate. His enthusiasm for the crusade moved some deeply, failed to sway others. The quarreling became violent and the assembly broke up in a riot. Demetrius Zvonimir himself was killed in the melée.*

Thus a brilliant reign, inaugurated under the highest auspices, ended in a tragic downfall. Up to this point the military career of Demetrius Zvonimir had been one of continued success and increasing effectiveness. In a time of general upheaval and in the face of almost constant attack by forces of the German emperor, Venice and Byzantium, he had created a strong political situation for his kingdom. His alliance with Norman Italy opened a new chapter in the long fight for Croatian independence from the Venetian control. Unfortunately, this chapter of Croatian-Norman cooperation closed too soon. Zvonimir's friendship and alliance with the

---

* There are several legends connected with the death of Zvonimir. Some of them have no knowledge of the national assembly, in which he met violent death. Moreover, by some historians the whole episode is subjected to doubt.

great Gregory VII had been the chief asset of his reign.

Contrary to his military experience of the recent past, he was swayed by the inspiration of Urban II from the orbit of traditional Croatian policies to the support of Emperor Alexius. The Croatian people could join him in the first, but refused to follow him in the new course of assisting an enemy even for the motives of the crusade. In this rapid change of his foreign policy lay Zvonimir's doom, and the future misfortunes of his nation.

Succession Claims

The sudden death of Demetrius Zvonimir created a new problem of succession. In the past dynastic struggles had brought the Croatian state to the edge of ruin. On this occasion the intervention of a powerful neighbor cost the political independence of the national kingdom.

There were two candidates contending for succession after Zvonimir's death. One was his widow, Helen-the-Fair, who claimed the crown as her lawful heritage. Some of the high nobility and the courtiers supported this claim, but were overborne by the supporters of Styepan II (1089-1090), the nephew of Peter Kreshimir. Styepan was duly raised to the throne, but death overtook him the following year.

Thus Helen could renew her claim without interference from the dynasty of Terpimirovichi. This time she secured the support of the major part of Styepan's party, and for all practical purposes she was now the ruler. Meanwhile the opposition became determined to settle the issue by armed force, and the clashes spread all over the country. Pressed on all sides by the tide of rebellion, the court faction decided to seek aid abroad and invite the intervention of Ladislaus (Szent Lázló, 1077-1097), brother of Helen, and king of Hungary. Ladislaus complied with the request, and in 1091 set out on a campaign to secure his "lawful heritage" of the Croatian crown. The partisans of Queen Helen controlled Pannonian Croatia, and the troops of Ladislaus met with no resistance (indeed the Hungarian king was received as a friend).

Intervention of Hungary

The fighting began near the coast in the mountain passes of the Iron Alps. Even here the progress of the invader was checked not by the national army of the Croatian State, but by the local forces of the tribes inhabiting the mountains. The Hungarians did not progress beyond these mountain ranges, although the objective of the king was to reach the seacoast and occupy the Dalmatian towns. In the midst of his campaign, Ladislaus was called back to Hungary to check the invasion of the Kumani, a nomadic horde. After the death of Vladimir of Kiev they swooped down to the Carpatian ranges from the great steppes of Russia.. Thus the Dalmatian part of Croatia was saved from the Hungarian conquest, but Pannonian Croatia or the territory between Gvozd and Drava remained in the power of Ladislaus. The king left his nephew Álmos (1091-1095) in control of the territory and charged him with the task of extending the Hungarian power over Dalmatia and Bosnia. Furthermore, he strengthened his hold over the occupied territory by establishing the diocese of Zagreb as a new tie between Croatia and Hungary.

While he was still campaigning in the Iron Alps, Ladislaus sent envoys to Rome asking Urban II to approve his claim to the heritage of the Croatian lands. The Holy See refused, however, whereupon Ladislaus joined forces with Henry IV, emperor of Germany against Urban II. Byzantium as might have been expected sided with the pope, thus stiffening the national faction in Dalmatia to organize its own forces for the recovery of Pannonian territory from the Hungarian rule. This national party rallied around the figure of Peter (1093-1097), the last member of the national dynasty. This Peter is commonly known by his last name of Svachich, although some historians derive his origin from the tribe of Kachich, taking him for a nephew of King Slavats, and son of Prince Rusin Kachich. Under the able leadership of Peter, the national life of Croatia was invigorated. The Hungarian Álmos had to abandon Pannonia and return to his uncle Ladislaus. Thus the political sovereignty of Peter was established over the whole territory north of Gvozd and south of the Drava river.

The Death of Peter Svachich

After his accession to throne the young Hungarian king Kálmán (1095-1116) conceived the ambitious plan of conquering Croatia and thus completing the undertaking begun by his uncle

Ladislaus. The international situation favored this plan, because both Byzantium and Western Europe were deeply involved in preparation for the First Crusade, while the Croatian forces had not yet recovered from the civil war. Early in 1097, Kálmán equipped a large army and entered Croatia. Peter was forced back toward the sea, and a decisive battle was fought south of the lower course of the river Kulpa along the northern slopes of the Iron Alps (Gvozd). The battle ended with disaster for the Croatian forces; King Peter himself was slain on the battlefield. Since 1097, the mountain range Gvozd is called Petrov Gvozd, or Petrova Gora. The victorious Hungarian armies pursued their course toward the sea, and occupied the coast and the Dalmatian towns without difficulty.

Alhtough the Hungarians overran and occupied the country, their victory would have been ephemeral if it had not been attended by moves of political wisdom. An uprising in Croatia at an opportune moment could have shaken off the foreign yoke, especially in view of the vulnerable position of Hungary proper after the defeat of Kálmán's armies by the Russians and Kumani at Przemysl in Galicia in 1099. Kálmán* therefore sought conciliation with Croatia, and offered a compromise to the Croatian nobility by which they would retain their ancestral privileges under the sovereignty of the Hungarian king.

When the way had been prepared by Kálmán's envoys, the representatives of the twelve Croatian tribes living in the territory between Gvozd and Neretva met with the king and elected him their lawful sovereign, with the title of king of Croatia and Dalmatia.** As a condition for this election the king was to respect the privileges of a special Croatian-Dalmatian diet, and accept separate coronation as the Croatian king. In turn the nobility was to prove its loyalty by supplying a small cavalry force to the king in case of war.

After this agreement both the noblemen and the king went to the city of Biograd-on-the-sea,

where Kálmán was crowned and invested with the title: *Rex Damatiae et Croatiae*. With his oath he guaranteed all the public and constitutional rights of the Croatian state. By this new constitutional structure Hungary and Croatia were henceforth to have a common king, but to continue as separate kingdoms bound together by the person of the sovereign, who supplied the organic link to the new commonwealth. In recognition of the relationship the kings of Hungary assumed after the reign of Kálmán the hereditary title: *Rex Hungariae, Dalmatiae et Croatiae* (King of Hungary, Daimatia and Croatia).

This union between the crownlands of Croatia and Hungary continued until October 1918, when it was dissolved by the Act of the Croatian Diet in Zagreb. There is much controversy in the historical literature as to the nature of this tie. Some Hungarian writers claim conquest pure and simple, and treat the Croatian territory as the "provinces" (tartomány) or "annexed lands" (csatolt ország) of the crown of St. Stephen, i.e. Hungary.

Experts in constitutional law hold different views. The practice of crowning the kings separately with the crown of Zvonimir was replaced in the course of time by a simultaneous coronation as king of Hungary and Croatia. Later, during the accession of the Anjou and Polish kings and after election of the Hapsburgs, the sovereigns carried the title of all their other possessions and claims.

On the other hand, the royal power during the reign of the Árpád dynasty and that of the Angevin Charles Robert was but nominal, and real authority was exercised locally by powerful oligarchs and barons. While they were on friendly terms with the king, harmony prevailed throughout the land, and both parties assisted each other in the conduct of foreign policy. In the meantime, the barons could engage in mutual struggles or organize opposing factions and the kings would not interfere in their domestic quarrels. The language of the realm was Latin as it was in most parts of Europe, and problems of nationality were nonexistent. The gravest problems arose in the domain of religion and in the feudal organization of the times. The following pages of this work will throw some light on these matters.

---

* The name *Kálmán* defies every attempt to set up a Hungarian etymology. It is probably a contraction of Colomannus, as reflected in the Croatian form: *Koloman*.

** This arrangement is usually called *"pacta conventa."*

Chapter XIV

ORGANIZATION OF THE CROATIAN STATE DURING THE NATIONAL DYNASTY

Early Middle Ages

THE first national and official name of the state was Croatia or the Croatian State (regnum Croatorum). In course of time another, more ancient name of the area became associated with the first. That was the name of Dalmatia which came into use during the eleventh century when the imperial maritime cities were attached to Croatia. From that time on the name of the state as it appears in official documents is Croatia and Dalmatia. The Byzantine writers were accustomed to refer only to Croatia (Chroaton Chora, Chroatia), while the popes preferred the name of Dalmatia. Alongside these two, the name Slavonia gained currency abroad. Thus, the "Croatian State," the only national name used at that early period, was designated also by two other names which in the long run obtained a geographical significance.

The frontiers of the Croatian State changed frequently. Having settled down in a part of the old Roman Dalmatia, the Croats did not immediately organize a unified state, but carried on in several separate regions and groups, forming Pannonian Croatia, Dalmatian Croatia, Narentan Province and Bosnia. Among all these areas the most important at first was Dalmatian Croatia which during the Roman rule, had been the center of ancient Dalmatia. Tomislav was the first to assemble a large number of Croatian areas under one rule. However the frontiers of the Croatian State were widest by far during the reign of Peter Kreshimir IV. In 1089 Bosnia broke away from this complex, but at the beginning of the eleventh century the Narentan District was annexed permanently. The frontiers of the Croatian kingdom, at the time of Koloman (Kálmán), ran approximately along Neretva River up to the Rama, and from the headwaters and central course of the Verbas to the confluence of the Bosna and Sava, and further along a line connecting the town of Brod with the lower Miholatz, to the Drava. Along the Drava River it extended to the Styrian-Carinthian border heights, where they descended to the sea near the city of Rijeka (Fiume). Among the coastal islands Kerk, Tsres, Rab, Pag, Hvar, Brach and Vis were Croatian.

Ethnical Elements and Social Organization

The people or nation which founded this kingdom was Croatian. By the Westerners it was frequently called also "Slav" (Sclavi). Alongside the Croatian ethnic element lived the Romance population, inhabiting the Dalmatian cities. They were called Romans (later also Latins and Wallachians), but gradually merged with the Croats so that by the eleventh century there were a large number of Croats settled in Zadar, Split and other cities.

The social organization was that of free and attached persons, or serfs. Attached persons (servi, ancillae) were living not only in the maritime cities but also on the large estates. Forfeiture of freedom came as a result of the purchase or sale of an insolvent debtor, or by voluntary surrender (especially to the Church), or through capture in war. The social position of the attached persons was hereditary. An attached person or serf could be freed by the public statement or legacy of his master. The free men divided into three classes: peasants, citizens and noblemen. In the old Croatian State the peasant enjoyed full ownership rights of his land and was on equal footing with the resident of the city. The citizenry was divided into two classes, that of the noblemen, whose family traditions were rooted deep in the Roman past, and that of the ordinary citizenry. The nobility also was subdivided into higher and lower strata. Conspicuous in the ranks of the higher nobility were the banus, the counts and Royal Court dignitaries while most others belonged to the lower nobility.

Both classes of nobility were in the retinue of the Court and escorted the Croatian ruler on all state occasions. From among their number came the chief dignitaries of the state, and by the will of the people they could be elevated to the throne. The source of the honors, especially those attaching to the counts (Zhupani), was not the grace of the ruler, but the tribal system. By the end of the eleventh century a number of

important families and clans had come into prominence along the seacoast and inland. We have already in this story met the scions of the Kachich, Svachich, Shubich, Kuryakovich, Nelipich, Vukchich and other powerful clans.

Religious Life

Soon after their Christianization, at the beginning of the ninth century the Croats were favored by the establishment of an autocephalic diocese, with its seat in Nin (Nona). This bishopric outranked all the others combined in territory and through the prestige which accrued to it from its independence became a serious rival to the archdiocese of Split. Seeing their authority undermined the Dalmatian bishops in 923 urged the pope to extend their jurisdiction, and especially that of the archbishop of Split, over the Croatian territory. This arrangement was sanctioned at the first Split Council and the bishopric of Nin was abolished. By the third decade of the tenth century the suffragans of the archbishop of Split were the bishops of Osor, Kerk, Rab, Zadar, Skradin, Ston, Dubrovnik. Kotor. Duvan and Sisak.

Important changes took place in the 11th century when new bishoprics were set up at Trogir (before 1000 A.D.), Knin (around 1040 A.D.) and Biograd (by 1058 A.D.) when the old bishopric of Skradin was vacated and transferred there. The diocese of Nin was reestablished in 1076, while in Bar (Antivari) a new archbishopric was instituted in 1089 which extended its authority over all Bosnia.

At about the same time the diocese of Ragusa was elevated to the status of archbishopric. The diocese of Cattaro from the eleventh to the fourteenth centuries was subject to the archbishopric of Bari in southern Italy. The most extensive and wealthiest diocese on Croatian territory was that of Knin, the authority of which extended north to the Drava River and reached east throughout the Pozhega district. Its bishop had the title of the "Bishop of Croats," after the pattern of the old bishop of Nin.

The archbishop of Split was elected at a council by the local clergy and citizenry of Split, together with the suffragans of the archdiocese. The election had to be unanimous. In the same way local bishops were elected by the will of the clergy and people. The archbishop was consecrated usually by the pontiff himself, or by his authorized representative. The bishops were consecrated by the archbishop of Split. At the consecration of the archbishop the pope vested him with the pallium, as an insignia of the prelate's authority to participate in the higher administration of the affairs of the Church.

The chief right of an archbishop was to call the provincial synod, act as its chairman, submit matters for discussion and promulgate its decisions. The provincial synod usually met in the Cathedral of Split; sometimes in other cities. The councils were attended by bishops and abbotts, while the matters under deliberation included problems of science, morals, discipline of the clergy and interests of the laymen. The decisions of the council were confirmed by the Holy See.

Activities of a powerful lay clergy were supplemented by numerous ordained clergy in the Croatian State. At that time only one monastic group, that of the Benedictines, was known in western Europe. A Benedictine monastery was built in 850 by Prince Terpimir near his palace at Klis and gradually the monasteries of the order became common throughout Croatian territory. Prefect of such an institution was the abbot, whose office was held in high esteem throughout the Croatian State.

Political Organization

Up to the beginning of the tenth century the Croatian State was headed by a Duke (Dux), and thereafter by the King. The supreme power, especially the royal power, was hereditary. However, the throne could be occupied under some circumstances by the king's brother, or by a son of the latter. Furthermore, the king could be elected, in case the situation warranted such course. The king was considered the representative of divine power on the earth: "King by Grace of God." This power was received, by general consent of the age, through the process of crowning, which at that time was essentially an ecclesiastic ritual. The royal insignia were the crown, the scepter, golden apple and sword. The Croatian rulers did not have a fixed capital, but resided in various localities of their dominion where they kept their own households. Their favorite residential places were the towns of Nin, Klis, Bihachi, Knin, Biograd and especially Solin (Salona).

The Court was modelled on the Merovingian and Carolingian pattern. The sovereign's escort consisted of court dignitaries. In the ducal period these were the clan chiefs (Zhupani) or counts. The court Zhupan (*palatinus jupanus*) was assisted by the chamber count (*camerarius*), the marshal of the royal horse stable (*cavallarius*), the royal shield bearer (*armiger*) and the royal mace bearer (*maceccha*). Later the royal court was expanded by establishment of the Chancery, in charge of *Comes Curiae* and creation of the Chamberlain's Office (*Comes postelnicus*); by that of wine-cellarers (*comes vinotoch*) and a crew of herd supervisors (*comes vola*). The maior domus (*djed*) looked after the income of the Court, while the judge (*regalis curiae iudex*) represented the king in settling disputes and in the general administration of justice.

There were also other officials and attendants of lower rank, all of them performing assigned functions similar to those introduced at the western European courts. The language used at the court was Croatian, while the royal charters and other documents were written in Latin.

Throughout the ninth century the duke shared his power with the clan chiefs (Zhupani). At the beginning of the national Croatian monarchy there was only one banus, who was entrusted with the administration of the inland districts of Lika, Kerbava and Gata. During the reign of Peter Kreshimir IV there were at least three bani: those of Croatia, Slavonia and Bosnia.

The Zhupani or counts were at the head of Zhupaniya or counties and these were made up frequently of a number of smaller districts (Zhupa). In the tenth and eleventh centuries there were seventeen counties occupying the coastal area and the adjacent inland territory. No reliable data are available on the number of these administrative districts in Bosnia or in Pannonian Croatia. However, there is no doubt that such administrative units did exist there.

Civil Affairs

The banus, counts and bishops constituted the Royal Council. Popular assemblies were held when deliberation on matters of national importance was called for. Local meetings or congregations made decisions on matters of local or regional interest.

The counts or district chiefs were represented by the vice-counts, and these by their captains in the administration of civil affairs in their respective districts. The supreme administrative, military and judicial authority was exercised directly by the king. However, he acted in the presence of, and in conference with his chief counsellors. In absentia, the royal power was exercised by his representatives, specifically by the Zhupani.

All disputed matters and litigations were decided usually by word of mouth, and in short procedure, after the witnesses and parties to the suit had been heard in open court. Subsequently the decision was confirmed in writing. Documents were issued by the Chancery of the Royal Court, headed by the bishop of Knin (Croatian bishop), while at a more remote period records were kept by the Court chaplains. The documents were written mostly in Latin and some few in the Croatian language, recorded in the Glagolitic script.

Fiscal Matters

The income of the Crown came in the first place from the tribute paid by the serfs who lived on the lands of the King. Royal estates were numerous, especially in the maritime province contained between Trogir, Split and Omish. Inland the most extensive royal estates were around Knin. Earlier in the ducal period collection of this revenue was in charge of the Chamberlain of the Court, while during the monarchy the fiscal affairs were managed by *Comes Postelnicus* as head of the royal treasury. Another source of royal revenue was the tax levied on all land owned and cultivated by the Croatian nobility and clergy, monasteries and churches. In fact, this tax was paid by the serfs for the account of their masters. By special grants of the king both noblemen and corporations (monasteries and churches) were frequently exempted from taxes. As a result of this the levies made on the serfs became the income of their owners. In return the noblemen assumed the obligation to supply the king with a number of cavalrymen in case of war.

When receiving the crown of Croatia and Dalmatia, Koloman granted exemption from land tax to twelve Croatian tribes residing between the Gvozd mountains and the Neretva, probably in line with a tradition that went back to the national dynasty.

Further income of the Crown came from the tribute paid by the Venetians (from about 890 to 995) for navigation privileges in the Adriatic, and also from "peace and amity taxes" levied on the Dalmatian cities still under the suzerainty of Byzantium. Penalties assessed against various offenders, and violations such as breach of contract, unlawful appropriation of land, etc., constituted another source of revenue. Custom duties, and port fees collected from foreign vessels, were among other items of royal income. Finally, an honorary tribute was levied from the magnates whose castles the sovereign and his escort visited on his journeys through the land. This consisted of gifts and accommodations offered to the king and his retinue. It was a heavy tribute, but it carried social prestige for a clan or corporation.

The Croatian rulers did not mint their own coins, but used the Byzantine gold and silver currency, as did Venice, Serbia and Bulgaria during the reigns of Simeon and Samuel. Moreover, the trade was carried on by direct exchange of goods and the taxes were paid in kind by produce and livestock (wheat, wine, oil, salt, cheese, bread, hogs, goats, sheep) and especially by marten pelts.

Armed Forces

The royal income was spent mostly on the upkeep of a strong army and navy. The king was the supreme commander, declared war and concluded peace. The military power on land and sea was very considerable even in the time of the dukes Terpimir and Domagoy, as the successful war against Bulgaria and the capture of Bari indicate. Later on, during the reign of Tomislav and Peter Kreshimir, it was much greater. From the second half of the eleventh century the Croatian navy was headed by the vicar of the duke of the Neretva district.

Autonomy of the Dalmatian Cities

The ancient Dalmatian cities enjoyed autonomy throughout this period. Gradually the new cities like Biograd and Shibenik, that had been built by the Croatians themselves, were granted the same privilege. The head of the city was a prior elected from among the city noblemen or patricians. He was confirmed at first by the emperor of Byzantium, and later by the Croatian king. For this reason the priors of Zadar or Split were the grandees of the kingdom. The most powerful magnate was the prior of Zadar, usually selected from the Madii family, kin of the Croatian dynasty. The prior was head of a city council consisting of judges, tribunes and notaries, acting as a steering committee or originating body for the enactment of laws and decrees, which in due course were submitted for approval to the Municipal Assembly by way of "Conlaudatio populi." This municipal assembly was attended by the bishop, clergy, nobility and citizens. The administration of justice followed the canons of the Roman law.

Education and Culture

The cities were centers of education and the arts, both fostered by the clergy. Every monastery of the Benedictine Order had its own library replete with manuscripts and precious illuminated texts. The members of the Order were under obligation to read them and digest them during their retreat. Gradually the monks engaged professionally in the education and training of youth, both for civil careers and clerical orders. In their schools the chief subjects were Latin grammar and logic. But the domestic Croatian literature was also cultivated in the native language, and in the Glagolitic script. From the eleventh century onward the Cyrillic script was also used in native manuscripts. The Glagolitic script was given a special angular form in Croatia, and for this reason it was called Croatian Glagolitsa. A large number of church books were written in Glagolitic. The best known specimens of this type are the missals, many of them neatly illuminated.

Architecture made great strides both in the religious and secular domain. The churches were for the most part small round buildings with a dome, while the altars and other parts of the church were decorated with figures of animals, carvings of symbolic birds and various types of geometrical ornamentation. Typical of this type of ornamentation are the plaited three-band decorative elements. Of these buildings the most important is the church of St. Donatus in Zadar. This structure was erected at the beginning of the ninth century on the foundations of a still older building. Such were also the round chapels of St. Nicholas and Holy Cross near Nin, the church of St. Barbara in Trogir and that of the Holy Trinity near Split.

All these churches were built in the ninth and tenth centuries and are preserved to this day. Many others are still extant, but badly neglected, while others were demolished by the Turks.

By the eleventh century the trades and crafts were flourishing. The chief industrial city was Split, where gold and silver smiths were abundant.

On the whole, Croatia of the eleventh century was a truly western country under the immediate cultural influence of neighboring Italy.

Chapter XV
UNION OF CROATIA WITH HUNGARY

The Reign of Koloman (1102-1116)

NOW that he was the crowned king of Croatia, Koloman decided to assert his sovereignty also over the Croatian cities of Zadar, Trogir and Split, and likewise over the islands of Rab, Tsres, Osor and Kerk. Such a course would in ordinary times have been bound to bring him into direct conflict with the emperor of Byzantium, the actual sovereign of these cities, and also with Venice, their immediate "protector."

In the year 1104, however, the youthful John Comnenus, son of the Byzantine emperor Alexis, married the Hungarian princess Piroshka (renamed Irene), daughter of the Saint-King Ladislaus. As a result of this dynastic tie friendly relations were established between Koloman who was a cousin of Piroshka, and her father-in-law Alexis. About the same time Robert Guiscard's son Boemundus, duke of Antioch and Tarentum, planned a new attack against Durazzo and the schismatic emperor and began to recruit crusaders in western Europe. In order to ward off this threat Alexis and Koloman made an alliance against Boemundus. Through this alliance, and because of the family relationship, strengthened further by political ties between the two sovereigns, Alexis, during a campaign in Asia Minor, agreed that his friend and ally Koloman should occupy the Dalmatian cities and islands. This arrangement was naturally a stunning blow to Venice. But being commercially and otherwise* tied up with Byzantium, Venice grudgingly submitted to the decision of Alexis, biding her opportunity to regain the lost possessions.

In the spring of 1107 Koloman set out with his army for the seacoast. Several Hungarian bishops and grandees accompanied him in this campaign. The king first aprroached Zadar, as the most important of the recalcitrant Dalmatian cities, and summoned it to surrender. But the citizens decided to offer resistance. Koloman began to invest the city and surrounding it from the mainland he pounded at its heavy walls with powerful siege weapons.

* Venice was allied with Byzantium against the Southern Italian Normans who threatened her trade.

Under such circumstances John, the bishop of Trogir, entered the beleaguered city from the sea and attempted to persuade its defenders to come to terms with the king. Shortly after, Koloman also sent messengers to Zadar, urging the citizens to surrender and to make peace with him "under the best conditions." The citizens accepted the offer by which Koloman guaranteed Zadar and its Church all the ancient privileges inherited from Byzantium. He confirmed this pledge with his own oath and that of the Hungarian churchmen and noblemen from his entourage. After this the citizens of Zadar took an oath of loyalty to the new ruler and received him in the city with great pomp.

Similar scenes were enacted in other cities. In the company of Bishop John, Koloman proceeded along the coast. The city of Trogir opened its gates without resistance, whereupon the king issued a decree similar to that of Zadar and lavishly endowed the church of Trogir. Thence he proceeded to neighboring Split. This city at first hesitated to recognize Koloman but when the king began to prepare for siege operations it surrendered, and through the intercession of its archbishop Crescentius, obtained a bull similar to that given to Zadar and Trogir.

After this Koloman returned to Zadar where the Croatian banus Ugra had assembled thirteen vessels. Embarking a fairly large land army, he landed on the island of Rab, which surrendered after some hesitation. In the same manner the islands of Tsres, Osor and Kerk were occupied as well.

Assembly Before Zadar

After the surrender of the cities and islands Koloman made a significant move of friendship toward his new subjects. He summoned all the Dalmatian citizenry to an assembly held in an open field before Zadar, and took a public oath that he and his heirs would at all times protect and respect the old self-rule of the Dalmatian cities, granting them full freedom to elect their own magistrates and bishops. The royal pledge was confirmed by a similar oath taken by all the Hungarian churchmen and civil dignitaries who were present in his escort and army.

Still another constitutional enactment took place at this assembly. In assertion of the political independence of the Croatian-Dalmatian kingdom, Koloman's six year old son Stephen was proclaimed a separate king of Croatia and Dalmatia. Contemporary church inscriptions in Zadar refer to Stephen as "our king" alongside Koloman as "King of Hungary, Dalmatia and Croatia." Regardless who the title-holder of sovereignty was, the power was actually in the hands of the Croatian banus Ugra. The military, judicial and administrative power which he exercised in Croatia and Slavonia was now extended also over the newly acquired cities and islands. Thus Koloman fully achieved his purpose, and having restored peace and order in his new possesions, he returned in 1107 to Hungary.

Municipal Privileges

The privileges which Koloman gave in his own name and that of his successors to the Dalmatian cities, were quite extensive. They provided for exemption from all manner of taxes, including the onerous "peace tax" which had been paid since the time of Emperor Basil I (about 822) for the undisturbed possessions of the Croatian lands in the rural districts. Koloman gave the people this "royal peace" without compensation. Besides that he guaranteed their ancient self-government rights in all the municipal affairs, including the election of their "prior" (mayor) and bishop. Through resort to the autonomous local courts they were relieved from seeking justice elsewhere, to the exclusion of the royal court itself.

At the same time the king was moderate in his claim of revenue, which he restricted to the collection of port fees from foreign vessels. Two-thirds of these fees went into the royal treasury, while the balance was distributed between the prior and local bishop. Furthermore, the Dalmatian citizens were exempted from the "royal visit tax." Neither should the members of the king's escort be quartered forcibly in the homes of private citizens. Compared with similar provisions in other European countries, the Dalmatian franchises were most liberal and comprehensive.

Boemundus at Durazzo

By the end of 1107, the Norman duke Boemundus led an army of 34,000 men against the Byzantine coastal city of Durazzo (Drach). His attack, however, was repulsed, and his army was encircled by the forces of Emperor Alexis. After a year of fruitless struggle Boemundus was forced to sue for peace. With the aid of Venetian galleys the forces of Koloman invaded Norman Appulia in the spring of 1108, laying waste the land of Boemundus. But after three months of marauding and pillaging they returned to Dalmatia. At the conclusion of peace between Emperor Alexis and Boemundus in Durazzo, two of Koloman's ambassadors were present. One of them was a Croatian.

Struggle with Germany

Through a quarrel with his brother Álmos, Koloman soon had to match his power with that of Henry V, emperor of Germany. The success of Koloman in Croatia had irritated Álmos to such a degree that he sued for aid in Germany, but failing to obtain it, temporarily was reconciled to his position. However, when Koloman took the Dalmatian cities and islands, and proclaimed his son Stephen as Croatian-Dalmatian King, Álmos set out again to sue for Polish and German aid with which to attack his brother. In Germany the news of the capture of the Dalmatian cities had been received with misgivings, since Croatia and Dalmatia had been considered part of the Western Roman Empire since the times of Charlemagne. Upon the request of Álmos, Henry V set out at the head of his army to invade Hungary, justifying his campaign with Koloman's attack against the maritime provinces. Late in the fall of 1108 Henry V laid siege to the city of Pozhun (Pressburg; Pozsony; Bratislava), but having achieved nothing, had to retreat in haste. Thus, under the walls of Pozhun Koloman not only defended his newly acquired Dalmatian cities and islands from the powerful Germans, but definitely and for a long time to come, put an end to the German attacks against Hungary.

Blinding of Álmos and Béla

After the failure of Henry V's campaign, Álmos again made peace with his brother, but once more only for a short period of time. Koloman, meanwhile, became gravely ill. In 1115, worried over some new intrigue of Álmos directed against the throne and life of Stephen, now 14, he seized his brother and the latter's nine year old son Béla by surprise, and ordered

them blinded. After this crime both Álmos and Béla were imprisoned in the Monastery of Doemoesh (not far from Vátz) where they remained in seclusion until the death of Koloman on February 3rd, 1116. Thereupon, aided by influential friends, Álmos went to Byzantium where he was well received by Emperor Alexis and his son John, husband of his cousin Piroshka—Irene. Álmos committed his blind son Béla to the friendly care of trusted friars at the Péchvárad Monastery, who attended him with such devotion that King Stephen up to the end of his life, could not learn his whereabouts.

Álmos was not the only family liability of Koloman. The king married twice: in 1097 he married the Norman princess Busilla, who bore him Stephen. In 1112 Koloman married for the second time. His new wife was the Russian Euphemia, daughter of the grand duke Vladimir II Monomachos of Kiev. This marriage was not a happy one, and in the next year Koloman sent Euphemia home, charging adultery. In Kiev she gave birth to a son Boris Kolomanovich, who was raised entirely in the Russian manner. Relying on the power of Kiev, Boris became a grave threat to his Hungarian kin.

Koloman's Reign in Croatia

Very little is known about the activities of Koloman in Croatia after his occupation of the Dalmatian cities. The absence of any record of complaints or strife in Croatia and Dalmatia during his reign indicates that his rule was benign. The most important fact about his reign is that he again united the Croatian territory from Drava to the Adriatic Sea and turned it over to the Croatian banus for administration. From that time forward the banus became the chief representative of royal power in the land. It is quite certain that during Koloman's reign, if not earlier, three important administrative districts (Zhupaniya) were organized which have endured to this day: Varazhdin, Krizhevats and Zagreb counties.* Apparently much build-

*Several smaller districts and tribal areas date back to the very beginnings of the Croatian State. For example, south of Sava River, Podgorye; across Kupa River: Goritza and Gora; along the Una River—the district of Dubitza; and on the opposite bank of Una—the Vodichevo or Voditza district. Then there was the Sana district in the river valley of Sana, and the Verbas district in the valley of the lower course of Verbas River, with its center in the town of Verbas (near the present-day town of Banyaluka).

ing activity went on during Koloman's reign. A highway connecting the towns of Koprivnitza and Chazma in the Drava region, and a bridge spanning the river, were identified by the name of Koloman long after his death. He encouraged the settling of the Hungarian nobility in the dense forests of Slavonia, a process that gained momentum as time went on. The king himself had extensive estates in Slavonia.

During the reign of Koloman the tax system in Slavonia was reorganized. From the time of the Franks the tax had been paid in that country with marten pelts. This custom probably went all the way back to the Slavic antiquity. Koloman ordered the payment of taxes in silver, at the rate of twelve silver denaria. Even though paid thenceforth in metal, this tax retained its old name of "marten tax." The tax collectors were assisted in the collection of taxes by a special military force assigned for this purpose.

*Stephen II (I) — (1116-1131).

Koloman's son Stephen II (I) ascended the throne at the age of fifteen. He was no longer a child to be placed under tutelage, but neither had he reached that degree of maturity which would make a wise and disciplined ruler. So the young king plunged into a course of dissipation which destroyed his health and bodily fitness. Thus the change on the throne of Hungary and Croatia brought in its wake a drastic readjustment in the international situation, since the neighbors of Stephen were only too eager to profit by the errors of the youthful king. In the first place they tried to extend their own frontiers at the expense of Hungary and Croatia. Yet the youthful Stephen bravely faced the situation and avoided serious injury on one hand by resort to diplomacy, and on the other, by effective use of armed force.

Having ironed out his differences with Austria and Bohemia, Stephen turned his attention to Croatia, where Venice still hoped to recover the Dalmatian cities and islands seized by Koloman. Since Koloman had won Dalmatia through the connivance of Byzantium, the Venetians

* From the time of St. Stephen, the first Hungarian king, to that of Kálmán (Koloman) a number of Árpád House members occupied the Hungarian throne, without any connection with Croatia. That is why the later rulers appear in the Croatian Constitutional Law with one serial number less than in the Hungarian succession order. This rule ceases to operate after the accession of Angevines.

strove in turn for the favor of the emperor. An opportunity soon presented itself through the family feud at the Hungarian Court. Princess Piroshka (Irene), whose influence at the court of Byzantium was a powerful one, she being the wife of the heir apparent, supported the party of Álmos in opposition to Koloman. When she heard that Álmos and his son Béla had been blinded by Koloman, she used her influence with Alexis to support the Venetians. The result was a change of policy which brought on a long and bitter struggle between Stephen on the one hand, and the allied forces of Venice and Byzantium on the other.

In August 1115, with the consent of Byzantium, the Venetian doge Ordelafo Faledro captured Zadar. However, the municipal castle, garrisoned by Croatian troops under the command of banus Kledin, could not be taken. In this campaign the doge occupied Trogir and Split, as well as the islands but his attack against Biograd failed.

The easy victory of the doge was due largely to the infirmity of Koloman, and his preoccupation with his feud with Álmos. Thus the defense of his maritime province was badly neglected, so that with the exception of Biograd and the municipal castle of Zadar, no other place along the coast was protected by his troops.

In May 1116, the doge again put to sea in the direction of Dalmatia. On this occasion he was aided both by the Byzantine and Roman empires. On the 29th of June, 1116, a great battle was fought under the walls of Zadar in which the Croatian banus Kledin was defeated. The doge seized the municipal castle and soon afterwards neighboring Biograd. Having captured Shibenik as well, and demolished its fortifications, the doge returned to Venice in triumph. Thus, in 1116, the Republic of St. Mark had in its power not only all Byzantine Dalmatia but also two Croatian cities: Biograd and Shibenik.

Stephen was occupied in the meantime with his Czech and Austrian affairs, and only in the following year (1117) was able to rush with his forces to Dalmatia and Croatia. The tide now turned. Soon Ordelafo Faledro, the victorious leader of the previous campaigns, was badly beaten, and died from wounds incurred in battle. The new doge Domenico Michieli sued for a five year truce, which was granted to him by Stephen (1117-1122). But after the lapse of the truce period Stephen renewed the campaign (1124) and in a victorious dash recaptured the cities of Biograd, Shibenik, Trogir and Split. The islands and city of Zadar, however, were denied him.

Stephen came down to Croatia acting as a benevolent ruler. He confirmed the privileges given by Koloman to Trogir and Split, and attended to some constitutional matters. The situation was favorable for the king's dispositions, because the main Venetian force had been tarrying in the Holy Land since 1122, engaged in the siege of Tirus. But in May 1125, the doge Dominico Michieli returned from the East and again invaded Dalmatia. In the course of this campaign he recaptured the cities of Split, Shibenik and Trogir, and demolished Biograd to its very foundations. Thus Stephen's success of the preceding year was reduced to naught. The situation was now aggravated by a dispute between Stephen and a much more dangerous enemy than Venice, Emperor John Comnenus Kalojohannes (1118-1143), the gifted son and sole heir of the late Alexis I.

Byzantine Empire in the 12th Century

Throughout the 11th and 12th centuries Byzantium still was the most important empire or political government in Europe. It still held extensive areas in Asia Minor and the Balkans, plus fragmentary holdings in Italy. It drew its force mainly from a loyal and rich citizenry. Its military, financial and legal institutions were so perfected that western Europe looked to them for inspiration. Its industry, especially its crafts, stood out unchallenged; the glamor of its letters and arts continued untarnished, and its commerce spread all over the known world. Heir to a vast treasury, and in command of an excellent army John Comnenus strove with great ambition and adroitness to revive the ancient Byzantine claims and dreams of world domination.

Fortunately for Stephen's kingdom, Emperor John was preoccupied with other affairs during his first ten years in office and could not throw all his forces against Stephen. Nevertheless, he egged on Venice to the conquest of Dalmatia and laid difficulties in the way of the Hungarian-Byzantine trade along the Danube. His wife Irene (Piroshka) received the blinded duke Álmos and little by little the court became a haven for the Hungarian rebels. These were dissidents and malcontents of all description, who tried to persuade the Byzantine court to

overthrow Stephen and raise Álmos to the throne of Hungary and Croatia. The emperor encouraged these Hungarian emigres and assisted them in many ways, but while he was occupied elsewhere with more urgent business, he was not in a position to descend in the field with all his forces against Stephen.

War with Byzantium

On the other hand, Stephen did not underestimate the peril threatening him from Byzantium. Having renewed friendly relations with the margrave of Austria, the prince of Bohemia and Emperor Henry V of Germany, he made an attempt to contact all the enemies of Byzantium, and especially the south Italian Normans and Serbs, who also were fighting Byzantium for their independence. When Stephen had brought his army into fighting readiness and made proper arrangements with his allies, he demanded that Emperor John expel from his empire all the Hungarian refugees, including his uncle Álmos.

Naturally, John refused to comply. In retaliation Stephen sent his army across the Sava in 1127 and captured the cities of Belgrad and Branichevo. Encouraged by his initial success, he proceeded south to the cities of Nish and Sofia, but near the Bulgarian town of Plovdiv the emperor forced him to retreat. In the meantime, Stephen demolished Belgrad to its foundations. Furthermore, he had the stones of that ruined city ferried across the Danube in order to lay the foundation of the present-day town of Zemun at the confluence of the Sava and Danube.

A bitter but indecisive struggle continued for two years. Finally the opponents came to terms on a status quo basis (1120) making the course of the Sava and Danube boundary line of the empire. The treaty did not provide for the rights of either Duke Álmos, who died in 1127, nor those of his son Béla, for no one suspected that he was alive.

In the meantime Stephen returned from the campaign with broken health and everyone in his entourage realized that his days were numbered. The agony of the king was heightened by the fact that he had no children, and the Árpad dynasty was about to become extinct. Then he heard the news that the blind Béla was still alive. The king promptly took him to his court and by royal proclamation made him his successor. He also arranged for his marriage with the Serbian princess Helena, daughter of the grand duke Urosh.

Early in March, 1131, Stephen died and was buried in Oradia Mare (Nagy Várad), an ancient city of Transylvania.

Béla (Adalbert), the Blind (1131-1141)

Because of his blindness Béla could not perform military or polital duties of any importance. In his time the practical exercise of the royal power was in the hands of his trusted men, and especially of his wife Helena. His own person was merely a symbol of legitimacy based on his descent from the Árpad dynasty.

Even in this respect he had a serious contender in the person of Boris Kolomanovich, son of Koloman and Euphemia of Kiev. Boris came to Hungary to claim the throne of his father. But the archbishop of Ostrogon (Esztergom) as primate of Hungary refused to recognize the legitimacy of his birth as a descendant of the Árpad dynasty. Boris now went to the court of Emperor John Comnenus for assistance. He was received with great honors, and the emperor gave him an imperial princess in marriage. Thence Boris proceeded to Poland where he collected an army, at the head of which he crossed the Carpathians and broke into Hungary in the year 1132. However, he lost the decisive battle and abandoned further attempts to overthrow Béla.

During the short reign of the blind king there was no conflict with Byzantium, but in the continuing struggle with Venice he recovered all of Dalmatia, with the exception of the city of Zadar and the islands (1133).

For some unexplained reason Béla took the title of "rex Ramae" (king of Rama), which was interpreted as "king of Bosnia." Since there was no war with Bosnia, and consequently no conquest of that country, nor any constitutional act on record by which Bosnia had submitted to the king of Croatia or Hungary, some have explained it as an act of inheritance, which is also subject to doubt. Whatever the origin of this title, it was seized upon by the later kings of Hungary in making their claims upon Bosnia, and in enforcing them.

Geyza (Géza)—(1141-1162)

The blind king died in February 1141. He left three sons. Geyza, Stephen and Ladislaus.

Geyza, as his first-born, succeeded him on the throne, while Stephen was given the title of duke of Croatia, and Ladislaus that of duke of Bosnia. All three being minors, the royal power in Hungary and Croatia was exercised by their uncle, banus Byelosh, while banus Borich ruled in Bosnia.

At that time the situation for Hungary and the southern Slavic countries was very unfavorable, since Germany and Byzantium combined forces to effect their conquest. The new emperor Emanuel Comnenus (1143-1180) advanced claim to all the countries which in time past had been within the confines of the Eastern Roman Empire. By this he meant Serbia, Croatia, Dalmatia, Hungary (Pannonia) and the south Italian Normandy. In making this claim Emanuel referred to the principle of seniority, which was universally applied among the Slavs, and prevailed also in Hungary. According to this law, not the son succeeds the father on the throne, but the oldest member of the royal family. In order to ward off the impending menace, the court of Ostrogon concluded a new military alliance with the Serbs and Normans.

The war began in 1146 with a German invasion, but the German armies were beaten and fled and banus Byelosh following in hot pursuit caught and crushed them on the banks of the Layta River. In the next year (1147) when the troops of crusaders passed through Hungary on their way east, Boris Kolomanovich joined their ranks in order to get to Byzantium. He was cordially received by Emperor Emanuel. In 1150 a rebellion broke out among the Serbs, who were assisted by the Hungarians and Croats, but, the emperor defeated the allies on the banks of the Tara River.

The following year Emanuel broke into Hungary and Croatia, captured Zemun and devastated Sirmium. In 1152 Geyza made him a peace offer, which Emanuel accepted. But in 1154 the war was renewed. In the course of the fighting, incidentally, Boris Kolomanovich lost his life. Peace was concluded soon after (1156). In the treaty Geyza profited not only by favorable terms, but also by dissolution of the alliance between Germany and Byzantium. Moreover, Geyza entered into an alliance with Frederic Barbarossa. This favorable situation was upset when Geyza's brothers, first Stephen and then Ladislaus picked a quarrel with him and fled to Byzantium. Emperor Emanuel received them with joy and promptly made up his mind to use them in a showdown with Hungary and Croatia.

Dynastic Strife

Geyza I (II) died on the 31st of March, 1162. He left the throne to his son Stephen IV (III). But Emanuel Comnenus set out in the field with a strong army, and forced the new king to yield the throne, on the principle of seniority, to his uncle Stephen. However, the Hungarian magnates refused to accept this Stephen, deciding in favor of his elder brother Ladislaus I (II) (1162-1163). Ladislaus died soon after his enthronement (January 14, 1163), and the Estates finally recognized Stephen V (IV) (1163), son of Béla, as their sovereign. The Croats being the first to take the assault of Byzantium, supported the succession claims of the emperor's favorite. But the extravagance of the new king soon provoked a rebellion, and the people drove him from the country. After this, Stephen IV (III) (1163-1172), son of Geyza, returned to the throne. This change precipitated a brief war with Emperor Emanuel, but peace was soon restored. In the terms of peace the emperor agreed to withdraw support from Stephen V (IV), while King Stephen IV (III), in return, ceded Sirmium to the emperor. Further, the king agreed to send his brother Béla to Byzantium for education and turn over to the emperor the administration of Béla's heritage, namely Croatia south of Velebit, and Dalmatia.

So Béla went to Constantinople where the emperor betrothed him to his daughter Maria and having no son of his own, proclaimed him successor to the Byzantine throne. In spite of that Stephen refused to give up Béla's heritage. Moreover, in fall of 1163 he came to Croatia and Dalmatia, where he confirmed the privileges given by his predecessors to the Dalmatian towns, and in all probability had himself crowned Croatian-Dalmatian king. Because of this move a new war broke out in 1164, and Stephen was forced once more to cede the Croatian lands to Emanuel. However, the peace was only of short duration because the ex-king Stephen V (IV) provoked a new war, in the course of which King Stephen IV (III) took from Byzantium the province of Sirmium with the town of Zemun which he had recently ceded to Emanuel.

Byzantine Overlordship in Croatia

During the siege of Zemun in 1165 the ex-king Stephen V (IV) died from poisoning. In the meantime, Emperor Emanuel set out at the head of a powerful army against Croatia and Hungary. With one half of his forces he went to Sirmium and took Zemun by storm, while he sent the other half into Bosnia, Croatia and Dalmatia, which were quickly conquered by the imperial prince, John Dukas. Stephen IV (III), in panic, sued for peace. By the terms of the treaty he again obligated himself to cede Béla's heritage to the emperor. However, soon he found a strong ally in Venice, and a new war was under way in 1166. In the course of this campaign Stephen quickly reoccupied the Croatian lands, and granted the city of Shibenik the same privileges which Split and Trogir had obtained from King Koloman. Stephen's treachery aroused Emperor Emanuel, and he now decided to fight it out to the bitter end. The imperial forces were successful, and in 1169 Byzantium extended its sway over Sirmium, Bosnia, Croatia, south of Kerka River and Dalmatia, with the exception of Zadar and islands, which were under Venetian authority. At the head of the administration in Byzantine Croatia the emperor placed Constantine, a relative who was very circumspect in his dealings with the Croats, respecting both their property and the Catholic faith. In the meantime Emanuel became the father of a son who was given the name Alexis. Thereupon he not only voided Béla's rights to the succession, but also cancelled his daughter's betrothal to Béla, giving him in her stead an obscure princess from Antiochia. In the meantime, Stephen IV (III) suddenly died in 1172 and the young duke returned to Hungary where he ascended the throne under the name of Béla II (III).

His sway extended over Hungary and Croatia from the Drava to the Kerka. The authority of Byzantium continued in the rest of Croatia until the death of Emanuel, September 24, 1180, when the power of the Byzantine Empire began the long and gradual decline toward its disintegration and downfall.

Chapter XVI
THE DECLINE OF BYZANTIUM AND ASCENDANCY
OF THE HUNGARIAN-CROATIAN RULERS

King Béla II (III)—1172-1196

AFTER the death of Emanuel the Byzantine authority was promptly voided, not only in Sirmium but also in southern Croatia and Dalmatia. After the bitter experience of foreign domination the Croatian-Hungarian State alliance was solidified along the lines laid down in 1102 by Koloman. In compliance with this tradition, Béla II (III) allowed his son Emeric (Imre) to be crowned king of Hungary and separately king of Croatia-Dalmatia during his own lifetime. At the same time he ceded to him all the Croatian kingdom from the Drava to the sea, as his independent administrative territory. In Bosnia banus Kulin, an appointee of Emperor Emanuel, reigned from 1170 to 1204, apparently as a vassal of Béla, while the Serbian great zhupan Styepan Nemanya remained close to the Hungarian court as its old political ally.

After the death of Emanuel great disorders broke out in the Byzantine empire. This made it possible for the Balkan peoples, and especially for the Serbs and Bulgars, to extricate themselves from under the Byzantine overlordship. On the ruins of the Low Empire Béla II (III) conceived the ambition to assume the former rôle of Byzantium. By his plan Béla provided new channels for the Hungarian policy, but at the same time incurred the hostility of the Serbs and Bulgars. This hostility and the imperialistic ambitions of the Hungarian kings continued up to the time of the Turkish invasions, and, to a certain degree, became the very instrument of the latter. Just as Emperor Emanuel turned the strife over the succession in Hungary to his own advantage, now Béla and his successors were stirring up trouble and fanning religious strife in the Balkan peninsula for their own political ends.

In the meantime, the city of Zadar was returned to Béla in 1180, but a new war broke out in 1181. For a period of ten years the Venetians steadily pounded at the city, but Zadar stood firm, and repulsed all attacks, both from land and sea. This forced the doge Henry Dandolo to sue for a truce, which was continued for a long time, without, however, resulting in a peace.

Feudalization of Croatian Nobility

The protracted and fierce struggles which the Croatians of noble birth conducted against the foreign invaders, both Byzantines and Venetians alike, became conducive to far-reaching internal reforms. In acknowledgment of the merit of these Croatians, the king gave them liberal grants under the terms of feudal nobility. So it appears that in 1193, King Béla II (III) conferred upon Bartolus, son of Domnius (Duyam), a nobleman from the island of Kerk, possession of the county of Modrush, in recognition of his loyal and valiant exploits during the war. The rights of ownerships were to pass on to his successors. In exchange for this grant, the beneficiary was expected to serve in the king's army within the frontiers of the State with the force of ten soldiers in heavy armor, while abroad this obligation was limited to four heavily armed soldiers. However, this service was restricted only to occasions when the entire Croatian army was summoned by the king. This grant was the foundation of the historical destiny of the Croatian family known at the beginning of the 15th century as the Frankopani. About the same time King Béla confirmed to Miroslav, count of Bribir, a member of the Shubich clan, the ownership of the county of Bribir-Babonitsa. Count Stephen of the Babonichi clan was likewise made the owner of the entire area between the Una and Sana rivers in northwestern Bosnia. With these royal patents the ancient noblemen became king's vassals. Thus, among the Croatian nobility representing the chiefs of the ancient tribes and clans, feudalism was introduced after the western European pattern. From that time on the Croatian nobility was set on equal footing with the Hungarian nobility, thus more closely cementing the constitutional ties between Croatia and Hungary.

Reforms of Béla II (III)

The reign of Béla II is very important and significant both for Hungary and Croatia, not

only because of the events abroad, but also for internal reforms. Béla was the first king since the time of Koloman to be professionally trained in the capital of a great and well-administered world power. He made the court a place of splendor and introduced royal ceremony and customs, lending it an outward glamor. At this time the coronation took on the character of a constitutional act, a sort of inaugural for the exercise of royal power.

Béla's fiscal policy was rational and conscientious. The king acted as a conscientious guardian of state property. On the basis of his Byzantine experience he introduced order in financial administration and turned the minting of coins into a source of royal income. He developed the salt mines, making the trade in table salt a state monopoly in Hungary and Slavonia. Due to these dispositions he was able to provide an annual cash income of nearly two million dollars.

A permanent Office of the Chancellor was established in 1193. Briefs were introduced in trial courts. Taught by the bitter experience of seniority rule, Béla restored primogeniture as the governing principle of succession. Moreover he abolished the practice by which the king's brother obtained authority over the Croatian kingdom as a special duchy, and transferred this right to the first-born son of the king before his accession to the throne. All this was against the wishes of the Croatian nobility, which insisted on the principle of secundo-geniture, with a view to establishing a Croatian branch of the Árpad dynasty.

King Emeric (Imre)—1196-1204

Emeric was bent on pursuing the policy of his father, but his younger brother Andrew interfered with this resolve, and in 1197 instigated a rebellion, demanding Croatia and Dalmatia as his lawful heritage. Having defeated the king in battle, Andrew became Duke of Croatia and soon assumed royal power. He became an independent ruler from the Drava to Neretva and had a brilliant reign. He undertook successful campaigns in the Hum area (Herzegovina) and Serbia, appointed bishops and archbishops, issued patents, successfully administered justice and surrounded himself with a glittering court and escorts.

Andrew was attended also by the banus of Croatia, who undoubtedly had been appointed by himself. But the fortunes of war did not always attend his banners and in the continuous struggle with his brother Emeric, Andrew was finally defeated. Deserted by his supporters, he was imprisoned in the Croatian town of Kneginyats near Varazhdin. In the meantime the sickly king Emeric was oppressed by worry over the future of his family. In order to secure the throne for his only son Ladislaus during his lifetime, he had him crowned by the archbishop of Split as the separate king of Croatia-Dalmatia, and in 1204 by the archbishop of Kalocha as king of Hungary. All this took place during Emeric's lifetime.

Destruction of Zadar by the Venetians (1202)

During the period of civil wars raging in Croatia and Hungary, the fourth crusade was organized in western Europe. On their journey to the Holy Land the crusaders had to use the Venetian galleys for transportation. Naturally, they had to pay the cost of passage to the ship owner. But most of the crusaders were lacking the necessary means and agreed to serve the Republic for their fare. So doge Henry Dandolo used them to capture and demolish the Christian city of Zadar. This act took place in November, 1202. The Holy See protested and threatened to excommunicate Dandolo; but in vain. In the following year Dandolo captured Constantinople, and the Venetians set up the weak Latin empire on the ruins of Byzantium.

The inhabitants of Zadar reconstructed their city, with the aid of Prince Domaldus, scion of the Svachich clan, but since they could obtain aid neither from King Emeric nor from Duke Andrew, in 1205 they again surrendered to Venice on oppressive terms.

Encroachments on Bosnia

About that time Emeric began to interest himself in Serbian matters and in 1202 he assumed the title of king of Serbia. Then he turned his attention to Bosnia, where the heterodoxy of the Bosnian Church offered him a convenient pretext to interfere in Bosnian affairs, the first of

many Hungarian kings to do so.* When he called banus Kulin to account for his leanings to the Bosnian heresy, he initiated a chain of episodes which we cannot follow at this time, but which will be related in another volume of this work.

Andrew (Endre) I (II)—1205-1235

Shortly before his death Emeric made up with his brother Andrew. The king was succeeded on the throne by his son, Ladislaus II (III), a minor. After eight months of reign (1204-1205), this Ladislaus was overthrown and Andrew I (II) ascended the throne. Andrew's reign was long and eventful, for he ruled from 1205-1235.

With his accession to the throne Andrew I put an end to the strife among the various members of the royal house. These struggles, frequently connected with foreign wars, had greatly undermined the authority of the king. In place of the power of the sovereign, that of the ecclesiastic and lay dignitaries came into prominence. But Andrew was not a ruler of a stature to cope with this menace. Profligate and undecisive, he made his lot worse by submitting to the influence of his entourage, which was mostly of foreign origin. Bertold, the youthful brother of Andrew's wife, Gertrude, a German princess, was appointed archbishop of Kalocha and later was made also banus of Croatia.

Provoked by this challenge, some of the Hungarian magnates assassinated the queen in 1213 in the forest of Pilish, near Budavár, at the end of a hunting party. Her brother Bertold managed to escape. King Andrew mourned over Gertrude for some time but finally forgot her and in 1216 married Yolanta, sister of the Latin emperors Baldwin and Henry. Feeling that his authority was at a low ebb, Andrew attempted to raise his prestige by a successful campaign in Galicia. At the beginning of 1217 he had his son Koloman crowned king of Galicia. Two years later, Koloman was captured by the Russians

---

* In Bulgaria, Serbia and Greece the heterodox sects such as the Bogumils and others had also come into prominence, but they were gradually absorbed by the Orthodox Church of each country. In Bosnia, on the contrary, the native faith became identified with the struggle for independence because of the Hungarian encroachments upon the sovereignty of that nation. Thus, in the sectarian movement of Bosnia we have to distinguish the religious movement from the political element and see in it a desperate effort on the part of the Bosnians to defend and preserve their independence.

and kept in prison for two years. In 1221 he was set free, but all the efforts of Andrew to extend his sway over the Transcarpathian regions failed.

Andrew's Campaign in the Holy Land

To his failure in Galicia, Andrew soon added another one. It so happened that Andrew's father, Béla II, had made a vow to campaign in the Holy Land, and on his deathbed passed on the pledge to Andrew. In spite of his previous misfortunes and failures, Andrew decided to carry out the promise given to his father. In return for the transportation of his company to the Holy Land, he renounced his rights to Zadar (1216) in favor of Venice. Before setting out East he appointed Ponzio de Cruce, a knight templar, his vicar in Croatia, and the archbishop John of Ostrogon (Esztergom) in Hungary. Then in the summer of 1217 he set out through Zagreb to the sea. In Zagreb at that time the new cathedral was completed, and its consecration took place in the presence of the king, who on that occasion confirmed all its ancient privileges.

On his journey to the Holy Land, Andrew was accompanied by numerous Croatian noblemen, including members of the Babonich clan. They all embarked on board the Venetian ships at Split, and were carried to the coast of Palestine. The crusade of King Andrew is only a minor episode in the gigantic struggle between the Christian and Mohammedan world and was concluded without any notable success. Andrew returned to Europe by way of land through Constantinople and in place of trophies he carried with him some hallowed relics which he acquired during his stay in the Holy Land.

The Golden Bull

After his return home Andrew found his country in a state of anarchy, chiefly because of the greed and depredations of the high nobility. On one occasion he complained that it would take him fifteen years to restore order in the land. Preliminary to his major moves, he let his elder son Béla be crowned as the "younger king" of Hungary (rex Hungariae junior) and made him at the same time duke of Croatia. After this he began to seize the estates of noblemen who of recent years had been robbing the State of its landed property. Yet, he went a great deal further to meet the emergency. So when he debased the currency, spent the treasury funds recklessly

and pawned the revenue sources to usurers, the lower nobility rose against him and his counsellors in rebellion. The malcontents came mostly from the military class and were headed by the king's son Béla. Through the mediation of Stephen, Bishop of Zagreb, father and son composed their differences, but the embittered Hungarian and Slavonian arm-bearing nobility forced Andrew to issue, in 1222, the "Golden Bull" (i.e. Magna Charta).

The Golden Bull had two objectives. In the first place it was an attempt to break the overlordship of the high nobility and thus to raise the power of the king. Further, it aimed to guarantee the rights and freedom of the lower nobility. By its form the "Golden Bull" was at the beginning only a privilege, while later on it became by far the most important public law, and the foundation of the constitution. Indeed, up to the dissolution of the Hungarian-Croatian union in 1918, the Hungarian-Croatian kings at their coronation took the oath of allegiance to the provisions of the "Bull."

In its preamble this document, consisting of thirty-one articles, stresses the need of a sweeping reform in the kingdom. The single provisions are specified in their proper sequence. The king or his vicar, the palatin, must hold a solemn trial court on St. Stephen's day (August 20) in the city of Székesfehérvár to which all the arm-bearing noblemen shall have access in order to present their grievances. The king cannot imprison any such nobleman or confiscate his possessions for the benefit of some grandee, unless the trial court finds him guilty. Further, the king cannot arbitrarily collect tax from the noblemen, nor can he enter their villages or homes without their consent. Outside the boundaries of the State the nobility will fight only at the king's expense and even the magnates are entitled to upkeep at the king's expense in case of an offensive war. However, in case of invasion, they all must hasten to the defense of the country without compensation.

Only the palatin, banus and the judges of the Royal Court may be vested with two honors at the same time. On the other hand, foreigners cannot obtain any office, except upon consent of the Council of the State. Tithes should not be paid to bishops in money but in kind, usually with wine and wheat. The newly minted coin will be valid only for the period of one year. Jews cannot be employed at the coin mint, in salt stores and customs house. Also a number of fiscal provisions are inserted in this document. The most important is Section 31 of the "Bull" guaranteeing execution of the foregoing provisions. It fixes the right of both higher and lower nobility to raise separately or in common a rebellion against the king, should he or any of his successors infringe on these institutions. They can do so either by word of mouth or with arms in hand, without becoming liable for high treason.

Among other prelates who signed the momentous document was the bishop of Zagreb, Stephen. The "Golden Bull" was effective only in Hungary and northern Croatia, up to the Gvozd mountains, but did not apply to southern Croatia extending from the Gvozd to the Neretva River.

Croatian Oligarchy

As the high nobility of Hungary increased its powers at the expense of the king, the same strife within the royal family became conducive to exaltation of the Croatian nobility, especially in the area between the Gvozd mountains and the Neretva. Here various clans had so effectively increased their power that in their own districts they had become actual sovereigns supporting a whole army of poor men. With its gradual opposition to the Hungarian Court, the Croatian oligarchy performed a true national service by strengthening the local traditions and preventing submission of Croatia to Hungary. Beginning with the first decade of the 13th century ascendancy of the oligarchy in Croatia continued until 1348 when King Ludovic I finally succeeded in breaking the power of the Croatian oligarchs. This struggle of the king with his peers was concluded in Hungary by the father of Ludovic, Charles I.

In addition to the Frankopani, princes of Kerk (Veglia), who in 1225 obtained in addition to the Modrush district, that of Vinodol also, the Bribirian princes of the Shubich clan came into prominence. The chief of this clan was Prince Gregory. The Svachich clan, with its chief prince Domaldus, controlled a vast area, while the Kachich clan, with Prince Malduch as its head, was in possession of the stronghold of Omish and the entire seacoast from Split to the mouth of Neretva River. Because of priority claims upon Split a bloody feud arose between the Shubich and Svachich clans, in which Prince

Domaldus finally succumbed. On the other hand, Prince Malduch caused, with his Omish subjects, so much damage to shipping and struck so many serious blows at the coastal towns and especially at Split that the papal legate, Acontius, had to intervene as a peace mediator in 1221.

In the meantime Duke Béla started again a quarrel with his father and became a rival ruler in 1226, while his younger brother Koloman, the titular king of Galicia, replaced him in 1226 as duke of Croatia. Both King Andrew and Duke Koloman tried to win over the Croatians to their cause, but failed to make much headway in their policy. The challenge of the Croatian barons came in spite of the fact that King Andrew appointed by the end of Béla's administration in 1225, two separate bani, one for the "entire Slavonia" up to Gvozd, and the other for Croatia and Dalmatia or "maritime regions." The rebellious Croatian barons were headed by Prince Domaldus of the Svachich clan, and he started a civil war both on land and sea, in which he was eventually defeated (1229).

After settling the domestic differences in Croatia, Koloman turned his attention to Bosnia, where at that time banus Matey Ninoslav was ruling (1230-1250). In pursuit of the imperialistic Hungarian policy throughout the Balkans Koloman had a plan to subject Bosnia directly to his authority. He found abundant reasons for meddling in the Bosnian internal affairs as a crusader against the Church of Bosnia, to which even banus Ninoslav adhered.

King Andrew promoted the plans of his son Koloman by assigning to him supervision of Bosnia and had this decision confirmed by Pope Gregory IX. Consequently, the Croatian duke began to act both with suasion and armed force. When his army broke into Bosnia banus Ninoslav and his co-religionists pretended loyalty to the Catholic Church, upon which Koloman retired (1234). But no sooner had the duke left Bosnia with his army, than the banus and his subjects embraced the "Bosnian Church" again. From that time on it became customary that as long as the Catholic armies were on the Bosnian soil the natives would declare themselves Catholics, but as soon as the aliens left the country, they again espoused openly their native faith.

Last Days of Andrew

Despite the privileges promised in the "Golden Bull," the situation in Hungary did not improve.

Andrew continued his lavish spending and the usurers again obtained lease on the State revenue. This provoked a new storm of indignation but this time the ecclesiastic magnates joined hands with the barons as leaders of the rebellion. So, in 1231 Andrew was forced again to issue the "Golden Bull", which literally repeats the provisions enacted in 1222, but with a clause removing the right of "armed resistance." In its place the king and his sons declared that in case of disloyalty to the Constitution they would submit to the judgment of archbishop of Ostrogon, who would have the power even to excommunicate them for cause. And indeed, in the next year (1232) Andrew became subject to this penalty, for the archbishop Robertus excommunicated both him and Hungary from the Church. Andrew promptly took a solemn oath that henceforth he would respect the provisions of the Golden Bull, and he and his kingdom were spared the anathema.

After this humiliating experience, Andrew again provoked his entourage when shortly after the death of his second wife Yolanta in 1233, he married in May, 1234, the youthful Beatrice, niece of the Margrave of Azzo and Este-Ferrara.

Andrew (Endre) I (II) died on the 21st of September, 1235, and was succeeded on the throne by his son Béla.

Reign of Béla III (IV)—1235-1270

Béla was about thirty years of age when he ascended the throne. A man of great foresight and energy, he made up his mind to restore the prestige of the king, which was now at a low ebb. This could be achieved only by breaking the power of the oligarchs. In the long line of rulers descending from the House of Árpád he was undoubtedly the most brilliant.

From the first days of his reign Béla III (IV) went through some odd experiences which became a source of serious trouble. Queen Beatrice, Andrew's widow, declared one day that she was to become a mother, and therefore was entitled to a proper position at the royal court. Otherwise, the childless dowager queens were expected to leave the court. After this revelation Béla had Beatrice surrounded with guards, but she slipped out and fled to Germany, where she gave birth to a son, Stephen, the Posthumus, known to history as the father of Andrew II (III), the last scion of the Árpád dynasty. From Germany Beatrice went to Venice where she placed herself

and her son under the protection of the Republic, but neither Béla nor Koloman recognized Stephen as their brother. On the contrary, they declared him the fruit of his mother's adultery, and son of the former palatin Dionysius.

The third week after his father's death, Béla had himself crowned a second time in Székes Fehérvár, this time as king of Hungary and Croatia (October 14, 1235). The date is worth notice for it was the last time the separate ceremony for the crowning of the Croatian-Dalmatian king was celebrated. Whatever the cause of this change, it was of immense consequences for the constitutional status of the two countries.

Upon his ascension to the throne, Béla set out to introduce order and discipline at the court. In order to stress his unlimited power and to humiliate the nobility, he decreed that with the exception of the bishops and chief dignitaries of the State, no one could be seated in the presence of the king. Still more afflicting was the king's order that no one, not even the magnates of the highest rank could make an oral complaint or ask the king for immediate decision. Henceforth, only petitions in writing could be submitted to the Chancellor, who would pass on them after a due lapse of time. In view of the general illiteracy which prevailed at that time, this was a serious handicap for the courtiers. But the heaviest blow administered by Béla against the barons was his decision that all the estates and offices dispensed by his father would have to be returned to the Crown. Also any estates acquired by illegitimate means would have to be restored to their rightful owners. Thus, many estates changed hands both in Hungary and Croatia.

Campaigns and Dispositions of Duke Koloman

Béla's brother Koloman, the duke of Croatia, had a brilliant career as a general, administrator and sponsor of religious institutions. Throughout his life he kept a keen eye on developments in Bosnia. Seeing the lapse of that country into the native heresy, he entered it with his troops and bound banus Ninoslav to renew his former pledge of loyalty to the Catholic faith. Then in 1237 he conquered the Hum province (Herzegovina), which was governed at that time by prince Tolyen.

After his victories Koloman set out to put the affairs of the Bosnian Church in order. For the benefit of the newly appointed bishop of Bosnia, the Dominican Pousa, in 1239 he built the Cathedral of St. Peter, with its Chapter in the town of Berdo near Serayevo. He also endowed this diocese with tithe and gave it the town of Djakovo, with an extensive adjacent area in Slavonia and Sirmium.

Since the Bosnians began soon to menace the position of the bishop, Pousa transferred the seat of his diocese from Berdo to Djakovo, which has ever since been the administrative center of the Bosnian Catholic Church. This readjustment took place between 1242 and 1252.

In addition to Bosnian affairs Duke Koloman was engaged also in regulating the Croatian Church matters. Since the archbishopric of Split had become unduly impoverished, Duke Koloman came in 1240 upon the idea of uniting it with the diocese of Zagreb, which would be removed from under the jurisdiction of the archbishop of Kalocsa. The archbishop of Split, Gunzelius, concurred with Koloman's plan, but the project never went through, on the one hand because of reluctance of Pope Gregory IX to decide this question in a hurry, and on the other, because of the advance of the Tartar hordes, which menaced both Hungary and Croatia.

Tartar Invasion

At the beginning of the 13th century the Mongolian chief Temujin united the various tribes of his race north of China, and proclaiming himself genghis-Khan, "the most powerful Lord." He soon conquered China, Central Asia and Persia. Some of his armies broke into eastern Europe, where they defeated the united Kumani and Russians in 1223 on the banks of the Kalka River, not far from the Sea of Azov. After the death of Genghis in 1227 his son Ogotay succeded him on the throne. Batu-Khan, a nephew of Ogotay, took over the power in eastern Europe and planned to expand it far to the west.

As the Tartars advanced about 40,000 Kumani fled with their Khan Kuten toward central Europe, and asked King Béla (1239) for refuge in Hungary. Béla acceded to their wishes, subject to their conversion to the Christian faith. As the news of this deal reached the Tartars, they summond King Béla to return to them their Kumanian "subjects." When the king rejected their request, they decided to break into Hungary.

Unfortunately there was a general tendency to minimize the Tartar peril in Hungary. So when the Hungarian Estates met in Buda in February, 1241, bitter complaints were raised against

the Kumani. The king's opponents demanded that they be expelled from Hungary and the aroused populace, suspecting that the Kumani were secret Tartar spies, broke in the house of Kuten Khan and killed him. Aroused by the murder of their leader, a part of the Kumani left Hungary and through devious routes reached their homeland plundering and devastating the countryside all along the way.

The Hungarian Disaster

In the meantime Batu-Khan assembled in the neighborhood of Kiev an army about 150,000 strong, and descended through the Carpathian passes into northern Hungary, while his kinsman Kadan broke in from the southern end into Transylvania. Being able to put in the field no more than 60,000 men, including the Croatian forces under Duke Koloman, Béla went to meet the enemy. On Shayo River, near the city of Mishkoltz, a bloody battle was fought on April 11, 1241. In this battle the army of the king suffered a decisive defeat and was dispersed in all directions. The king managed to escape through the Carpathian mountains and by way of Nyitra and Pozhun he fled to Austria, seeking refuge at the court of the duke Frediric II of Babenberg. However, his brother, Duke Koloman, gravely wounded in the battle, died before he could reach the sea in the Slavonian town of Chazma. At this point the duke of Austria took advantage of the king's misfortune and forced Béla to cede to him three frontier countries. Disappointed by this reception, Béla proceeded with his family to Zagreb whence he pleaded for aid with various Christian rulers, all of whom turned deaf ears to his entreaties.

The Tartars Invade Croatia

In the meantime the Tartars devastated all of Hungary along the left bank of the Danube, killing all who came within their reach. It so happened that the winter in that year was exceptionally cold and the rivers were frozen. This made it possible for the Tartars to cross the Danube at the beginning of February, 1242, and split into two forces: one body of troops commanded by Kadan, turning south in pursuit of King Béla, and the other, under the leadership of Batu Khan, heading for Ostrogon, Székes Fehérvár, Veszprém, Gyoer and other Hungarian cities.

With his forces Kadan crossed the Drava River, reducing towns and hamlets on his way, and

especially Zagreb, where the recently completed Cathedral of St. Stephen was badly damaged. In hot pursuit of Béla, Kadan hurried to the sea coast where the king with his family and many grandees sought refuge alternatingly in the well-fortified strongholds of Klis, Split, Trogir and the neighboring islands. Many Croatian noblemen came to the defense of the king at this time, such as Prince Styepko of Bribir, the son of George and the princes Frankopani of Kerk (Veglia), who won Béla's undying gratitude. Kadan descended with his forces upon the coast, but all his efforts to capture the fortified cities and seize the king were unsuccessful.

By the end of March, 1242, the Tartar commander received from Asia the news that in Karakorum, a city of Mongolia, the supreme Khan, Ogotay, had died. Concerned about the succession to the throne, Kadan and the other Tartar leaders, both in Hungary and Croatia, decided to return home. One column went through Bosnia, Serbia and Bulgaria to southern Russia, sowing murder and devastation all along the way. Another column reduced the vicinity of Ragusa, set Kotor on fire, and through Bulgaria broke through the lower Danube where it joined up with the troops of Batu-Khan, who arrived there from the borders of Austria.

The epic of the Tartar invasion impressed itself deeply on the mind of the Croatian people, and became a prolific source of folklore, the legends of which have been frequently taken for historical facts.

Reconstruction in the Wake of the Tartar Hordes

The horrible visitation that befell central Europe demolished in one year what had been building for centuries, both in Hungary and Croatia. The land was laid waste, the surviving population hiding in the forests and mountain retreats so that far and wide not a living soul could be seen. The state organization was shaken to its foundations. Since the land had not been cultivated, famine broke out, followed by pestilence. Increasing the misery of the people were bands of robbers and packs of hungry wolves roaming through the land. A graphic picture of these horrors is given by the contemporary historian and chronicle writer, Archdeacon Thomas of Split.

Informed of the withdrawal of the Tartars, King Béla left Dalmatia in the summer of 1242.

On his journey home he was accompanied by the princes of Kerk who lent him large sums of money. He returned first to Zagreb, and then went on to Hungary. The king quickly convinced himself that the work of reconstruction had to be started from the bottom. With great zeal and energy he tackled the task, and progress was gratifying. First he repaired the administrative apparatus, restored personal security and respect for property. He did all he could to alleviate the suffering of the population. Then he strengthened the defenses of the country, for another Tartar invasion was to be feared. Indeed the Tartar peril was permanent since they controlled all the territory east of the Carpathian mountains.

His experience in Croatia convinced the king that only well-fortified cities could offer a measure of security, and reliable refuge in case of emergency. At that time there were only a few strongholds in the open country. While mountainous Croatia was well fortified, level Slavonia remained open to attack. For this reason Béla did everything to induce the high clergy and the lay nobility to build their own fortifications, while the old ones he had repaired and reinforced at public expense. The court took an active part in the general construction work. The king built up Budavár and the queen took the initiative in fortification of Vishegrad, not far from Ostrogon. In the northern Croatia, too, many fortifications were built. Among them the most important was Kalnik, near Krizhevats, Medvedgrad near Zagreb, and Lipovats near Samobor.

Rise of the Royal Free Cities

In order to swell the population of the devastated country, the king decided to invite foreigners, especially Germans to settle there, offering many inducements. Most of these newcomers were craftsmen, who would settle only in towns and trade centers. In this manner the so-called royal free cities came into existence. The residents had a municipal government of their own and freely elected the city judge who performed the functions of a mayor up to the middle of the 19th century. They also elected the assistants of the judge, the parish priest, and in litigations they could appeal directly to the royal court.

An important privilege of the city residents was their free disposal of legacy. Attracted by these privileges many lower noblemen and free peasants settled in the towns. Together with the older city population they formed the Croatian municipal element. The citizens took part also in the defense of the country. Thus, they surrounded their cities with heavy and high stone walls and turrets, while able-bodied citizens served as soldiers or even horsemen in the royal guard. In 1242, on a hill near Zagreb, the first royal free city of Gradetz was founded. At about the same time also the free municipalities of Samobor (1242), Krizhevtsi (1252) and Yastrebarsko, were founded.

War with Venice

In 1242 Béla again felt himself strong enough to seize the three Hungarian counties which he had ceded to Frederic of Babenberg, duke of Austria under duress in 1241. Soon after he engaged in fighting with Venice on account of Zadar, which rebelled against the Republic early in 1242, upon the arrival of the king at the seacoast. However, the army of the Croatian duke and banus Dionysius was defeated in the summer of 1243, near Zadar, and consequently the city fell again into the hands of Venice. In view of this the majority of citizens migrated to the nearby Nin, which was made a base of operations against Venice. Confronted with this failure, Béla made peace in 1244 with the Republic of Venice, renouncing to Zadar, while the doge, in his turn, bound himself not to support the claims of "a certain Lombardian Stephen 'alleged son of King Andrew'" who at that time resided in Venice and for whose benefit Beatrice demanded, after the death of Duke Koloman, the Croatian duchy.

As a result of this arrangement, the citizens of Zadar composed their differences with Venice in 1247, under very oppressive terms. From this time on they had to accept an emissary of doge as their city chief. Further, they could no longer contract marriage with Croatians, and on top of this, the Venetians took over the administration of all the city revenue, and began to dispose arbitrarily of the merchant marine of Zadar. They also enlisted by force men capable of bearing arms.

Civil Wars in Croatia

The chief reason why Béla yielded to Venice so suddenly and to such an extent should be sought in the civil war that was then raging

in Croatia. It was necessary at all cost to prevent Venice from interfering in the struggle which arose from the old quarrel of Trogir and Split over Ostri village. The citizens of Split considered it their own, even though it was donated by King Béla to the citizens of Trogir. The grant was made by an especial patent in which their rights and possessions were specified (May 16, 1242). The struggle between these two cities broke out immediately after the departure of the king to Hungary, and soon, others, including high nobility, joined in the affray. Thus, two factions emerged: the Trogir faction or royalist party, headed by Prince Stepko, and the Split faction or anti-royalist party. Right at the beginning it became obvious that the Trogir faction was the strongest, especially on the sea. And for this reason the citizens of Split sought and found allies in the Omish clan of Kachich, the town of Polyitse, Prince Andrew of Hum (Herzegovina) and the Bosnian banus Matey Ninoslav. The latter seized upon the occasion to exploit the weakness of Hungary and Croatia after the Tartar invasion, the best he could. The armed intervention of the Bosnian banus was for the king the best proof of the seriousness of this strife in Croatia and he sent the banus Dionysius with a strong army to subdue Split, while he himself set to field with another force in a campaign against Ninoslav.

In summer, 1244, the royal armies scored success in both directions. The duke and banus Dionysius forced the city of Split to surrender and then made peace with Trogir, which renounced Ostri. In addition, Split bound itself to select a royalist for prior, deliver six hostages and once again take oath of loyalty. In his turn, King Béla forced Ninoslav into submission. Furthermore he confirmed the patent issued by his brother Koloman to the Bosnian Church, endowing it with the town of Djakovo and tithe collected in the northern provinces of Bosnia. For the execution of this order the king made banus Ninoslav responsible. From that time on and up to the death of the banus (about August, 1245), peace was firmly established in Bosnia. In the meantime Béla had his five year old son Stephen crowned "the young king" of Hungary, and concurrently raised banus Dionysius to the office of palatin.

War for the Babenberg Heritage

After settling the matters in Bosnia and Croatia, Béla went to war with the Austrian Duke Frederic of Babenberg. In a battle fought at Wiener-Neustadt, Duke Frederic, the last Babenberg descendant, lost his life. Thus all the country from Bohemia to the Croatian frontier including both Austria and Styria remained without a legal ruler. Now both the Austrian neighbors, King Béla and the Bohemian king Otokár Přemysl II, contended for the inheritance. The long bitter and indecisive struggle was ended by the intervention of Pope Innocent IV through whose efforts peace was concluded in the year 1254 in the city of Pozhun. By the terms of the peace the king of Bohemia obtained Austria proper, while all of Styria (from Semering south) was ceded to Hungary.

Thereupon Béla appointed his son Stephen, "the younger king," governor of Styria and assigned the Croatian duke Stephen to advise him. But the Styrians, exasperated by the Hungarian rule, soon were in general rebellion. The rebels forced the young Stephen and his counsellor to leave Styria and proclaimed as their sovereign the Bohemian king Otokár Přemysl (1259). This incident ended in another Bohemian-Hungarian war, in which the Bohemian troops defeated the Hungarian forces near Kroissenbrunn on the Morava River in 1260, after which Béla had to renounce his claims to Styria.

As a guarantee for a permanent peace the two kings agreed that the younger son of Béla should marry Otokár's niece, Kunigunda. Later on this marriage actually took place so that the blood-ties between the Árpád and Přemysl dynasties were to become instrumental in establishing harmony between the two countries. However, the peace did not last long, for in the declining years of Béla's life the king of Bohemia, after taking possession of Carinthia and Carniola, strove to take over western Slavonia also. True, the Croatian Zagorye and the whole Samobor region were, by the time of Béla's death in 1270, actually in Otokár's possession. The native partisans of the Bohemian king built a fortification over Samobor as a bulwark for the defense of the southern frontier of Otokár's state.

Growing Power of the Oligarchs

The Tartar invasion deflected the policies of King Béla from the course he was about to follow at the beginning of his reign. Up to the time of the Tartar scourge the king used all his authority to check the growth of oligarchy, but after the invasion he reversed his own policy.

In exchange for military service he made liberal grants to his barons, giving them not only single estates, but entire districts, and authorizing them to build fortified strongholds on their estates. Thus Béla achieved his immediate goal but also increased considerably the power of the barons and magnates, who now were enabled to keep little standing armies destined not only to defend the king and country, but also, and primarily, to promote the private interests of the grandees.

In order to counteract the power of the oligarchy, the king tried to attach to the Crown the citizens and their guilds, while his own servants in the royal cities were raised to the status of nobility. Furthermore, he made them owners of the Crown lands which they had been cultivating in the past. In addition, the king won the towns of the grandees by fair exchange for their possessions. By this transaction the king made an attempt to acquire and hold as castra regia (royal towns) all the more important strategic points in the country. But all these measures were mere palliatives, without effect upon the root of the evil. Controlling vast economic and military resources, the grandees became overbearing and presumptuous, both toward the king and lower nobility. By enclosing small estates within their huge domains, the barons forced less fortunate knights and squires into a state of vassaldom. Some organized their forces into robber gangs and from their strongholds successfully challenged the power of the king himself.

The might of the oligarchy was greatly increased by the strife between King Béla and his son Stephen. Stephen was impatient for power. At the age of 23 he compelled the king to cede 29 counties to him as crown prince (1262), but even this did not long content him. He seized the banate of Macsó (Machva or Northern Serbia), and a new civil war broke out in Hungary between the followers of father and son, ending in 1265 with victory for Stephen. From this time forward he exercised royal powers within his own extensive domains, and the land of Hungary was divided between two kings with their separate courts and administrations.

At the same time the king's younger son Béla ruled independently and with full royal authority in Croatia. His reign extended from 1261 to his death in 1269.

The "Golden Bull" had by now been entirely forgotten, and each king strove to win over the powerful barons by further grants of land and serfs. All Croatia stood firmly by the old king. In recognition of their loyalty and support during the Tartar invasion, King Béla endowed many noblemen with extensive estates.

Administrative Changes

In the latter part of his reign (around 1260) Béla reorganized the administration of Croatia by a number of significant and effective changes. First he provided a single rule for all the lands of the Croatian kingdom. In accordance with this disposition, he appointed a duke of royal blood to govern this extensive area, with the title: dux Totius Sclavoniae, Croatiae et Dalmatiae." In his administrative duties the duke was assisted by two bani: the Slavonian and Croatian-Dalmatian banus, the latter being called also the banus of "maritime provinces."

In the absence of a duke of royal blood, which was most frequently the case, supreme authority belonged to the Slavonian banus, with the title of "banus of all Slavonia." The Croatian-Dalmatian banus had to submit to him and the title he bore was quite often that of the "sea coast banus." By this division of administrative authority, foundation was laid for splitting the kingdom of Croatia into two separate political and administrative areas: the kingdom of Croatia-Dalmatia proper, and the kingdom of Slavonia as a separate entity. This situation was to continue into the 16th century.

With a view to defending the Hungarian and Croatian frontiers from Serbia, Béla founded by the end of his reign the banate of Machva, reaching well into the present-day northwestern Serbia, south of the Sava and between the Drina and Kolubara Rivers, with its administrative center not far from the present-day town of Valyevo. For the purpose of increasing the income of the banus and for strengthening his military arm, Sriyem and Vuka counties were later attached to this banate. On the other hand, the county of Pozhega became fiscal domain of the Queen from 1264 on. As a result the Croatian provinces slipped gradually from under the authority of the Slavonian banus into the Hungarian sphere of influence. This again became conducive to their incorporation into the Hungarian complex, a trend which was conspicuous especially in the 15th and 16th centuries, up

to the battle of Mohách. During a struggle for succession to the throne in Bosnia, after the death of banus Matey Ninoslav, Béla made a similar disposition in the areas south of the Sava, dividing the country into three parts after the pattern we have already discussed.

Last Years of King Béla's Reign

At about the same time Duke Béla was presiding over the Croatian kingdom but, being a minor, he carried on under the regency of his mother, Queen Maria. Duke Béla and his mother resided in Zagreb and Knin surrounded by a brilliant court. He remained under the tutelage of his mother until 1268, and then began to rule independently. The next year however, he suddenly died. Thus, another member of the Árpád family was removed form the stage.

Another important event of that year was the betrothal of Maria, daughter of King Stephen V (IV) to the royal prince Charles of Naples. Later on Stephen's son and successor Ladislaus married the Neapolitan princess Elizabeth of the House of Anjou. Thus the blood-ties between the Árpád and Anjou dynasties became close enough to enthrone the Angevin branch in Hungary and Croatia when the line of male descendants from the House of Árpád was broken off. In the meantime King Béla IV (III), hero of the Tartar campaigns, died on the 3rd of May, 1270.

Origin and Fortunes of the Anjou Dynasty

On such relatively insignificant matters as the intermarriage between the Árpád and Anjou families many epoch-making events depended not only in Croatia and Hungary, but also in Poland and Lithuania. For this reason a closer acquaintance with the Anjou branch of the Capetian dynasty of France will help us to obtain a clearer view of political relations in medieval Europe.

The founder of the Anjou dynasty was Charles, prince of Anjou, son of Louis VIII of France, and brother of the Saint-King Louis,

the famous leader of two crusades (1248-1254; 1270). Louis VIII had four sons, the youngest of whom was Charles. Since Louis' oldest son was to inherit the crown of France, the father endowed his younger sons with extensive fiefs. Robert was given the province of Artois, Alphonse obtained Poitou and Auvergne, while Charles was endowed with the duchy of Anjou. The fortunes of Charles were further improved by his marriage with Beatrice, heiress of Provence. Then during the struggle of the papacy with Manfred (1258-1266), usurper of the Sicilian throne, Charles of Anjou was offered the kingdom of Sicily as a papal fief. The struggle with Manfred and his supporters was a bitter one, but Charles won a decisive victory in the battle of Benevento (1265). Manfred himself was killed in the battle. Thus, Charles became the unchallenged king of Sicily in the year 1266. He soon established himself as a dominant power in the Mediterranean, defying the Byzantine emperors, Arabic Sultans and kings of Castille and Aragon alike.

The great Angevin founder was followed by a line of descendants all of whom left a deep imprint in the history of Europe. His son Charles II, king of Naples (1285-1309), was the husband of Mary, daughter of King Stephen VI (V) of Hungary and Croatia. From this marriage came Charles Martel whose son was Charles I, king of Hungary and Croatia (1301-1342), and whose grandson was Louis I the Great (1342-1382), king of Croatia, Hungary and Poland. Both the daughters of this Louis became queens. Mary, wife of Sigismund, inherited her father's throne, while Hedvig, wife of Włodźisław-Jagiello, was elected queen of Poland. Their son was Włodźisław I Varnenchik (1440-1444), and grandson Vladislav I (1490-1516), successor of Mathias Corvinus. The latter's son Louis II (1516-1526) fell in the battle of Mohach.

From a side branch of Charles Martel's family came Charles II of Durazzo, king of Naples and short-lived king of Croatia and Hungary (1386). His son was Ladislaus (1386-1414), king of Naples, Croatia and Hungary who treacherously sold Dalmatia to Venice for 100,000 ducats.

Chapter XVII
EXTINCTION OF THE ÁRPÁD DYNASTY

Last Members of the Árpád Dynasty

STEPHEN V (IV) was a man of violent temper, ambitious and ruthless. After his victories over his father, he invaded Bulgaria. The death of Béla in 1270 made him the sole and undisputed ruler over a once more united Hungary. Shortly thereafter he quarreled with the Bohemian king, Otokár Přemysl II, over the conquest of Carinthia and Carniola by his powerful neighbor. The war continued with changing fortunes until May, 1271, when a battle of decision was fought in the area contained between the town of Moshon and the creek of Rabtsa, west of Gyoer. In this engagement the forces of Otokár were repulsed but not defeated. Thereupon the rulers came to terms: King Stephen renouncing all his claims to Austria, Styria, Carinthia and Carniola, while Otokár promised that he would not support the pretender Stephen Posthumous, son of King Andrew I (II). In the meantime Stephen Posthumous died in Venice, leaving behind his widow, the Venetian Tomasina Morosini, and a son, Andrew the Venetian.

During Stephen's reign the princes of Kerk became the masters of the city of Sen in 1271, while Joachim Pektar was the maritime banus. In the summer of 1272 Stephen decided to pay a visit to Naples by making a trip through Dalmatia. On his journey he took along his elder son Ladislaus in order to show the lad the world. Soon he discovered that the task of a mentor was a trying one, and left the child in the abbey of Topusko, while he himself proceeded on his journey south. For this neglect of his paternal duty he had to pay dearly, for on his arrival at Bihach on Una he was stunned by the message that his son had disappeared from the Topusko monastery. The boy had been kidnapped by banus Joachim Pektar, probably in complicity with Queen Elizabeth, a Kumanian by birth.

On hearing the news Stephen immediately returned. His anxiety and the fatigue of the search undermined the king's health and forced him to return to Budavár. His followers continued to search for the prince, and found him held in the town of Koprivnitsa. They laid siege to the town, but in the meantime King Stephen died, early in August, 1272.

Ladislaus III (IV)—(1272-1280)

With the king's death the siege of Koprivnitsa was lifted while the banus Joachim Pektar hastened with the prince to Székes Fehérvár, where he was received by his mother Elizabeth. Here he was crowned as Ladislaus III (IV) (1272-1290). He was known by the name of his mother's kin, therefore the "Kumanian." Up to Stephen VI (V) the prestige of the king in Croatia was untarnished, but after his death there was an almost complete dissolution of the royal authority.

The oligarchs asserted their power. At first Ladislaus' youth, then his weakness and extravagance reduced the royal power to a vanishing point. The over-confident oligarchs now began to quarrel and fight among themselves for the office of banus and possession of the large estates. New families of magnates came into prominence. The Giessingen barons, emigrees from Germany were granted extensive estates in the county of Krizhevats. Then the Gut-Keledi clan, likewise a German family, also occupied large estates in the counties of Zagreb and Krizhevats around Koprivnitsa.

The native princes of Babonichi of Voditsa, later on of Blagay, were the masters of the entire province from the Carniola frontier to the river of Verbas, with important towns along Kupa River and the Sana. The princes of Kerk established themselves along the seacoast from Tersat down to Sen, extending east to the foothills of Gvozd (Kapela). Finally, the Bribirian princes from the clan of Shubich, were masters of the district of Bribir and swayed over the Dalmatian cities, with the exception of the Venetian Zadar.

Conditions in Croatia

While King Ladislaus was a minor, his mother, Queen Elizabeth, took over the reign. Her chief advisor was the banus of Slavonia, Joachim Pektar, who later became treasurer of the kingdom. Joachim was replaced in the office of

banus by Matthews of the Chak-Trenchin clan. His administration is remembered by the fact that on the 20th of April, 1273, he called the first Slavonian parliament. According to the extant records, this "general congregation" deliberated on judiciary matters, administration of justice, military obligations and taxes.

In Croatia and Dalmatia Prince Paul of Bribir, son of Prince Styepko became again "maritime banus." In Slavonia Mathias Chaky was replaced by Henry, the Giessingen. But Henry himself became a rebel and in an uprising against Ladislaus and his mother, lost his life. Now the king's younger brother Andrew was appointed Croatian duke. Yet being a minor, the actual ruler was his mother Elizabeth. Not even this change could prevent the outbreak of a Croatian rebellion under the leadership of Babonichi princes. The movement was aimed chiefly at the queen's advisor, Joachim Pektar, and did not subside until this man lost his life (1272). With his death soon every vestige of the Gut-Keledi clan was wiped out in Slavonia.

Battle on the Moravian Field

In the meantime, important changes took place in the neighboring Austria. In 1273 Rudolf the Hapsburg was elected German king, and he immediately summoned the Bohemian king Otokár to return the Babenberg heritage to Germany. Since the Bohemian king refused to comply with Rudolf's request, war broke out which ended in the battle on the Moravian Field (August 26, 1278). In this engagement Rudolf was aided by the Hungarians, and thus defeated his opponents while Otokár met a hero's death on the battlefield.

As a result of this battle the Hapsburgs became masters of the old Babenberg possessions, and immediate neighbors of the Bohemian, Hungarian and Croatian kingdoms. They were now in a position to meddle in the internal affairs of these three states and they did, with the aim of uniting them into one single realm under the Hapsburg standard. They actually achieved this ambition, but only after centuries of effort and under the stress of unusual developments.

Even after the death of Joachim Pektar peace was not restored in Croatia and Dalmatia. The situation became still more muddled after the death of Duke Andrew in the summer of 1278.

King Ladislaus was at that time the only legally recognized member of the Árpád dynasty since the Court steadily refused to admit the dynastic legitimacy of Andrew the Venetian, son of Stephen. In the meantime, the Giessingens and Babonichi were joined in the quarrels by the princes of Kerk, while in Dalmatia the Venetians attacked the Kachich clan of the Omish area and wiped it out completely.

However, banus Paul of Bribir put up a short defense in his stronghold of Omish (1280). This was an ideal situation for Andrew the Venetian to enforce his claims to the Croatian duchy. Moreover, he was aided by the Giessingen clan which raised in 1289 a rebellion against King Ladislaus, and invited Andrew to Croatia. Escorted by his uncle Albert Morossini, Andrew landed early in 1290 in the Venetian Zadar and set out north on a campaign of conquest. His venture was not propitious, for in the enclave of Drava and Mura Rivers, near the locality of Shtrigovo, he was made prisoner by some grandee who turned him over for safe-keeping to the Austrian duke Albert I, son of Rudolf of Hapsburg. But the wheel of fortune soon turned toward the young adventurer, for King Ladislaus was killed by his Kumanian kin. In the absence of a prince of the Árpád lineage, the Hungarian high nobility invited Andrew from Vienna to ascend the throne of Hungary.

Andrew II (III)—1290-1301

Soon after he established himself on the Hungarian throne, Andrew was confronted with the opposition of three powerful contenders, denying the legitimacy of his Árpád lineage. One of them was Rudolf of Hapsburg. This ruler insisted that King Béla III (IV) turned Hungary and Croatia over to the German emperor Frederic II for protection during the Tartar invasion (1241), thus submitting to German sovereignty. Accordingly, in August, 1290, Rudolf assigned both kingdoms to his son, Duke Albert of Austria.

Pope Nicholas IV was the second contender. The pontiff put forth the claim that both kingdoms were the lien of the Holy See, and that he alone had the authority to dispose of them. Queen Maria of Naples, sister of King Ladislaus III, claimed her own right to the throne, passing on this claim to her son Charles Martel. In her contention she was supported by the Pope and consequently Charles Martel was

crowned in Naples by the papal legate king of Croatia and Hungary in 1292.

In the meantime Andrew was legally crowned in Székes Féhervár and having the support of the greatest part of Hungary, quickly asserted his power in the face of opposition. First he settled accounts with Albert, the Austrian, as his most dangerous opponent, by declaring war on him and defeating him. Thereupon Albert renounced, by the peace treaty of Hinsburg, all his rights to Hungary.

However, it was far more difficult to settle the matter with the Court of Naples. Charles Martel was supported by almost all of Croatia from the Drava to Neretva, and even by John the Giessingen, banus of Slavonia. In view of this, Andrew, with his armed forces, crossed the Drava River, asserting his authority throughout. Yet on his way home from a successful campaign, he was treacherously seized by John the Giessingen and thrown into prison. After paying a huge ransom, Andrew regained his freedom in 1292. The king was now joined by the Babonichi clan which brought to Hungary the king's mother, Tomassina Morossini. She was promptly appointed duchess of Croatia.

Princes of Bribir

Both the Court of Naples and Andrew II (III) prized highly the friendship of the princes of Bribir, and especially that of banus Paul. In order to attach Paul to his side, King Charles II of Naples granted him in the name of his son Charles Martel, all Croatia from Modrush in the north, to Hum in the south. This ownership carried the right of inheritance, with the further provision that all Croatian noblemen who lived in that area became vassals of banus Paul and his successors. Outbidding the Neapolitan patent King Andrew did the same in 1293, giving Paul and his clan all of the Croatian-Dalmatian

banate and the title of banus as a hereditary honor. With these grants the princes of Bribir became the first magnates of Croatia, and the banus office became hereditary in their family, passing from father to son without any royal interference, or even approval.

At the same time the Babonichi princes made an effort to establish themselves as hereditary bani of Slavonia, while in Bosnia the princes of the Kotromanichi clan succeeded in founding their own dynasty.

Last Years of Andrew's Reign

After a short period of peace, the war flared up in 1295, in the course of which Zagreb and the nearby countryside became the scene of bitter fighting. The suburban royal town of Gradets stood by King Andrew, while the Kaptol (Chapter) stronghold of Zagreb supported Charles Martel. In that year (1295), however, Charles Martel died, bequeathing the Croatian-Hungarian crown to his son, Charles Robert. King Andrew himself had no son to succeed him on the throne, so in 1299 he proclaimed his uncle Albert Morossini as his successor. This attempt failed, for a general rebellion broke out in the country, and the Estates espoused the cause of Charles Robert.

George, the prince of Bribir, brother of banus Paul, went to Naples in August, 1300, and brought the young prince to Croatia. Shortly thereafter on January 14, 1301, Andrew was taken by death. With this event the male line of the House of Árpád became extinct. Upon the news of Andrew's death, banus Paul brought Prince Charles Robert to Zagreb, where he was received by Prince Ugrin of the clan of Chak-Ilok. Thence he was escorted to Ostrogon (Esztergom) and there in March, 1301, the young prince was crowned by Gregory, archbishop of Ostrogon, as Charles I, king of Hungary and Croatia.

Chapter XVIII

THE HOUSE OF ANGEVINS ON THE CROATIAN-HUNGARIAN THRONE (1301-1409)

Charles I (1301-1342) . Struggle with Rival Kings

CHARLES Robert was merely a boy, 12 years of age when Prince George of Bribir brought him from Naples. Almost all Croatia recognized him, but Hungary was divided into a number of factions. By marriage ties with the Árpád dynasty there were three claimants to the throne: the Neapolitan king Charles II, whose wife was the Hungarian princess Maria, daughter of Stephen VI; the Bohemian king Ventseslav II, son of the late Otokár Přemysl II and Kunigunde, grand-daughter of Béla III (IV) who passed on his claim rights to Ventseslav; and Otto of Bavaria, son of Béla's daughter Elizabeth.

The majority of Hungarian magnates, headed by the palatin Mathias Chak of Trenchin decided in favor of the Bohemian prince Ventseslav. They brought him to Székes Fehérvár and crowned him as Ladislaus V (1301-1304), king of Hungary. In consequence a bloody civil war broke out between the supporters of the two kings. Pope Boniface VIII himself cast the weight of his office in the struggle with such determination that Ladislaus V left Hungary in 1304, giving up the fight.

Thereupon the Hungarian Estates proclaimed and crowned Otto of Bavaria as their king. He actually ruled from 1304 to 1308, although his faction was weak. Since his strongest support came from Transylvania he went there to pay a visit to Ladislaus Ápor, whose daughter he intended to marry. But that high-handed magnate took him prisoner and seized the crown of St. Stephen, which Otto always carried with him. When he regained his freedom, Otto returned in 1308 to Bavaria, renouncing all claim to Hungary and Croatia.

The third rival of Charles came from Serbia. The Serbian ex-king Styepan Dragutin* was connected with the House of Árpád by his wife Catherine, daughter of King Stephen VI (V). He entered into an agreement with the Transylvanian duke Ladislaus Ápor, by the terms of which his son Ladislaus would marry the duke's daughter, receive the crown of St. Stephen and

* Lit: Stephen Charles.

become crowned king of Hungary. This intrigue was checkmated by the successful campaign of Charles in Sirmium, in which Prince Paul of Gara won distinction and established the historical fortunes of his family. Thus the Ápor episode was brought swiftly to its inglorious end.

Papal Interference

Meanwhile the Holy See sent Cardinal Gentilis to Croatia and Hungary, in order to prepare the way for peace. Early in November, 1308, Gentilis arrived at Budavár and by his wise and tactful bearing soon won over the chief opponents of Charles. He also had the Estates called, where he began to explain the right of the Holy See to the Hungarian-Croatian throne. But when during his explanation loud murmurs and shouts betrayed the hostile state of mind of the assembly, the Cardinal promptly changed his argument and conceded to the Estates the right of free election.

Thereupon Charles was elected by acclamation and generally recognized as legitimate ruler and sovereign. This move also ended forever the papal claim to the crown of Hungary and Croatia. However, the problems connected with Charles' enthronement were not yet at an end, for the crown of St. Stephen was still in the hands of the Transylvanian duke Ladislaus Ápor. Hence Cardinal Gentilis consecrated a new crown, having first declared the old one null and void. So Charles was crowned for the second time in Budavár on June 15, 1309, by Thomas, archbishop of Ostrogon. At the coronation Archbishop Peter of Split represented Prince Paul of Bribir while Henry Giessingen, banus of Slavonia, and the brothers Stephen John and Radoslav Babonichi also sent representatives to witness the ceremony.

Yet in the eyes of the people a coronation with a substitute crown did not have the glow of legitimacy. By old tradition three conditions were prerequisite to a valid crowning: first the crown of St. Stephen; second, Székes Fehérvár as the place of the coronation, and third, the presence of the archbishop of Ostrogon to perform the ceremonies. Therefore, it became nec-

essary to recover the hallowed crown of St. Stephen from the hands of the brigand. After much haggling and upon the delivery of ransom money, Duke Ápor finally released the relic. Charles was then crowned for the third time in Székes Fehérvár with the venerated crown of St. Stephen. The ceremony was performed on the 27th of August, 1310, again by archbishop Thomas of Ostrogon. Only then did Hungary recognize Charles I as king in due form.

But peace was not restored. The grandee Mathias Chak of Trenchin refused to recognize the young king, and challenged his power for another ten years. Only the death of Mathias in March, 1321, dispersed the forces he had gathered. Even then the disorders continued. Felician Zakh, a Hungarian magnate, attempted to strike the king down with his sword in April 1330, but failed in the attempt. With the death of this seigneur, peace was finally restored in Hungary, and Charles finally became a full-fledged ruler in his kingdom.

Banus Paul and Zadar.

While in Hungary the oligarchs were gradually trampled down by the king's rising power, developments in Croatia tok a different course altogether. Here Charles I was never able to consolidate his power fully. The Croatian magnates and nobility recognized him as their king, but they were carrying on in their own dominion quite independently. Foremost among these were the princes of Bribir, especially their senior, the Croatian banus (banus Chroatorum) Paul, and since 1299 also "Sovereign of Bosnia." The authority of banus Paul extended at the beginning of the 14th century from the mountain ranges of Gvozd to the Neretva, and from the sea to the Bosna River. Only Venetian Zadar was not in his possession. But he decided to extend his sovereignty over that important port also.

Developments in Italy favored his plans. So when Pope Clement V excommunicated the Venetians because of their seizure of Ferrara, and released all the Venetian subjects from their oath of loyalty, the banus succeeded in persuading the rebellious Zadar to stage an armed insurrection against Venice (1311). However, in the middle of the war, which lasted for three years, banus Paul died (May, 1312). According to some, he was assassinated by the Bosnian heretics. He bequeathed to his son Mladen the title of banus, together with his extensive dominion.

Banus Paul ranks among the greatest men of Croatian history, wise, deliberate and resolute. He nearly restored the might of the national Croatian rulers, uniting the largest portions of the Croatian State. For two centuries Paul and his son Mladen were considered by historians as independent rulers. Mladen (1312-1322) was, in fact, a highly educated and courageous man, but hot tempered and impetuous. Although the situation favored his course, he failed to complete the war with the Venetians to his advantage and Zadar was again forced to surrender (September, 1313) to Venice. This time, however, the terms of submission were less Draconian than those in the past.

Downfall of Banus Mladen

Mladen's failure in the Zadar affair tempted Venice to bring about his downfall altogether. Soon the Republic found suitable men in Shibenik and Trogir, who early in 1322 raised a rebellion against Mladen and surrendered both cities to Venice "for protection." In a further move the Venetians promoted a strife among the factions of Croatian nobility, with Duke Nelipich of the clan of Svachich as the leader of the malcontents. The group was joined by Paul, brother of Mladen, who was promised the office of banus. From this intrigue a civil war broke out in Croatia, and King Charles decided to take advantage of the situation. Consequently, he sent aid to the opponents of Mladen through the banus of Slavonia, Ivan Babonich, while he himself made a trip to Croatia. Late in the fall of 1322, banus Mladen was defeated by his enemies in the battle of Liska, near Trogir.

In the meantime, Charles himself arrived at Knin and summoned the Estates to a parley, which was attended by Mladen under royal safe conduct. There he was treacherously seized by the king and taken to Hungary. Details of this event are not clear. While the extant sources disagree about his captivity, Mladen never returned from Hungary, and it is assumed that he was put to death by the ungrateful king who owed his very throne to Mladen's family.

The title of Croatian-Dalmatian banus was now conferred upon John Babonich, banus of Slavonia. The Bosnian banate was also removed

from the authority of the Bribir princes. Stye-pan Kotromanich was appointed banus of Bosnia, and made a vassal of the king.

Duke Nelipich

When he appointed Ivan Babonich as the sole banus of the Croatian lands, King Charles directed him to restore the royal power in that country as it had been in the past. The banus not only failed to achieve this task, but aroused the Croatian magnates to such an extent that they joined in a defensive alliance against the king, entered into an agreement with Venice, and captured the royal city of Knin. The leader of the resistance was the same Duke Nelipich who had fought Prince Mladen, whose political power and ambitions he now inherited. Disappointed by his failures, the king dismissed Ivan Babonich, but his successors, Nicholas Omodeyev (1323-1325) and Mikats Mihalyevich, were even less successful. Not even the royal decree of 1325, by which Charles strove to restore the ancient glamor of the name banus, and to raise his authority above that of the grandees, proved effective. The magnates took this patent as a challenge to their own power, and Duke Nelipich answered it in 1326 by striking a fatal blow at the army of banus Mikats in a decisive battle, thus frustrating the king's attempt to subdue the Croatian barons.

As a result of this defeat all southern Croatia, from the districts of Lika and Kerbava down to Tsetina River, became free and out of the reach of royal power. Only the princes of Kerk, whose previous grants were confirmed by Charles, and further expanded in 1323 by the gift of Gat and Drezhnik counties, with a number of sizeable towns, remained loyal to the king as did of course Slavonia, with her banus Mikats.

Another consequence of the victory of Nelipich was the seizure by Venice of the coastal area from Zermanya River to the mouth of the Tsetina. The Venetians managed to persuade the citizens of Split and Nin (Spalato and Nona) to surrender to Venice "for protection."

Skradin and Omish (Scardona and Almissa) were the only free cities in this Venice-controlled territory remaining in the possession of the Bribir princes. Taking advantage of the general confusion, the Bosnian banus Stephen Kotromanich detached from Croatia the entire area between the Tsetina and Neretva rivers, including the districts of Imotski, Dumno, Livno and Glamoch, setting up from these Croatian counties a province named "the Western Lands" or "Tramontane." Over the rest of Croatia Duke Nelipich ruled as a sovereign, establishing his residence in the stronghold of Knin. He spent most of his time in feuding with his enemies, especially the princes of Bribir and raiding the Dalmatian cities. He died in 1344.

Last Years of Charles' Reign.

Charles I reigned peacefully in Hungary and Slavonia, and lived amid pomp and glamor never witnessed before in the courts of Temeshvar and Vishegrad. Even in Zagreb he built a royal residence. In Slavonia the banus Mikats Mihalyevich (1325-1343) ruled with an iron hand. For example he crushed the resistance of the powerful Babonich clan and seized their town of Stinichnyak (1327) for the benefit of the king.

In spite of his domestic problems King Charles did not neglect the field of foreign policy, for he aspired to the crowns of Naples and Poland. In fact, when his uncle Robert, king of Naples, remained without a son, the younger son of Charles, Andrew, was bethrothed with Robert's granddaughter Johanna. Then the young man was sent to Naples for education as the future occupant of the throne. At the same time Charles' elder son Ludovic was trained to occupy the throne of Poland besides that of Hungary and Croatia. Charles' wife Elizabeth was the sister of the Polish king Kazimir, another childless monarch, who obtained in 1339 the promise of the Polish Estates to elect Ludovic as his successor.

In the south Charles scored another important success with the capture of Belgrade in 1319, which, up to its seizure by the Turks, remained a bastion of Hungarian power in the Balkans.

At his death (July 16, 1342) Charles I left behind three sons: Ludovic, Andrew and Stephen.

Ludovic I, the Great—1342-1382
End of the Croatian Oligarchy

Still a boy 17 years of age, Ludovic inherited a vast dominion, with all its power and problems. Full of enthusiasm, determination and reliance on his good fortune, he plied to his immediate tasks. And indeed, after many wars and campaigns this ruler gave his state a compactness and significance which it never possessed before. For this reason the Hungarian

historians call him Ludovic the Great (Nagy Lajos).

The young king set immediately to untangling the complicated Croatian situation. This task was simplified a great deal by the passing of the powerful Duke Nelipich (1344). The duke's widow Vladislava of the Gussich clan took over the vast dominion as the guardian and caretaker for her young son John Nelipich. At the king's behest banus Nicholas of the Hahold clan invaded Croatia in the same year (1344), advanced to the walls of Knin and began to storm it. But the heroic Vladislava, fighting "like a lioness" repulsed the attacks. However, seeing that she would not be able to hold out indefinitely, she entered into negotiations with the banus, following which he left Croatia.

Aroused over this rebuff, King Ludovic set out at the head of an army 30,00 strong. Upon arriving at Bihach on the banks of the Una River the king pitched camp with his host. As the news of this movement reached Vladislava, she came with her son Ivan to the king's camp, took the oath of loyalty and surrendered her stronghold of Knin. Ludovic acquitted her of the "lifetime treason" of her husband, and confirmed her son Ivan Nelipich in all his ancestral possessions, including the city of Sen, and the Tsetina district. Thus, the power of the Nelipich clan was broken and from then on its members became loyal subjects of the king.

Loss of Zadar and War with Naples

Upon the news of the king's arrival at Bihach, the city of Zadar declared its loyalty. This move of the rebel city led to a new war with Venice, in which Zadar sustained a long siege. Yielding to the frantic appeals of its citizens for aid, King Ludovic came to Zadar with an army, 100,000 strong, in the summer of 1346. But the campaign failed, because through the treachery of banus Stephen Kotromanich, and his own poor generalship, he lost the battle. Embittered over his defeat, Ludovic left Zadar to its fate, and returned to Hungary. Moreover he made a truce with Venice for eight years (1348). In the meantime, the citizenry of Zadar, exhausted from starvation and disease, surrendered under oppressive terms after two years of heroic defense.

During his stay before Zadar Ludovic managed to compose his differences with the princes of Bribir. Prince George, son of Paul, and

brother of banus Mladen, surrendered to Ludovic the well-fortified and important town of Ostrovitsa, and received in exchange the town of Zrin in Slavonia. Thus Prince George became the founder of the famous Zrinski family. Through the loss of their key stronghold, the power of the Bribir princes fell to a low ebb. Moreover, the branch that remained in Croatia soon died out, gradually losing its former prestige and significance. With the collapse of the Nelipich and Bribir clans, the oligarchy of the Croatian magnates came to an end. In consequence, Ludovic restored the royal power in Croatia, which had practically ceased to exist there since the reign of Ladislaus III (IV), the Kumanian.

The chief reason why Ludovic sacrificed the cause of Zadar and made an eight year truce with Venice was the assassination of his brother Andrew at Aversi, near Naples. Realizing that he would never get the satisfaction he desired through negotiations, he set out at the head of his army to Naples, conquered the entire kingdom and put to death all those guilty of the assassination of his brother. Only Queen Johanna, considered the chief offender, escaped his wrath (1348). But when Ludovic returned to Hungary, new disorders broke out, calling for another campaign overseas. Rather than squander his forces on Naples, which he could not hold forever, he gave up further plans of conquest and finally ceded the kingdom of Naples to Queen Johanna in 1352.

Marriage Tie with the Bosnian Dynasty

During the first years of Ludovic's reign and his preoccupations with Croatia, Venice and Naples, the Serbian king Styepan Dushan acquired a large territory at the expense of Byzantium and raised his state to such a height of power that in 1346 he proclaimed himself emperor (Tsar) of all Serbians, Bulgarians, Albanians and Greeks." Then he directed his ambition toward the conquest of the Hum district (Herzegovina), which together with Bosnia, was the province of the banus Styepan Kotromanich, a vassal of Ludovic I. Dushan broke into Bosnia but the resistance was stubborn and he withdrew in 1350.

Adding to the prestige which now accrued to Stephen Kotromanich came the betrothal and marriage of his daughter Elizabeth to King Louis I in 1353. Stephen, however, did not

long survive this climax of his career, and left the Bosnian throne to his gifted nephew Tvartko, at that time a youth of 15 (1353-1391). Then late in December, 1355, the great Serbian tsar Styepan Dushan fell a victim to the Black Plague. After his death the Serbian State began to disintegrate. The dissolution of the Serbian power brought the kings of Hungary temporary relief, although this respite was attended by the prospect of a disaster that was to befall the Christian nations of the Balkans and central Europe.

Second War with Venice

As the eight-year truce expired, Venice gained possession of the stronghold of Skradin and was bent on seizing the cities of Klis and Omish. This forced Ludovic into a final showdown with the Republic. He started a campaign for the liberation of all of Dalmatia, including the islands and towns. In order to assure victory, he planned to conduct the operations not only in Dalmatia and Croatia, but to invade also Serenissime's Italian possessions, in order to separate the island-city from the mainland. In execution of his plan the king began to organize a great army in Zagreb, pretending that he was about to wage war against Serbia. Suddenly he turned west and declared war on the Republic (1356).

Caught unprepared, Venice offered to return all the Dalmatian cities except Zadar. But the king rejected the terms and the war went on for two years. In Croatia and Dalmatia the army was led by the banus Ivan Chuze of Ludbreg. Split and Trogir promptly surrendered, while the other cities soon followed suit. Resistance was offered only at Zadar, where fierce battles were fought. At the same time Ludovic's armies campaigned successfully in the north of Italy, and the Republic finally gave in. The peace treaty of Zadar (February 18, 1358) ended the war. By the terms of this covenant Venice renounced all her Dalmatian cities and islands from the Bay of Quarnero to the city of Drach (Durazzo). Thus, Kotor and other coastal cities became free, while the doge gave up his title "duke of Dalmatia and Croatia," which the heads of the Republic had borne since 1,000 A.D. Through this settlement the Dalmatian cities and islands were returned to their legal king and the Croatian kingdom, while the Venetian authority was suppressed along the Croatian coastland for a long time to come.

Balkan Wars

Having defeated Venice and regained the Dalmatian cities, Ludovic turned south in pursuit of the Balkan policy of conquest laid down by Béla II (III). In the spring of 1359 he declared war on the Serbs. After the death of Tsar Styepan Dushan, Serbia had split up into several small principalities so that Dushan's son and successor Styepan Urosh (1355-1371) no longer had the power with which to substantiate his imperial title: "Emperor of the Serbs and Greeks." Through the invasion of Serbia, in the course of which he reached the Rudnik mountain range, Ludovic secured the Machva province. But otherwise he did not achieve any important success and he came into conflict with the Bosnian banus Tvartko.*

After his campaign in Bosnia, Ludovic made plans to attack Bulgaria. The opportunity came after Emperor Alexander died and the power in Bulgaria was divided between his two sons, Shishman and Stratsimir. The first had his capital in Ternov, and the other in Vidin. Since the brothers were quarrelling, Ludovic conquered the Vidin part of the empire without difficulty, taking prisoner the emperor Stratsimir himself (1365).

Encouraged by his success, Ludovic founded a Bulgarian banate between the Danube and Balkan mountains in the west with Vidin as its capital. Stratsimir spent his years of captivity in Slavonia. In 1369 Ludovic made peace with the captive emperor, restoring to him western Bulgaria and making him his vassal.

In the year 1370 Ludovic's uncle, King Kazimir of Poland passed away. The Polish Estates honored their promise of 1339, electing Ludovic their king. Amid pomp and celebration he was crowned as king of Poland on the 17th of November 1370. Thus, he became one of the most powerful monarchs in the Europe of his day. His power reached from the lower Vistula on the Baltic Sea to the port of Kotor on the Adriatic. With the exception of a small number of Hungarians and Germans, all his other subjects were Slavs. Among theme were Croats, Serbs, Slovaks, Ukranians and Poles. Hence he is mentioned by many as the first Pan-Slavic

* These events will be more fully discussed in Volume II.

ruler in history. But all this was ephemeral. While Ludovic was extending the frontiers of his realm, an ominous power appeared in the Balkan peninsula, which in less than a century would become by far the most dangerous foe of both Croatia and Hungary. This power was that of the Ottoman Turks.

The Third War with Venice

In his declining years Ludovic engaged in a new war with the Republic of Venice. In 1378 a war broke out between Venice and Genoa over their interests in the East. Genoa went to Ludovic for aid, and he promptly set out with an army in order to weaken and humiliate the rival of his power on the Adriatic. Hostilities were carried on again, mostly on Italian soil, while the Venetian galleys confined themselves chiefly to devastation of the Dalmatian coast. Finally peace was concluded in 1381 in Torino. By the terms of this treaty the Serenissime Republic confirmed all the provisions of the peace of Zadar (1358), and in addition, bound itself to pay a yearly tribute of 7,000 ducats to the Hungarian-Croatian king.

Venice was saved from worse humiliation by the disorders in Naples. Since Queen Johanna refused to recognize the Roman Pope Urban VI, and became an ally of the Avignon pope Clement VII, Urban VI excommunicated her from the Church and deprived her of her throne. Thereupon King Ludovic sent an army to Naples under his relative Charles of Drach (Durazzo), duke of Croatia,* who dethroned Johanna and proclaimed himself king of his native country in 1381.

King Ludovic died on September 11, 1382, leaving behind two minor daughters, the elder of whom was Maria, bride of the Bohemian prince Sigismund of Luxemburg, son of the emperor Charles IV. The younger daughter was Hedwig, the future wife of Yagiello and the sainted queen of Poland.

Dynastic Troubles in the Anjou Family (1382-1409)

Shortly after the death of Ludovic I the Hungarian magnates crowned his elder daughter Maria (1382-1385) as if she had been Ludovic's son ("Coronata fuit in Regem"). Since Maria was only 12 years of age, her mother Elizabeth

* From 1369 to 1376.

Kotromanich acted as a regent. She was a simple and ambitious woman, fond of intrigue. Her chief advisor was the Hungarian palatin Nicholas of Gara (Gorjanski), an intelligent but selfish man.

The first task of the queen mother was to see how she could acquire the Polish throne, as well as the Hungarian-Croatian throne for Maria. But the Polish Estates rejected her decisively since they no longer wanted their sovereign to reside in the Hungarian capital. However, they were willing to place the younger Hedwig on the Polish throne, and after lengthy negotiations they crowned her queen of Poland. Thus they separated Poland from Hungary. The next year Hedwig was married to the Lithuanian prince Włodźisław Yagiello, founder of the Polish dynasty of Yagielloni (1386).

Strife in Croatia

Throughout this period important and serious changes were taking place in Croatia, where the centralistic policies of both Anjou kings and the enthronement of a woman caused widespread disaffection. This strife came as a boon for the expansionist policy of the Bosnian king Styepan Tvartko, for he aspired to the whole territory south of Drava River. As soon as he heard of the change on the Hungarian throne he sent emissaries to some of the Dalmatian cities and certain Croatian magnates. The first to accept his invitation was the prior of Vrana, Ivan Palizhna, but the Dalmatian cities and most Croatian barons turned deaf ears.

When the plans of Tvartko became known in Budavár, palatin Nicholas Goryanski offered a defensive alliance to Venice which was declined. At this juncture the queen mother Elizabeth decided to go herself to Croatia and effect a compromise with the malcontents. Upon the news of the queen mother's coming to Croatia, Ivan of Palizhna raised a rebellion in Vrana. However, the aid which he had expected from Bosnia failed to materialize. Vrana had to surrender and Ivan Palizhna escaped to Bosnia, while Maria and Elizabeth installed themselves and a glamorous retinue without further opposition at Zadar.

By the end of November, 1383, the Croatian barons appeared reconciled to the crown and a brief lull followed. After this palatin Nicholas effected a compromise with the king of Bosnia, ceding to him the city of Kotor in 1385.

Rebellion of the Horvat Brothers

The capricious and unpredictable rule of Elizabeth and Maria created disaffection not only among the magnates of Slavonia but in Hungary as well. The malcontents were headed by the Horvat family of Vuka county. Outstanding leaders of this clan were Paul, bishop of Machva, and Ladislaus. They were joined by many Hungarian barons, including two officials of the royal court: Judge Nicholas Széchy, formerly Croatian banus, and the treasurer Nicholas Zambó.

Confronted with the league of the malcontent Slavonian and Hungarian magnates, the Court first attempted a conciliation through palatin Nicholas of Gara. A compromise was arrived at by the treaty of Pozsega, signed in May, 1385, but this arrangement was not of long duration, and when the nobility became convinced of the lack of sincerity and good faith on the part of Elizabeth and the palatin, it decided to find another sovereign in the person of the king of Naples, Charles of Durazzo (Drach), the only surviving male member of the Anjou dynasty. He was also the only foreign prince acquainted with the laws and constitution of Hungary and Croatia.

Exactly at that time Maria's fiancé, Sigismund of Luxemburg, broke into Hungary with a large army and proceeded to marry the 15 year old Maria. Having achieved his purpose he again returned to Bohemia.

In the meantime Bishop Paul Horvat went to Naples and invited Charles of Durazzo to take over the throne of Hungary and Croatia. Charles was willing and went to Hungary, where the parliament in Budavár elected him king. The young queen Maria renounced her throne and Charles was crowned in the year 1385 in Székes Fehérvár as king of Hungary and Croatia.

Charles II and Maria

Charles of Durazzo assumed the name of Charles II, but his reign was limited to a few days because in February, 1386, Queen Elizabeth and the palatin Nicholas Gara had him assassinated by Balázh Forgách, a Hungarian magnate, in the royal palace itself. Once again the youthful Maria was on the throne (1386-1395).

Elated over the success of their intrigue, Elizabeth and Maria made an excursion to Slavonia in order to pay a visit to Nicholas Gara, who was reinstated in the office of palatin. The assassin, count Balázh Forgách was a member of the party, together with a number of trusted grandees. They all headed for the town of Gara, residence of the palatin, but they never arrived there. Early in the morning of July 25, 1386 as they left the neighboring town of Djakovo, the royal party was ambushed by the forces of the Horvat brothers and their friends. A fierce fight ensued, in the course of which palatin Nicholas of Gara, Balázh Forgách and other courtiers were killed, while Elizabeth and Maria were taken prisoner.

The women were then sent to the seacoast, and kept in Novigrad, near the town of Nin. There Ivan of Palizhna, their custodian and the banus of Croatia, had Elizabeth strangled before the eyes of her daughter Maria. The life of the young queen was spared. This took place toward the middle of January, 1387. It was done, many believe, upon the insistence of the Court of Naples, in revenge for the murder of Charles of Durazo.*

King and Emperor Sigismund (1387-1437)

Informed of the tragedy of Djakovo and Novigrad, Sigismund hastened to Hungary where a party of the peers elected him their king and immediately crowned him in Székes Fehérvár. Sigismund made it his first task to deliver his wife Maria from the Novigrad prison. For this purpose he entered into an agreement with the Republic of Venice and the latter sent him a fleet of vessels with which to invest Novigrad from the sea. On the land side the stronghold was besieged by the troops of Prince Ivan of Kerk (Frankapan) and an army sent by Sigismund. After a long siege, banus Ivan of Palizhna released the queen early in June, 1387 under the condition that his own troops be allowed to withdraw from the stronghold unharmed.

At the same time the king's army, headed by Nicholas (Gara) Goryanski, son of the assassinated palatin, fought so successfully in southern Hungary and Slavonia that the Horvat brothers, Styepan Tvartko and the Serbian prince Lazarus, had to retire their forces into

---

* Because of political division of the Croatian territory, frequently one and the same event produced a different effect on each side of the frontier. Therefore, in presenting certain important events and developments, it was necessary to review them in their new political setting. In such cases repetition is marked with the symbol *Cf.* and the page-number of the related episode.

Bosnia. In this struggle the youngest Horvat brother, Ladislaus, was killed.

Both the surviving brothers became active in Bosnia under King Tvartko, who relied on their wisdom and generalship until his death in 1381. His successor Styepan Dabisha sought conciliation with Sigismund and in 1393 signed a peace treaty in Djakovo, by the terms of which Sigismund was to inherit the Bosnian throne in case of Dabisha's death. They further agreed to the fate of the Horvat brothers, who were thus finally seized by Sigismund. As his prisoners they were sent to Hungary, where the king took a cruel vengeance upon Ivanish, tying him to the tails of two horses, and having his body torn apart. The fate of Bishop Paul is unknown, but he was probably incarcerated in some cloister where he is believed to have died in 1394. With the death of these two national heroes, the rebellion in Croatia was crushed.

Disaster at Nicopolis (1396)

The expansion of Turkish power in the Balkans came about simultaneously with the sedition in Croatia, the developments in Bosnia and the Serbian disaster at Kossovo (1389). Sigismund himself was alarmed at the Turkish conquests and sought and obtained aid from Germany, England, Poland and France. With an army of 40,000 men he turned against Sultan Bayazid, who at that time was making preparations for the siege of Constantinople. The purpose of Sigismund's campaign was to destroy the Turkish power in Europe. Crossing the Danube near Orshova he came to Nicopolis on the Danube, and laid it under siege. On September 25, 1396, however, Sultan Bayazid appeared with a superior army and completely destroyed the Christian forces. Sigismund saved his own life by boarding a barge and sailing down the river to the Black Sea. There he rested for a short period and at the beginning of the next year (1397), he returned through Constantinople and Dubrovnik to Hungary. The Ottoman victory at Nicopolis consolidated the Turkish power on the Balkan peninsula for many centuries to come.

End of Volume I.

1

The science of anthropology not only confirms the speculative conclusions of philosophers, but also gives us more definite details about the importance of man's symbiosis with flora and fauna, as well as of relations between the individual and the group.

According to the medical branch of the physical anthropology, the transformism of the human body comes as a result of endogene and exogene causes, that is, of the internal effect of the hereditary cell elements, and the external effect of the natural surroundings.[1] This progression ascertained over all the continents of the world, is discussed in most treatises on anthropology, and in a number of special works published on this subject.

Among the exogenic factors which result in changing the anthropographic characteristics of man, are those which come from his natural surroundings, whether geographical or social. The physico-geographical factors refer to physical surroundings such as are provided by nature itself. In distinction from these, the anthropo-social factors are the product of human life and work. The consistency and configuration of the terrain, the climate and biographical aspects form the physico-geographical factors of the natural environment. By way of contrast the anthropo-social elements move within the limits of the social and spiritual culture of man.

2. Transliteration

In transliterating words derived from a large number of languages used in this work, the writer attempted to reproduce the phonetic structure of the foreign elements, through resort to nearest sounds of English. A brief outline of transliteration rules is presented below.

1) Affricates

Whether in Roman or Cyrillic letters, the Slavic affricates are transliterated into English by adding a mute *h* to the basic consonant. So the Slavic ć, č; ś, š; ź, ž, ż, appearing in Croatian, Slovenian, Czecho-Slovak and Polish, respectively, will be marked in English with *ch; sh* and *zh*, respectively. The sound of *zh* is the same as that of *s* in the words: *usual, pleasure, measure,* etc.

The same *zh* sound is used for the Czech *ř* and Polish *rz* in the prevocalic or intervocalic positions, otherwise, they are transcribed with *sh*.

2) Spirants

The general Slavic dental spirant *c* or Roumanian *ţ* are equated with *ts*.

The guttural spirant marked in Czech and Polish with *ch* is transliterated with *kh*.

3) The Glide-sound *j* and Palatals

The Croatian, Slovenian and Serbian (Cyrillic) *j*

have the same value as German *j*, or English consonantal *y* as in: you, year, yell, etc.

The palatal consonants such as *t', l', l, lj, ń, nj*, appearing in various Slavic languages are equated with the plain consonants *t, l, n,* rejecting the palatalizing symbol.

4) Syllabic Liquids: *l* and *r*.

The syllabic *l* appearing in Czecho-Slovak is relieved by insertion of *e* before *l*, i.e., by changing the word into its Polish form.

Since the syllabic *l* changes in Slovenian and Serbo-Croatian into *u* while in Polish and Russian is relieved by insertion of *e*, respectively *o*, no further problem is encountered with its transliteration into English.

The syllabic *r* of Czecho-Slovak, Slovenian and Serbo-Croatian is relieved with insertion of *e*, i.e. by restoring the word in most cases to its Polish or Russian form, except for occasional Russian anaptyxis (cf S-Cr. *Drvo*, 'tree', Russian *derevo* /idem/, etc.) and occasional Polish preference for *a* (cf-S-Cr. *Tvrd* 'hard, firm', and Polish *twardy* /idem/).

In accordance with this, we marked the names: *Novo Brdo* with *Novo Berdo*, *Trst* with *Terst*, *Crna Gora* with *Tserna Gora*, *Krk* with *Kerk*, etc.

The only exception we make with the name of king *Tvrdko* calling him *Tvardko*, in accordance with the Polish form and generally established usage in the historical literature.

5) Cyrillic Letters

In transliterating Cyrillic characters we follow the phonetic rules established for Slavic languages using Latin alphabet. Wherever palatal dipthongs: я, ю, ь, е occur, they are reproduced with the English consonantal *y* followed by respective vowel, providing the combinations: *ya, yu, ya* or *ye*, with due variations under primary stress: *yo* or *o*, for ь and *e*.

The Russian short *u* is equated with the consonantal English *y*.

The guttural spirant *x* is rendered with English *kh*, except in Serbian where it appears as an aspirate, and is, accordingly, equated with *h*.

6) Hungarian

The vowel-system of this language offers considerable complications. Its alveolar-guttural sounds, even though denoted with the conventional graphic symbols of the Latin alphabet, follow entirely different phonetic patterns.

The most difficult is the simple vowel *a*, which comes closest to English *aw* as in *law, draw, crawl*, etc., but still better approximation of it will be the compromise sound between *law* and *low; draw* and *drole; call* and *coal*, etc.

Its open variety marked with an acute accent giving *á*, will bring us closest to the vowel appearing in the words: *calm, palm, barn, farm*, etc.

The Hungarian *ó* comes close to the monophthong *ow*. So *ló*, 'horse' sounds as *low; só* 'salt' as *show*, etc.

<hr/>

[1] A case in point is the theory of Franz Boas, who has confirmed the increase of dolichocephaly among the descendants of Jewish immigrants to this country, and that of C. Toldt, who has noted the intensive increase of brachycephaly in the northwestern part of the Balkans.

The Hungarian *ú* will be the long English *oo* as in *fool*, *stool*, *wool*, etc.

The Hungarian *é*, will come close to French *é*, except that it is an alveolar-guttural sound, acquired best by hearing.

The Hungarian *ö* and *ő*, and *ü* and *ű*, follow the respective German vowels, the umlaut symbols rendering the short and quotation marks the long values of the same sound

Relatively little change is observed in the consonants.

So: Hungarian *s* or *ss* is the English *sh*.

Hungarian *cz*, *ccz*, or *czcz* is marked with *ts*.

Hungarian *cs*, *ccs*, or *cscs* is *ch*.

Hungarian *sz*, *ssz*, or *szsz* is *ss*.

Hungarian *zs* is marked with *zh*.

Hungarian *y* is merely a palatizing symbol as Russian *ь*.

Hungarian *j* is the same as German *j* or English consonantal *y*.

So: *jó* 'good' sounds as *yoe*; *juh* 'sheep' as *yooh*; *jeles* 'distinguished, excellent' as *yellesh*, etc.

7) Ancient and Modern Greek

Each one is transliterated according to its phonetic rules.

8) Turkish

Spelling follows the modern Turkish alphabet, except that Turkish *c* is equated with English *dj*, and *ç*, with *ch*.

3. Geographical Names

Toponomy offers considerable difficulties. The same locality is sometimes called by two, three or four names according to the historical period, or the language in which it is referred to.

Here we present only those appearing more frequently in this volume.

1) Adriatic Area (Proceeding South).

Croatian	Italian
Gradež	Grado
Oglaj	Aquileia
Gorica	Gorizia
Trst	Trieste
Kopar	Capo d'Istria
Poreč	Parenzo
Rovinj	Rovigno
Pulj	Pola
Lošinj	Lussigno
Cres	Cherso
Krk	Veglia
Opatija	Abbazia
Rijeka	Fiume
Bakar	Buccari
Senj	Segna
Rab	Arbe
Zadar	Zara
Skradin	Scardona
Pag	Pago
Šibenik	Sebenico
Trogir	Trau
Split	Spalato, Spalatro
Solin	Salona
Omiš	Almissa

Otok Dugi	Isola Lunga
Hvar	Lesina
Sulet	Sciolta
Palagruž	Pelagosa
Brač	Brazza
Korčula	Curzola
Mljet	Meleda
Lastovo	Lagosta
Vis	Lissa
Pelješac	Sabioncello
Ston	Stagno
Gruž	Gravosa
Dubrovnik	Ragusa
Cavtat	Ragusavecchia
Herceg Novi	Castelnuovo
Kotor	Cattaro
Budva	Budua
Bar	Antivari
Ulcinj	Dulcigno
Skadar	Scutari
Drač	Durazzo

2) Other Areas

Zagreb — Zágráb (Hungarian) — Zagrabbia (Italian) — Agram (German)

Požun — Bratislava (Slovak) — Pozsony (Hungarian) — Pressburg (German)

Križevci — Kőrös (Hungarian) — Kreuz (German)

Esztergom (Hungarian — Ostrogon (Croatian — Gran (German)

Budim — Buda or Budavár (Hungarian) — Ofen (German)

Székes Fehérvár (Hungarian) — Stolni Biograd (Croatian) — Stuhl-Weissenburg (German)

Osijek — Eszék (Hungarian) — Esseg (German)— Mursa (Ancient)

Ilok — Újlak (Hungarian)

Iločki — Újlaki (Hungarian)

Mitrovica — Sirmium (Ancient)

Zemun — Zimony (Hungarian) — Semlin (German

Beograd (Serbian) — Belgrad (German) — Nándor Fehérvár (Old Hungarian)

Smederovo (Serbian) — Semendria

Niš (Serbian) — Naissa (Ancient)

Skoplje (Serbian) — Üsküp (Turkish)

Solun (Serbian) — Salonica — Thessaloniki (Greek)

Carigrad (Slavic) — Constantinople — Istanbul, Stanbul (Turkish)

Pontus or Pontus Euxinus — Black Sea

4.

The most revealing and illuminating work in this field has been that of the late Prof. Charles Goryanovich-Kramberger, the leading geologist and paleontologist of Croatia.

In a number of monographs published by the Croatian Academy of Science and other scientific institutions Dr. Goryanovich described and explained in Croatian, Latin and German the many fossils of the pliocene and pleistocene periods. His work on fossil fishes deals with specimens found in the cretaceous strata of the island of Hvar (Lesina) and Brach (Brazza), and with others discovered in the Isonzo valley and on Mount Lebanon in

Syria. He identifies among them a number of species going back to the Jurassic period. Among the finds on the island of Hvar he distinguishes 28 species. To 9 of these he assigns scientific names for the first time.

More interesting are his other works. In his monograph on "The fossil mammals of Croatia, Slavonia and Dalmatia" (1884) he makes a comprehensive comparative study of the fossil remains of all the mammals found in this area, while in his survey of proboscide fossils, he concentrates on the two families of Dinotheridae and Elephantidae. In the latter group he separates the sub-family of mastodons from elephants proper.

Two kinds of elephants are attested: *Elephas Antiquus* represented by two toes and five pisiform bones, found in the Krapina cave, and by 233 miscellaneous bones (up to 1912) of *Elephas Primigenius* discovered in numerous locations of the Danube-Sava enclave of Slavonia.

In his book on the "Fossil Rhinocerotides of Croatia and Slavonia (De rhinocerotidibus fossilibus Croatiae et Slavoniae, praecipue ratione habita Rhinocerotis Mercki var. Krapinensis)," Prof. Goryanovich provides a wealth of materials bearing on four kind of rhinoceroses living from the pliocene up into diluvium in various parts of Croatia and Slavonia. The oldest is *Rhinoceros Schleiermacheri* discovered at Brdovets, together with the bones of *Dinotherium giganteum* in the pliocene deposits. Somewhat younger is *Rhinoceros Etruscus*, the bones of which were found in the ferous gravel of the upper pliocene near Virovititsa in western Slavonia.

However, the most important is *Rhinoceros Mercki*, a contemporary of *Homo Primigenius* (Neanderthal man), and *Elephas Antiquus*, the oldest known variety of elephant in the Pannonian basin. Remains of this diluvial rhinoceros are represented by 320 bones (192 of them teeth) found in the Krapina cave alone. A still younger species, *Rhinoceros Antiquitatis*, is discovered near Varashdinske Toplitse. (Sulphuric Hot Springs), about 45 miles northeast of Zagreb, and in many places along the banks of the Sava and Drava rivers.

5.

See discussion of this aspect of anthropology in the work of Alessandro Gatti: L'Uomo (il suo corpo —la sua mente—la sua storia), Torino, 1934; p. 577 ff. Also Marcelin Boule: Les hommes fossiles, Paris, 1946, Chapter I.

6.

E. A. Hooton, "Up from the Ape," New York, 1931. Marcelin Boule. "Les Hommes Fossiles", Paris, 3rd. ed., 1946.

7.

For an illuminating analysis of neolithic culture and religion, see Ch. II and V of Christopher Dawson's "The Age of the Gods," London, 1928; consult also R. L. V. under "Religion" and other known authorities. See the bibliography.

8.

For more information on eneolithic and bronze ages see: Chapters IV and V of "Prehistoric Man" by Jacques de Morgan, London, 1927; Chapters XIV, XXI of "Prehistory" by M. C. Burkitt; Cambridge, 1925; and Chapter XIV of "The Age of Gods" by Christopher Dawson, London, 1928.

9.

"The tumuli are situated," writes Dr. Munro, op. cit. 132 f. "on the slopes of the rounded hills, where they are distributed in some twenty or thirty groups or cemeteries, each group numbering several hundreds. Their total number is estimated at 20,000— an estimation which is now regarded as coming far short of the real number—of which about 1,000 have been explored. They vary in length and breadth from 6 feet to 60 or even 120 feet, and in height from 14 inches to 12 feet. They are constructed of earth and surface stones gathered from the vicinity.

10.

For a list of prehistoric iron goods see: Jacques de Morgan, "Prehistoric Man," Chap. VII; and for religion: Chap. II-(Part 3);

For iron age cultures see: Christopher Dawson, "The Age of Gods," Chap. XVI.

11.

See: Prof. A. Ivachich in "Dalmacija" p. 49 and Arthur Evans "Through Bosnia and Herzegovina, etc.," p. 388.

12.

See: K. Jirechek, "Handelsstrassen und Bergwerke von Serbien und Bosnien, p. 1; Carl Patsch, "Historische Wanderungen im Karst, etc.," Chap. I.

13.

For detailed information on the history of these colonies see William Smith, "A Dictionary of Greek and Roman Geography," and Pauly-Wissowa's "Real Encyclopädie der kl. Alterthumswissenschaft" under each respective name.

14.

At the beginning of the 19th century L. Cassas and J. Lavallée published many engravings in their interesting book: "Voyage Pittoresque et Historique en Istrie et Dalmatie," Paris, 1802. G. Kowalczyk reproduced in 1910 about 40 plates of Adam's engravings.

15.

Interesting is the scholarly discussion of R. Munro, op. c., Chaps. VII and VII of Diocletian's palace, together with the ruins of Salona and Necropoles at Marusinac and Manastirine. A. L. Frothingham follows with his "Roman Cities in Italy and Dalmatia," 1910. Among the more recent tourist writers providing eyewitness impressions and attractive illustrations, should be mentioned: (1) Maude M. Holbach's "Dalmatia, the Land Where East Meets West," 1908; Chaps. V. and VI; (2) Hamilton Jackson's "The Shores of the Adriatic, the Austrian Side," 1908, Chap. XXI; (3) Mrs. Russel Barrington's "Through Greece and Dalmatia," 1912; pp.

130 ff; (4) Horatio F. Brown's "Dalmatia" (in colored pictures painted by Walter Tyndale), 1925; and (5) Geoffrey Rhodes: "Dalmatia, the New Riviera," 1928, Chap. VII and VII (the volume has many beautiful photographs).

Valuable scientific works on the subject have appeared in Croatian, Latin, German, Italian, French and Danish. An exhaustive bibliography up to 1925 is given by Don Frank Bulich, a well-known Croatian archeologist in his two works: "Razvoj arheoloshkih istrazhivanja i nauka u Dalmaciji Kroz Zadnji milenij," 1924; (Development of Archeological Investigations and Science in Dalmatia in the Last Millenium), and "Palacha cara Dioklecijana u Splitu," 1927 (Palace of the Emperor Dioclecian in Spalato). The volume of Hébrard-Zeiller also contains a copious bibliography.

16.

Through the work of Don Frano Bulich, the foundations of two cities, pagan and Christian Salona, have been brought to light. Much has been written about these finds, both in archeological and tourist literature. Although in English our first thought is of Robert Munro and his illuminating volume on the archeology of Bosnia, Herzegovina and Dalmatia, a more important book is that of Don Bulich entitled: "Development Archeological Investigations, etc.," which reports on the results of excavations up to 1925.

Nonetheless the information gained from Dr. Munro is quite impressive. From him we learn that archeological excavations in this area were initiated through the effort of Emperor Francis I of Austria, who visited Salona in 1818. This course of excavation continues, with some interruptions, to the present day. Dr. Munro visited the sites and gives a first hand account of his experiences there. After a rapid description of the ruins of the ancient pagan Salona, he passes to the discussion of the Christian tombs and churches in the necropoles of Monastirine and Marusinats, (See o. c., Ch. VII and VIII.)

Further, he visited the Museum of Spalato and carefully studied there the exhibits disinterred in Salona. So in August, 1893, he found listed by Dr. Bulich, curator of the museum, the following objects: 2,034 inscriptions, 387 sculptures, 176 architectural pieces, 1,548 fragments of terra cotta and vases, 1,243 objects of glass, 3,184 of metal, 929 of bone, 1,229 gems, 128 objects from prehistoric times, 15,000 coins; also a library of 1,377 works.

But since that time immense riches have been discovered and added to the already existing treasure house of pagan and Christian antiquities for Salona. Both Dr. Bulić in his bibliographic work and G. Kowalczyk in his folio volume present some neat and representative illustrations of the Salonitan monuments and grave goods. On page 47, o. c., Bulić presents a neat bas-relief of Mithra: "Sol Deus" and "Petra Genetrix." On p. 49 (Kow. plate 58) he presents an impressive bas-relief portraying the Israelites crossing the Red Sea. On p. 53 we see the foundations and ruins of the walls and towers of old Salona near the eastern gate (Porta Andetria)

fully disinterred. Page 57 gives a view of a pagan Roman cemetery enclosed by solid walls and divided into several sections, each of them housing a number of sarcophagi.

A most refreshing sight is presented by three illustrations of the amphitheater (pp. 61, 63 and 65) located close to the sea like the one in Pola. Here we see a number of heavy pylons, with arches, and the circular outline of the edifice. On page 91, Sudatorium or steam-room of the Roman thermae (hot baths) is pictured in its latest disinterment. On page 69 we see the Christian cemetery at Manastirine with the remains of the basilica of St. Domnius and other martyrs. Some of its columns have been set up in their original places. A closer view of the same edifice, with sarcophagi scattered all over the place, is given on p. 71.

The Christian Baptistery located near the northern gate of the city with two rows of parallel city walls can be seen on page 79. By way of contrast, page 83 presents the ruins as of 1902, before the excavations in Salona started. The sight presents a shapeless heap of stones resembling more an abandoned quarry than remains of any creditable architectural work. Two interesting pictures of the basilica of Sympherius and Esychius, the ruins of which are well preserved, appear on pages 85 and 87. All the basic structures, including the columns, are still on the site, however, damaged and scattered. Interesting is a framed mosaic group from the floor of that basilica, with the inscription revealing the names of its founders (p. 99). There is a beautiful picture of the floor of the basilica of St. Anastasius, in colored mosaic, almost fully restored.

An immediate contact of the ancient world with our own days has found its symbolic expression in the modern two-story building (p. 77) erected in Salona through the efforts of Dr. Bulich from the stones, materials, columns, sculptures and architectural decorations salvaged from the ruins of Salona. The building is used as a library, specializing in works on classical archeology.

While Kowalczyk produces some of the same pictures (p. 50 and 51), he provides also impressive details of these structures as found in the museum of Spalato. Such are the early Christian mosaics, with entirely new decorative patterns; somewhat crude, but novel capitals of columns and pilasters; statues; decorative vases; inscriptions and bas-reliefs of sarcophagi, including the famous sculpture of a boar hunt, numerous Christian symbols and other articles, up to the appearance of the purely Croatian art.

17.

We reproduce here the short article by Leonhard Schmitz, in William Smith's Dictionary of Greek and Roman Geography, p. 1014. "Sirmium, an important city in the southeastern part of Lower Pannonia, was an ancient Celtic place of Taurisci, on the left bank of Savus, a little below the point where this river is joined by the Bacuntius . . . The town was situated in a most favorable position, where several roads met, and during the wars against the Dacians and other Danubian tribes, it became

the chief depot of all military stores, and gradually rose to the rank of the chief city in Pannonia. Whether it was ever made a Roman colony is not quite certain, though inscription is said to exist to that effect. It contained a large manufactury of arms, a spacious forum, an imperial palace, and other public buildings, and was the residence of the admiral of the first Flavian Fleet on the Danube. The emperor Probus was born at Sirmium. The city is mentioned for the last time by Procopius, as being in the hands of the Avari; but when and how it perished, are questions which history does not answer. Extensive ruins of it are still found about the modern town of Mitrovtisa."

18.

R. Munro, o. c., p. 203 and 206 (plate 25) shows two Roman bridges near Mostar (*also o. c. p. 343). One of them spans the Buna. Another old bridge over that river, and the famous Mostar bridge over the Neretva, are probably also of Roman origin. (*See Sir Arthur Evans, through Ba. and H. etc. p. 344.)

19.

The two monographs of Carl Patsch, "Bosnien und Herzegovina in Römischer Zeit," 1911 and "Historische Wanderungen im Karst und an der Adria," 1922, display illustrations of ancient cultural objects found throughout Herzegovina and Bosnia.

20. *Mohammed and Islam*

Born of poor parents and orphaned at the age of nine, Mohammed (570-632) had to contend with great hardships in his early life. As a youth he plied the trade of a camel driver. This gave him an opportunity to visit many places with the caravans. He was eager to learn all he could from the merchants and seamen of distant lands. Thus he became acquainted with the teachings of Hebrews and Christians alike, and was fascinated by both. In spite of his descent from the fetish-worshipping tribe of the Kuraish, Mohammed became attached to the idea of one God, Allah. He insisted that this was the God of Jews and Christians alike. In his admiration for Christianity, Mohammed inclined to the Arian and Nestorian faith rather than to the orthodox teachings of the Church. Man's destiny and purpose in life and the whole complex of human relations in an organized society, attracted his attention. Above all he studied the teachings and lives of the prophets. After years of study and meditation, he became obsessed with a passion to teach and to convert other people to his way of thinking. He achieved that by a set of elegant and musical verses called *suras*, which resemble the proverbs of Solomon. Published by his disciples after the death of the prophet, these verses became known collectively as the Koran (Arabic: *AL Qran* 'Reading').

At first the number of Mohammed's followers was very small. It hardly exceeded a select group in his own household and among his personal friends. Among these were his first wife Khadija, his cousin Ali, the young and gifted Omar, and his closest friend and adviser, Abu Bekr. The rest of the Kura-

ish tribe and inhabitants of Mecca were either indifferent to him, or hostile.

The friction grew and Mohammed went into exile. This event is known as the Hegira, and the year 622 when the prophet and his little band of followers left for Yathrib, serves as the starting point for computation of time in the Moslem world. In Yahtrib Mohammed was well received and the inhabitants were willing to recognize him as their Messiah. The city was renamed in his honor Medina (City of the Prophet). Here Mohammed continued his ministry with still greater vigor and devotion. The scope of his religious outlook was widened by inclusion of social and political problems. Realizing that the success and dominon of a religion depended on the power of the state, he laid the foundation of a state that rested on the tenets of his faith. In this manner he could propagate his teachings both by persuasion and coercion, through resort to arms.

After eight years in Medina, Mohammed returned at the head of a victorious army to his native Mecca, and captured the city without striking a blow. The prophet's triumph was complete and the proud Kuraish accepted the new faith. Among other notables, Khalid and Amr Ibn al-Ras, great military commanders, became fervent followers of Islam. They were placed in command of the first great armies entrusted with the task of enforcing Islam in the neighboring lands.

The sudden death of Mohammed (632) was a heavy blow to the cause of Islam. Yet his work was done. A long line of descendants emulated the messianic ardor of the founder. Within less than a century the Orient, including Asia Minor, Eastern Europe, Central Asia and Western India, together with the north of Africa and southwestern Europe submitted to the rule of Islam. Under the leadership of the caliphs, titular successors of the prophet, the Holy War was pressed with utmost energy, so that the rapid succession of triumphs surpassed anything known in history.

21.

The term 'duke' is used here in preference to that of 'prince.' The Latin documents used consistently the term 'dux' omitting such synonyms as *princeps patricius, comes,* etc. It is further in line with the Venetian *doge* (Italian *duce*) 'duke, chief of the State,' the source word of the Croatian *dužd* 'idem.' The difference between the two terms should not be essential, because the Old Slavic *kùnendzu* (modern *knez*, Russian *knaz*, Polish *ksiendz, Ksienże*) is borrowed from the Old Germanic *kuning* 'prince, chief,' which developed into German Koenig, English king, etc. Obviously, in all of them we have the idea of ruler, chief of the tribe, sovereign.'

22. *Were St. Cyril and Methodius Slavs or Greeks?*

The epoch making work of the two sainted brothers, and its cultural effect upon the history of the Slavs, of necessity raises the question: "Of what race or nationality were these two great teachers?" And again: "What was the motive behind their strenuous and perilous work?" The right answer to these two questions may give the key for the solution of many

outstanding problems connected with their activity. There are two opposite views in answer to each of these questions. According to tradition they were Greeks, who late in life learned the Slavic language through two or more of its dialects. Similarly, as to the motive of their missionary work, there is a deeply rooted belief that they acted as emissaries of the Byzantine emperor, who was eager to spread his influence among the Slavs, and thereby to antagonize the Carolingian emperors, whose advance east had taken place at Byzantium's expense.

No doubt there is much in the way of circumstantial evidence to uphold these views. Substantial evidence, however, seems to point in another direction. Indeed, to say that the first Slavic translators of the New Testament were not Slavs is tantamount to asserting that Ulfilas, the Gothic translator of the Bible, was not a Goth; that Horace, the poet of Carmina, was not a Roman; that the authors of King James' version of the Testaments were not Englishmen. The anomaly of such an assumption is heightened by denying Slavic nationality to the inventor of *glagolitsa,* the first Slavic writing, which is admirably suited to the phonetic problems of the ancient Slavic language. The very fact that Cyril rejected the use of both the Latin and Greek writings as unsuited for the Slavic sound-structure, shows remarkable command of the Slavic language, at par with the superior talent and literary skill with which the language of the common people was used in the translation of the New Testament from the Greek originals. Therefore, if there is any foundation at all to the traditional belief that Constantine and Methodius were the first Slavic translators of the New Testament and other sacred texts, the story of their Greek origin must be discarded. No foreign-born person could have achieved such a linguistic miracle.

23. *Combination of Syllabary and Alphabetical Systems*

The mere specification of a few pertinent problems will show the hand of a master. In the syllabic system of sound notation a consonant is always attended by a vowel or diphthong. Such was the cuneiform writing of the Assyrians, Babylonians, Sumerians, Ancient Persians and others. In Sanscrit, the literary language of ancient India, the cuneiform writing was changed for a great variation of signs, but the principle of the syllabary was retained. Such is still the case in the Japanese and a large number of native languages in East India. In Sanskrit, for instance, the graphic symbol of any consonant carries with itself the vowel a, so that it is necessary to mark off the symbol with a special sign, if the vowel has to be eliminated. With a slight re-touch of the symbol the vowel *a* can be changed into *i, e, ai, o,* and *au.* In this manner the consonant *n* can with slight change of the character express the following combinations: *na, naa, ni, nii, nu, nuu, ne, nai, no* and *nau.*

The consistent use of such a system in Slavic would cause great difficulties and make the writing cumbersome. However, three classes of sound-groups called for adoption of the syllabary in Slavic. This is the combination of a vowel with the glide-sound *j* (y) forming such groups as *ya, ye, yu,* and *iye.* Another group is represented by combination of a vowel with a nasal (*m* or *n*) before a consonant, or at the end of the word. The last group arises by the combination of the first two, giving such syllables as *yam, yan, yem, yen,* etc. Both in the Glagolitic and Cyrillic script all these sound-groups are expressed with one single sign or graphic symbol. In this way two advantages were achieved. In the first place the writer's time was saved, and in the second the reader's attention was called to a grammatical momentum, owing to the fact that such syllables frequently had functional value or morphological assignment.

In its alphabetical part both *glagolitsa* and ancient *chirilitsa* commanded a larger variety of vowels and consonants than either the Latin or Greek writing. In addition to the regular stops represented by the labials (*p, b*), dentals (*t, d*) and gutturals (*k, g*), Constantine's system contained special symbols for the fricatives, affricates and palatals. So we find in it special signs for: *c, č, z, ž, s, š, ch, sc,* and *dz.* The palatal variations of the consonants(*tj, dj, gj, lj, nj, r, s,* etc.) have been brought out by the following pre-palatal syllable (*ja, ju, je,* etc.) or the semi-vowel b.

Creating order and symmetry in the vast sound-material of a language, which had never been studied before and analyzed by grammarians, could only be accomplished by a man of vision and scholarship, in whose mind the sound-harmony of the language has been vibrating with increasing fascination since the early days of his life. A product of thorough observation and acoustic details, the Glagolitic system did not rise over night in the mind of its maker, but matured in the course of a long period of time. Its merits are based on the shortcomings of both the Latin and Greek alphabets, which had to be negatived first, before the decision for the powerful synthesis had matured. The Slavs, and particularly Croats and Bulgarians, lost nothing by clinging to Constantine's invention for centuries. They gained much. On the contrary, they lost much when *glagolitsa,* under the pressure of foreign influences, went out of use.

Such is the brief history of this fascinating writing.

24.

For the clarifying of many points in this controversy the most important source of information is the meritorious work of Armin Vámbéri, a distinguished orientalist, entitled: A magyarok eredete (The Origin of the Hungarians). Among the scientific works of the more recent period should be consulted the excellent grammatical work of Simonyi, entitled "A magyar nyelvtan" (The Hungarian Grammar), which is translated into German under the title: "Die ungarische Sprache."

25. *Persecutions*

While the account of these grave events in the extant sources is fairly consonant, reference to some

details of the matter is subject to doubt. This whole movement impresses one with the determination of the weaker party to stand for its rights in the face of superior powers and strong opposition. It must have dawned on the minds of the leaders from the outset that their chances of success were slim. They were also conscious of the dire consequences which would befall them, should their efforts fail in the uneven struggle. Finally, their motives were noble, untainted with expectation of political or material gain. For this reason, the three men should be exempted from the suspicion of untruthfulness cast upon them by their opponents.

The claim was made by their enemies that after their return to Kerk, the three men falsely declared that Zdede had been consecrated by the pope and was made head of the Croatian Church. Literal acceptance of such an insinuation would deprive the three fearless champions of the national cause of intelligence, courage and pride, all of which they so magnificently attested amid risks and trials to the end. The only safe conclusions we may draw from such unsparing aspersions, is the hostility of the source to the idea of Slavic liturgy. Its prominence should be assigned to the class of those who, for political reasons, defamed even the character of St. Methodius, through whose kindly words the message of Christ became possessed of the mind and hearts of the people throughout the Slavic world.

E. Chapple & C. Coon. Principles of Anthropology, 1942 Chap. 5 &10).

E. Perrier. The Earth Before History; Man's Origin, and Origin of Life, 1925

E. Baily & J. Weir. Introduction to Geology. 1939

Dalmatia, London, 1920

Bosna i Hercegovina, 1922. Engineers' Memorial Book.

L. Dudley Stamp. A Regional Geography, Europe & Mediterranean, 1940.

Lóczy Lajos. A Magyar szent Korona országainak földrajzi stb. leírása. (Geographical Description of the Countries under Sovereignty of the Holy Hungarian Crown).
  I. A Társországok: Horvát és Szlavonország, Dalmátország (Companion countries: Croatia, Slavonia and Dalmatia).
  I. Bosnia és Herczegovina, (Bosnia and Herzegovina).

Cambridge Ancient History. Vol. I.

Stjepan Ratković, Zemljopisni pregled Banovine Hrvatske. Zagreb, 1941. (A Geographical Survey of the Croatian Banate).

Nikola Žic. Istra. Dio I. Zemlja (Istria, Part I. Country) Zagreb, 1936.

E. W. Berry. Paleontology; 1929

E. A. Hooton, Up from the Ape, 1931

J. de Morgan, Prehistoric Man (A General outline of prehistory); 1924.

W. J. Perry, The Growth of Civilization; 1924

V. G. Childe, The Dawn of European Civilization; 1925

Christopher Dawson; The Age of Gods; 1928; Chaps. VI. VII, VIII, XIII, XV.

Sir Arthur Evans, New Archeological Lights on the Origins of Civilization; 1917

Sir Arthus Evans, The Palace of Minos. 4 Vol. 1921-35.

Sir Arthur Evans, Through Bosnia & Herzegovina on Foot; 1876.

Sir Arthur Evans, The Earlier Religion of Greece in the Light of Cretan Discoveries; 1931.

The Cambridge Ancient History, 1925. Vol. III, Chap. VII and XXV.

L. Wilby, A Companian to Greek Studies, 7th ed. 1931.

A. Holm, History of Greece, 1894. Vol. 1, chap. XXI.

G. W. Botsford, Hellenic History; 1922.

W. Smith, Dictionary of Greek & Roman Antiquities, 2 vols. 1891.

O. Seyffert, A Dictionary of Classical Antiquities; 1895.

W. G. East, An Historical Geography of Europe. Chap. XVIII "The Danube Route-way," 374 ff., 1935.

M. Rostovzeff, A History of the Ancient World, 2 vols., 1940.

M. Rostovzeff, Social and Economic History of the Roman Empire 1926.

Theodore Mommsen, The History of Rome. (5 vols.) Translated by: W. P. Dickson, 1903. Vol. III, 264, 290 f; 426 f. Vol. V. 103, 284 f.

Theodore Mommsen, Provinces of the Roman Empire, 2 vols. Translated by W. P. Dickson, 1887. Vol. 1, Chap. VI "The Danubian Lands."

R. Munro, Rambles and Studies in Bosnia-Herzegovina and Dalmatia. Chaps. VI, VII, VIII 2nd ed.; 1900.

A. E. R. Boak, A History of Rome; New York, 1943.

M. Rostovzeff, A History of the Ancient World-II-Rome. Oxford, 1927.

Dio Cassius, History of Rome, 6 Vols. Translated by: H. B. Foster, 1905. Vol. IV, pp. 196-221.

C. Suetonius Tranquillus, The Lives of the Caesars. Translated by J. C. Rolfe, 1914.

J. Hindmarsh, The New History of Count Zosimus, Sometimes Advocate of the Treasury of the Roman Empire. London, 1684.

J. B. Bury, The History of the Later Roman Empire (395-565). 2 Vols., 1923.

J. B. Bury, The Invasion of Europe by the Barbarians, 1928.

Ch. W. Ch Oman, The Dark Ages, (476-918). 1901.

P. Villari, The Barbarian Invasions of Italy. 1902.

Tho. Hodgkins, Italy and Her Invaders. 8 Vols. 1885-99.

W. G. Holmes, The Age of Justinian and Theodora. 2 Vols. 1905-07.

A. Carr, The Church and the Roman Empire. 1902.

E. Hatch, Organization of the Early Christian Churches. 1881.

James T. Shotwell & Louise R. Loomis, The See of Peter, New York, 1927.

Kidd, Beresford, The Roman Primacy to A.D. 461.

Chr. B. Coleman, Constantine the Great and the Christian Church, New York, 1914.

N. H. Baynes, Constantine the Great and the Christian Church, London 1931.

J. B. Bury, A History of the Later Roman Empire from the Death of Theodosius I to the Death of Justinian (395-565) I-II London, 1923.

W. Holmes, The Age of Justinian and Theodora I-II., 2nd ed. London, 1912.

Sir Arthur Evans. Les Slaves de l'Adriatique et la Route Continentale de Constantinople. London, 1916.

F. Preveden, The Vocabulary of Navigation in the Balto-Slavic Languages. 1927. University of Chicago dissertation.

J. Bary, The Chronological Cycle of the Bulgarians, Byzantinische Zeitschrift 19. (1910)

A. Vasiliev, History of the Byzantine Empire. 2 vols. 1928-29.

Ch. Oman, Story of the Byzantine Empire. 1892.

Ch. Diehl, History of the Byzantine Empire. 1925.

I. Goldziher, Mohammed and Islam. 1917.

Sir W. Muir, "The Caliphate," its rise, decline and fall. 1915.

C. H. Becker, Christianity & Islam. 1903.

N. W. Pickthall, The Meaning of the Glorious Koran. (Arabic Text and explanatory translation). 2 Vols. 1938.

C. Stephenson, Mediaeval History. 1935-43-44.

J. B. Bury, The early history of the Slavonic Settlements in Dalmatia, Croatia and Serbia.

J. B. Bury, A History of the Later Roman Empire from Arcadius to Irene (395-800), 2 Vols., London, 1923.

Franjo Rački, Scriptores rerum chroaticarum ante 1200 a.d. 1880.

Hodgson, F. C The early history of Venice. 1901.

J. B. Bury, A history of the Eastern Roman Empire from the fall of Irene to the accession of Basil I (802-867). London, 1912.

I. Jirlček, Geschichte der Serben. Gotha, 1911.

G. Zenoff, Die Geschichte der Bulgaren.

John Farrow, Pageant of the Popes, London, 1943.

Attwater, Donald. A dictionary of the Popes, from Peter to Pius VII-1940.

G. Balashchev, Clement, the Slavic bishop, Sophia, 1898.

J. B. Bury, Life of Thomas the Slavonian. Byzant. Zeitschrift (1892).

Pastor, Ludwig, The History of the Popes (32 Vols.). 1891-1940.

Bower, Archibald, The History of the Popes (5 Vols.). 1749-1766.

Soranzo, Girolamo, Bibliografia veneziana. 1885.

S. Runciman, The Emperor Romanus Lecapenus and his reign. Cambridge, 1929.

August Theiner, Vetera monumenta Slavorum meridionalium, maxima parte nondum edita, etc. Vol. I-II. Zagreb, 1836-1875.

J. B. Bury, Roman Emperors from Basil II to Isaac
Komnenos. Cambridge, 1930.

C. Neuman, Die Weltstellug des byzantinischen Reiches
vor den Kreuzzügen. Leipzig, 1894.

J. B. Bury, Roman Emperors from Basil II to Isaac
Komnenos. The English Historical Review 4
(1889).

Živko Jakić, Poviest Srba, Hrvata i Slovenaca. Zagreb,
1929.

Deér, Jószef, A magyar törszövetség és patrimoniális
királyság Külpolitikája.

Jalland, Trevor G. The Church and the Papacy. 1942.

Milman, Henry Hart, History of Latin Christianity. 18
volumes. 1903.

Vj. Klaić. Poviest Hrvata (5 Vols.).

Note. The above represents only a part of the sources
used in this work. The full bibliography will appear as
a supplement to a later volume.

LIST OF DUKES AND NATIONAL KINGS OF CROATIA

1) *Dukes*

1. Visheslav	. . .	about 800- 810
2. Ljudevit Posavski	. .	about 810- 821
3. Vladislav	. . . .	821- 835
4. Mislav	. . . .	835- 845
5. Terpimir	. . . .	845- 864
6. Domagoy	. . . .	864- 876
7. Ilko	. . . . .	876- 878
8. Zdeslav (Sedeslav)	. .	878- 879
9. Branimir	. . . .	879- 892
10. Mutimir	. . . .	892- 910

2) *Kings*

1. Tomislav	. . . .	910- 928
2. Terpimir	. . . .	928- 935
3. Kreshimir	. . . .	935- 945
4. Miroslav	. . . .	945- 949
5. Michael Kreshimir	. .	949- 969
6. Styepan Derzhislav	. .	969- 995
7. Svetoslav	. . . .	995-1000
8. Goyslav	. . . .	1000-1019
9. Kreshimir Suronya	. .	1000-1030
10. Styepan (Stephen) I.	. .	1030-1058
11. Peter Kreshimir IV the Great	.	1058-1074
12. Slavats	. . . .	1074-1076
13. Demetrius Zonimir	. .	1076-1089
14. Styepan (Stephen) II.	. .	1089-1090
15. Peter Svachich	. . .	1090-1097

LIST OF KINGS ORIGINATING FROM THE HOUSE OF ÁRPAD

1) *Kings of Hungary Alone*

1. Saint Stephen (Szent István)	.	1000-1038
2. Peter (for the first time)	. .	1038-1041
3. Aba Samuel	. . .	1041-1044
4. Peter (for the second time)	.	1044-1046
5. Andrew (Endre) I .	. .	1047-1060
6. Adalbert (Béla) I .	. .	1060-1063
7. Solomon	. . . .	1063-1074
8. Géza I.	. . . .	1074-1077
9. Saint Ladislaus (Szent László) .		1077-1095

2) *Kings of Hungary and Croatia*

10. Kálmán (Koloman)	. .	1095-1116
11. II Istvan (Stjepan I)	. .	1116-1131
12. Blind Béla (Hung II., Croat I)		1131-1141
13. II Géza (Croat I)	. .	1141-1161
14. III Istován (Stjepan II)	.	1162-1173
15. II László (Ladislav I)	. .	1162-
16. IV István (Stjepan III)	. .	1162-1163
17. III Béla (Bela II)	. . .	1173-1196
18. Imre [Almericus] (Mirko)	.	1196-1204
19. III László (Ladislav II)	. .	1205-
20. II Endre (Andrija II)	. .	1205-1235
21. IV Béla (Bela III)	. . .	1235-1270
22. V. István (Stjepan IV)	. .	1270-1272
23. IV László (Ladislav IV)	. .	1272-1290
24. III Endre (Andrija II)	. .	1290-1301

CROATIAN-HUNGARIAN KINGS OF MISCELLANEOUS DYNASTIES

1. Vencel (Vjećeslav) (Czech)	.	1301-1304
2. Otto (Bavarian)	. . .	1304-1308
3. I. Károly, (Karlo-Robert) Angevine,	.	1308-1340
4. Nagy Lajos, (Ludovik I), Angevine .	. . .	1340-1382
5. Maria, (Angevine)	. . .	1382-1385
6. II Kis Károly, (Karlo Drački), Angevine	.	1385-1386
7. Ladislaus of Naples (Angevine)		1396-1400

LIST OF SERBIAN KINGS OF THE NEMANIDE DYNASTY (NEMANYICHI)

Founder: Grand Duke Stefan Nemanya, 1165 (?) - 1196

1. Stefan Pervovenchani, (Stephen, the First-Crowned)	.	1196-1228
2. Stefan Radoslav	. . .	1128-1234
3. Stefan Vladislav	. . .	1234-1243
4. Stefan Urosh I .	. . .	1243-1276
5. Stefan Dragutin, (Stephen Charles)	. .	1276-1282
6. Stefan Urosh II, Milutin .	.	1282-1321
7. Stefan Urosh III	. . .	1321-1331
8. Stefan Dushan, (since 1346 emperor)	.	1331-1355
9. Stefan Urosh IV, (also called: emperor)	. .	1355-1371
10. Vukashin, co-ruler	. .	1366-1371

LIST OF OTTOMAN EMIRS — until 1403

Emirs

1. Osman I Ghazi (the Victorious)		1299-1326
2. Orkhan Ghazi (the Victorious .		1326-1360
3. Mourad I Ghazi (the Victorious) Posthumously called Sultan		1360-1389
4. Bayezid I Ilderim (The Thunderbolt) . (Posthumously called Sultan)	.	1389-1403

Over the years that have passed in the preparation of this work, so many more than originally planned, many contacts have been made through correspondence and personal consultation, with a view to achieving a more thorough and accurate presentation of the subjects bearing on the history of the Croatian people. There fore I feel duty-bound to express to all concerned my deep gratitude for their interest and cooperation in this gigantic project.

In acknowledging my debt, my thanks go in the first place to the authors mentioned in the bibliography, whose texts I quoted in pertinent excerpts, either directly, or used passim and studied carefully for purposes of comparison. It goes without saying that in each instance I weighed the evidence most carefully and critically.

All this wealth of historical materials would have never come in my hands but not for the vast resources of the Library of Congress. The Administrative Office of the Library was accommodating with research facilities and the use of necessary materials.

Even with all the resources of the Congressional Library, many points of detail would have remained obscure to me, had I not been aided by numerous friends in Croatia and other parts of Europe who sent to me rare books, monographs and materials of inestimable value.

For their review of the work, and helpful comment, I am indebted deeply to the following:

Dr. Francis Ivanichek of the University of Zagreb; Zagreb.

Prof. Hamid Kreshevlyakovich of the University of Sarayevo; Sarayevo.

Dr. Ivan Esih of the Yugoslav Academy of Science; Zagreb.

Mr. Joseph Horvat, the noted Croatian historian; Zagreb.

Prof. Alberto Freixas of the National University of Buenos Aires; Buenos Aires, Argentina.

Prof. R. Fawtier of the University of Paris (Sorbonne) ; Paris.

Prof. Y. Renouard of the University of Bordeaux; Bordeaux.

Prof. André Vaillant, contributor to the periodical "Revue des Études Slaves"; Paris.

Prof. Werner Haegi of Basel University; Basel, Switzerland.

Prof. John R. Williams, Dartmouth College; Hanover, N.H.

Profs. Barnes and Siney, Western Reserve University; Cleveland, Ohio.

I am aloso deeply gratified for the encouragement given me by Prof. Pablo Martínez del Río of the National University of Mexico; Prof. Garrett Mattingly of Columbia University of New York; Prof. R. R. Betts, University of London; Prof. R. Morghen, University of Rome, Italy; Prof. A. E. van Giffen, University of Amsterdam, Holland; Prof. W. F. McDonald, Ohio State University, Columbus, Ohio; Prof. William Bennet, University of Notre Dame, Notre Dame, Ind.

Inspiring were the messages of commendation and encouragement sent to me by many scholarly Croatian readers, including Dr. Ivan Pernar, the former Yugoslav senator; Dr. Andrew Ilich, Bury, England; Rev. Dr. L. Ivandich, Windsor, Ont.; Dr. Giunio Zorkin, Nanaimo, B. C.; Dr. Ante Smith Pavelich, Paris, France; Dr. Andrew Artukovich, Los Angeles, Calif.; Mr. Ali Kadragich, Geneva, Switzerland; Mr. Antony Kocman, Munich, Bavaria; Prof. Ivan Meshtrovich, sculptor, Syracuse University, New York; and others.

A great deal of useful knowledge and pertinent information has been derived from consultation and discussions with the Very Rev. Dr. John J. Callahan, former President of Duquesne University; Dr. Martin André Rosanoff, former Dean of the Graduate School, Duquesne University; Prof. J. Dubois, Duquesne University; Dr. Count Julius von Sigmar, Duquesne Universtity, Pittsburgh, Pa.; with Dr. Marshall Newman, Asst. Curator, Division of Physical Anthropology of the Smithsonian Institution, Washington, D. C.; with Dr. Francis Ivanichek, during his connection with that institution; with Dr. Doris Cochran, Asst. Curator, Division of Reptiles and Amphibians; and Dr. Charles O. Handley, Asst. Curator, Division of Mammology of the Smithsonian Institution.

I am also indebted to Mr. Vincent D. Engels, an eminent American writer and head of the Editorial Section of the Office of Naval Intelligence, for his kindness in assuming the onerous task of critically reviewing the next-to-final draft of my work. He not only suggested revisions which resulted in my reorganizing the entire text of this volume, but also has aided me with

valuable suggestions from his experience in the publishing field so that I am now able to present to the public a much better copy than the advance typescript.

The illustrations appearing in the book come from two different sources: the Congressional Library Collection; and Anton Schroll and Company, art publishers, Vienna, Austria. But most of this material would have been unavailable, if not for the timely and effective coopera-tion of Mr. Joseph Kraja, executive director of the United Printing and Publishing Company, Younstown, Ohio. My sincere thanks to all of them.

Last   but not least, I remember with sincere appreciation, the unselfish and arduous work of Mrs. Svea Swartz and Miss Margaret Brooks, my transcribers, who conveyed the original text of this volume from sound-records to the printed page.

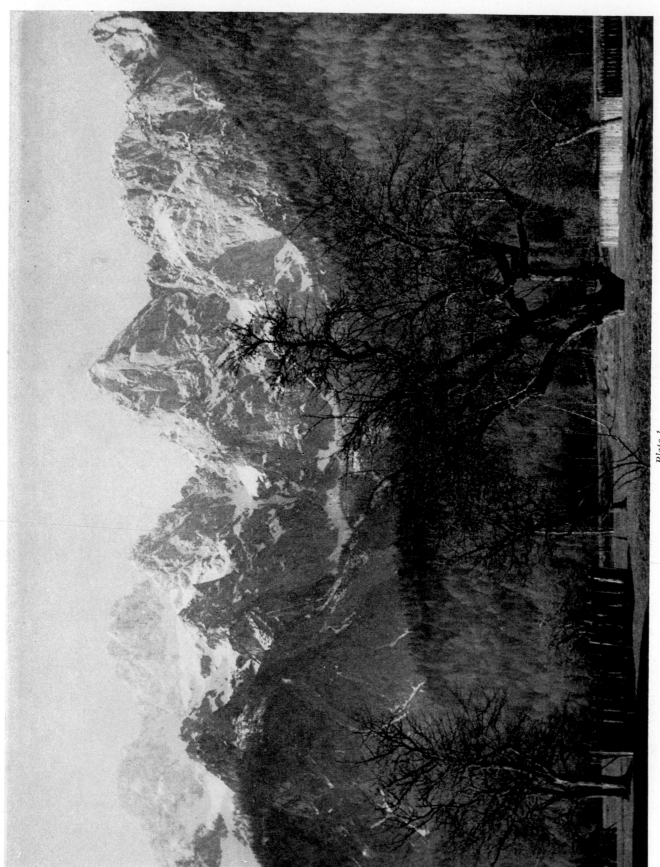

Plate 1.

Triglav (Three-heads Mountain), one of the rare scenic beauties of Europe, glorified in Croatian and Slovenian poetry. Its snows feed the head-waters of Sava, Drava and Mura, with their confluents, and eventually flow down the Danube to the Black Sea. (Anton Schroll & Co., Vienna.)

Engraving by courtesy of Mr. L. Katusin.

Plate 2.

The Velebit ranges spreading over the rocky Karst region and in places dropping abruptly in the sea. In Roman times these highlands were called Alpes Bebiae. For centuries they have inspired Croatian folklore and poetry. The central figure of this folklore is Vila Velebita (Fairy queen of Velebit) who is the symbol of Croatia as is Marianne of France.

Rugged views of the Velebit ranges show nothing at their summit but huge masses of rock and sparse growth of lichens. In these crags air currents originate which sweep down to the sea in the form of violent bura storms
(George Kufrin Studio, Chicago, Ill.)
Engraving by courtesy of Mr. A. Starchevich.

Plate 3.
As the Velebit drops down to the sea exposing its limestone slopes, it is traversed by coastal highways as the
one shown in this picture. (Anton Schroll & Co., Vienna.)
Engraving by courtesy of United American Croatians.

Plate 4.

Fishing hamlets and towns shelter in coves at the foot of the Velebit range. Among them is Jablanac shown in this picture. (Anton Schroll & Co., Vienna.)

Engraving by courtesy of Croatian Catholic Union.

Plate 5.

The Roman fort Clissium controlling the coastal area of Epetion (Stobrech), Spalato (Split), Tragurion (Trogir) and other nearby towns.

Under the name of Klis it became the trusted strong-hold of Croatian rulers. Later the Turks took it over and held it for centuries as a convenient bargaining point with Venice, which held the coastal area. (Anton Schroll & Co., Vienna.)

Engraving by courtesy of United American Croatians.

Plate 6.

A bura storm in the making over the Biokovo mountain and the town of Makarska at its foot. On the opposite coast of the sound is Korchula island, birthplace of Marco Polo. (Anton Schroll & Co., Vienna.)

Engraving by courtesy of Mr. Stanley Borich.

Plate 7.

Ombla river, one of the largest underground rivers in
Europe, known and glorified by ancient Roman writers,
ıssuing from a huge karst massif for its short surface run
into the sea. (Anton Schroll & Co., Vienna.)
Engraving by courtesy of Croatian Catholic Union

Plate 8.

The waters of the Adriatic agitated by a strong wind, probably of force 6 on the Beaufort scale. In the background a reef is seen, with a lighthouse atop. Numerous beacons and lighthouses protect the navigation of this coast from hidden hazards. (Anton Schroll & Co., Vienna.)

Engraving by courtesy of United American Croatians.

Plate 9.

Off the island of Hvar, there is a group of reefs known as "hell's islands" because of the unbearable heat prevailing there in summer. In the background is the island of Vis. In the waters between these islands the Italian navy in 1859 suffered a crushing defeat at the hands of Admiral Tegethof, Commander-in-chief of the Austrian Navy, which was manned mainly by Croatian sailors. Both the islands of Vis and Hvar rank among the oldest Greek colonies in the Adriatic. Their original names in Greek were Issa and Pharos. (Anton Schroll & Co., Vienna.)

Engraving by courtesy of United American Croatians.

One of the chief attractions to European tourists are the cascading Plitvitsa lakes of the Velebit ranges. Sixteen lakes are placed above each other discharging the excess of their water mass through thundering waterfalls. At their lowest cascade they form the head-waters of Korana river, a tributary of the Sava. (George Kufrin Studio, Chicago, Ill.)

Engraving by courtesy of Mr. Valent Susa.

Plate 11.

Vegetation on Trieste Bay, the northernmost portion of the Adriatic, shows Mediterranean characteristics. The park of Miramar castle near Trieste reveals a multitude of southern plants. (Congressional Library Collection.) *Engraving by courtesy of the Croatian Peasant Party of Canada.*

Plate 12.
The park of Lovrana, a sea resort near Abbazia on the still more striking characteristics of the Mediterranean
Quarnero Bay, along the southern coast of Istria, shows climate. (Anton Schroll & Co., Vienna.)
Engraving by courtesy of Mr. Zvonimir Kunek.

Sl. 1. Sl. 2. Sl. 3. Sl. 4. Sl. 5. Sl. 6. Sl. 7. Sl. 8. Sl. 9. Sl. 10. Sl. 11. Sl. 12. Sl. 13. Sl. 14.

Plate 13.
Artefacts of Mousterian culture found in the Krapina
cave. These are instruments and weapons of the Homo
Primigenius varietatis Krapinensis, an ancestor of the old
stone age. (Congressional Library Collection.)
Engraving by courtesy of Mr. Peter Stankovich, Winnipeg,
Man.

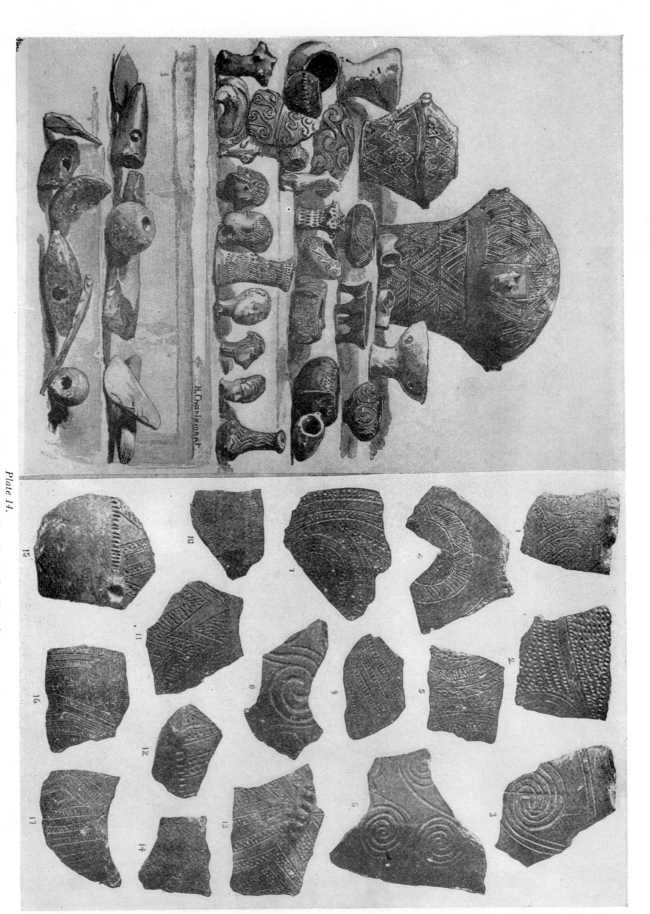

Plate 14.
Artefacts of neolithic industries found at the Butmir station of Bosnian lake dwellers. (Congressional Library Collection.)
Engraving by courtesy of Mr. John Jurinich.

Plate 15.

1) A cair or large mound of earth and stones laid over the remains of the dead. Probably a contemporary of the Glassinats tumuli in southern Bosnia.

2) Bronze utensils found in a metal age station of Bosnia. (Congressional Library Collection.)

Engraving by courtesy of United American Croatians.

Plate 16.

The Temple of Roma and Augustus still surviving the ravages of time as one of the chief archeological monu- ments of Istrian Pola, called by Romans Pia Julia. (Congressional Library Collection.)

Engraving by courtesy of Mr. John Bozwick.

POLA : L'ARENA. (Fot. Alinari).

Plate 17.

The amphitheater built in the second century in Pola, then called Pia Julia. It is used for various public performances to this day. Its site on the seashore coincides with that of the ruins of the amphitheater of Salona (Solin). (Congressional Library Collection.)

Engraving by courtesy of the Croatian Peasant Party of Canada.

Plate 18.
A Triumphal arch gracing the streets of ancient Pola.
(Congressional Library Collection.)
Engraving by courtesy of United American Croatians.

POLA : PORTA GEMINA.   (Fot. Alinari)

Plate 19.

1) "Porta gemina" or the twin gate of ancient Pola, still in a good state of preservation.

2) One of the outer gates leading through the massive Roman walls in the city. (Congressional Library Collection.)

Engraving by courtesy of Mr. Anton Klobuchar.

Plate 20.

1) A relic of ancient Jadera, at present Zadar. The city gate connecting the island city with the mainland.

2) Studies in detail by L. F. Cassas in 1802. (Congressional Library Collection.)

Engraving by courtesy of Mr. Frank Antich.

Plate 21.

Ruins of the amphitheater of Salona (Solin), sumptuous capital of Roman Dalmatia. (Congressional Library Collection.)

Engraving by courtesy of Croatian Catholic Union.

Plate 22.

Necropolis at Manastirine, a suburb of Salona, with both a Christian basilica built before the destruction of the pagan and Christian sarcophagi surrounding the ruins of the city. (Congressional Library Collection.)

Engraving by courtesy of Mr. L. Lukeshich.

Plate 23.

Reconstruction by Hébrard of Diocletian's citadel in its original form. If there were any doubt about the military nature of the huge structure, the sixteen bastions reinforcing the tall and heavy walls, should dispel it. The sea-level has receded, but in Diocletian's time it offered comfortable draft for the Roman galleys to anchor at the very steps of the building. (Congressional Library Collection. Engraving by courtesy of Mr. Valent Susa.)

Plate 24.

1) "Caius Aurelius Valerius Diocletianus, Imperator Romanorum," the most powerful ruler of history, who combined the power of Alexander the Great, with that of the Pharaohs of Egypt, Julius Caesar and Trojan of Rome, as well as that of Charlemagne.

2) Reconstruction of the Mausoleum or Temple of Jupi-

ter, in whose interior Diocletianus wanted to rest forever reposing in a sumptuous sarcophagus, surrounded by the statues of the chief Roman deities to guard his peace.

(Congressional Library Collection.)

Engraving by courtesy of the Croatian Peasant Party of

Canada.

Plate 25.

The present appearance of the Mausoleum which was converted with the advent of Christianity into the cathedral of St. Domnius (Sveti Dujam), and adorned with a lofty campanile, which had to be replaced due to wear of many centuries, with a new structure erected toward the end of the 19th century. (Congressional Library Collection. Engraving by courtesy of Mrs. Augusta Mertz.)

Plate 26.
The main entrance to the Cathedral viewed from two different angles. Still in the same condition as it was in the 3rd century. (Congressional Library Collection.)

Engraving by courtesy of Rev. V. Vanchik.

Part of the Door of the Temple to a Larger Scale

A

Part of the Soffit of the Cornice

B

Scale of Feet

Plate 27.

Decorative stone carvings enhancing the beauty of the main entrance of the Temple of Jupiter, now St. Dom- nius' Cathedral. Drawn by Robert Adam in 1763. (Congressional Library Collection.)

Engraving by courtesy of Mr. Mirko Grchich.

Plate 28.
Interior of the Mausoleum or Cathedral of St. Domnius
as it appears now. (Congressional Library Collection.)
Engraving by courtesy of Rev. V. Vanchik.

Plate 29.

Reconstruction by Niemann of the exterior of the private quarters of the emperor. (Congressional Library Mausoleum, with the adjoining entrance structure of the Collection.) vestibulum, the luxurious ante-chamber leading into the *Engraving by courtesy of Mr. Peter Stankovich, Winnipeg, Man.*

Plate 30.

Reconstruction by Niemann of both the Mausoleum and stylium, an elegant front hall of the vestibulum. (Con-
the Temple of Aesculapius, separated by the "sacred pre- gressional Library Collection.)
cinct" (frontyard of the latter) and the columns of peri-
Engraving by courtesy of United American Croatians.

Plate 31.

Peristylium as seen and drawn by Robert Adam in 1763. In his time it was used as a market place, with both vendors and buyers appearing in most interesting cos- tumes, here greatly reduced. (Congressional Library Collection.)

Engraving by courtesy of Mr. Simon Gabrek.

Plate 32.

The present condition of the outer hall surrounding the front part of the Mausoleum (Cathedral), with the columns supporting the horizontal entablature, in contrast with semicircular arcs of the peristylium. (Congressional Library Collection.)

Engraving by courtesy of Mr. Mark Kolak.

Plate 33.
Drawings of Hébrard of various chapters and cornices of
the Mausoleum stressing the remarkable designs of the
Roman stone-cutters. (Congressional Library Collection.)
Engraving by courtesy of Mr. A. Maltarich.

Plate 34.

The porta aurea (Golden Gate) barring the entrance to the palace from the east, as seen and drawn by Cassas in 1802. Three columns which were still standing on the consoles, have since vanished. (Congressional Library Collection.)

Engraving by courtesy of Mr. Ivan Kreshich.

Plate 35.

The present condition of the Temple of Aesculapius where Diocletian offered sacrifice to the deities of his empire. After its conversion to Christian worship it was called "Church of St. John the Baptist," and is used to this day as a baptistery. There has been much controversy about a low-relief, kept in the church, in which some see the figure of the first Croatian king Tomislav, sitting on a throne, and accepting obeisance of his subjects, while others see in it the figure of Christ accepting the worship of his faithful. (Congressional Library Collection.)

Engraving by courtesy of St. Nicholas Church, Pittsburgh, Pa.

Door of the Temple of Aesculapius

Scale of Feet

Plate 36.

A drawing by Robert Adam made in 1763, as he saw and reconstructed the frontispiece to the entrance in the Baptistery. Again we are fascinated with the beauty, precision and symmetry of the sculptural design. (Congressional Library Collection.)

Engraving by courtesy of Croatian Catholic Union.

Plate 37.

The western front of the palace facing the sea with its famous Portico which has since been walled in and turned into two-story high dwellings of squatters. Likewise parasitic are the buildings in front of the Portico, and on the roof of the Palace. This is all the work of squatters. (Congressional Library Collection.)

Engraving by courtesy of United American Croatians.

Plate 38.

A fascinating view of a squatters' town built on the vacant premises of an imperial palace. The squatters have so firmly established their ownership rights that several attempts to have the space cleared have failed. (Anton Schroll & Co., Vienna.)

Engraving by courtesy of Mr. Steve Grachanin.

Plate 39.

Cathedral of Kotor (Cattaro), chronologically and architecturally comes closest to Diocletian's Mausoleum, in spite of its two belfries which also bear the marks of the Romanesque style.

Below the ciborium altar richly decorated with stone carvings and low reliefs. (Congressional Library Collection.)

Engraving by courtesy of St. Nicholas Church, Pittsburgh, Pa.

Plate 40.
Campanile of the Cathedral of Rab, with Romanesque
features plainly in sight. (Congressional Library Col-
lection.)
Engraving by courtesy of St. Nicholas Church, Pittsburgh,
Pa.

Plate 41.

Cathedral of Shibenik, a noble structure of varying styles where the Romanesque and Renaissance patterns meet under the same roof. Here roof, too, assumed a semi-circular shape as a crowning glory of its architectural prototype in Split. No other roofing of this type in Croatian lands is on record. (Congressional Library Collection. Engraving by courtesy of Rev. L. Chuvalo.)

Plate 42.

Interior of the Cathedral with an equally semi-circular ceilings and tops of the apse over the ciborium altar. Elaborate columns are gracefully supporting the en- tablature resting firmly over the arched vaults. (Congressional Library Collection. Engraving by courtesy of Rev. L. Chuvalo.)

Plate 43.

Cathedral of Trogir, chronologically one of the closest descendants of the Mausoleum. Even though two intermediate stories of the campanile of a much later construction date, display the art of renaissance, the apsis, as shown above, is purely Romanesque. With its massive substance and graceful details, it reminds of the structures of Mausoleum in the neighboring Split. (Congressional Library Collection. Engraving by courtesy of Rev. V. Vanchik.)

Plate 44.

Cathedral of St. Anastasius in Zadar shows the wide front tower of Pisa the belfry of the cathedral carries columns of the cathedral of Pisa but the semi-circular shape of its with semi-circular vaults as its effective ornamentation. three entrances and the four stories of decorative columns assert its Romanesque style. Not unlike the inclining

(Congressional Library Collection. Engraving by courtesy of Mr. Paul K. Kufrin.)

Plate 45.

Cathedral of Dubrovnik shows features at variance with the style of classical Greek edifices. (Congressional Library Collection. Engraving by courtesy of Rev. D. Kamber.)

The graceful columns of its façade support the entablature with horizontal beams in the Romanesque structures.

Plate 46.

The cathedral of Hvar is still devout to the Romanesque architecture, a feature made evident especially by the decorative design of its belfry. (Congressional Library Collection. Engraving by courtesy of Rev. L. Chuvalo.)

Plate 47.

The cathedral of Korchula follows both the Romanesque and renaissance patterns. On the whole, the massiveness of the structure and elaborate artfulness of its details recall vividly its prototype in Split. (Congressional Library Collection. Engraving by courtesy of South Chicago Croatian Parish.)

Plate 48.

The impressive appearance of the Church of St. Blaise of
Dubrovnik owes its effect to the massive structure adorned
with several styles of decorations, among which some

Romanesque features are plainly in evidence. (Congressional Library Collection.)

Engraving by courtesy of Rev. V. Vanchik

Plate 49.

Far apart are the architectural designs and styles of church buildings and public edifices in Croatia and Slavonia. The new cathedral of Zagreb replacing one of the 12th century, is a pure Gothic structure embellished by the ornamentation devices of the Italian renaissance. (George Kufrin Studio, Chicago, Ill. Engraving by courtesy of South Chicago Croatian Parish.)

Plate 50.

Another exhibit of Zagreb's church buildings widely apart in style from those of the seacoast. The church of St. Mark is considered as a national shrine as the national emblems decorating its roof will indicate. (George Kufrin Studio, Chicago, Ill. Engraving by courtesy of South Chicago Croatian Parish.)

Plate 51.

Two great cathedrals of national fame. The upper shows the shrine of Maria Bistritsa, a place of pilgrimage from the western part of Croatia.

The lower picture shows the cathedral of Djakovo in Slavonia, erected toward the end of the 19th century through the effort of Bishop Strossmayer. The massive building shows a combination of styles, among which its Romanesque features are plainly visible. (George Kufrin Studio. Chicago, Ill. Engraving by courtesy of South Chicago Croatian Parish.)

Plate 52.
Interior of the basilica of St. Francis in Shibenik fascinating with its basic features and simple beauty. (Congressional Library Collection.)
Engraving by courtesy of Rev. Sylvio Grubishich, O.F.M.

Plate 53.

Interior of the Jesuits' church in Dubrovnik impressing with its baroque style of decoration. Yet, the semi-circular vaults reveal the architect's attachment to the Roman-esque tradition. (Congressional Library Collection.)

Engraving by courtesy of St. Nicholas Church, Pittsburgh, Pa.

Plate 54.

Interior of St. Mary's church in Zadar, the tragic victim witnesses the church was demolished in the aerial attacks of the Second World War. According to reports of eye- of the British airforce. (Congressional Library Collection.)

Engraving by courtesy of Rev. Anton Nizhich, T.O.R.

Plate 55.

A painter's concept of the coming of the Croats to the Adriatic in the seventh century. Apparently the artist was inspired by the closing lines of Xenophon's Anabasis, when 10,000 Greek fighters shout in ecstasy "Thalassa! "Thalassa" at sight of the sea, after their perilous journey over the numerous Caucasian mountain chains. Dabac Studio, Zagreb.

Engraving by courtesy of United American Croatians.

Plate 56.

Artist's conception of the second Church Congress at Split when organization of a Croatian Church was rejected by the Latin clergy. The painting is one of several historical murals adorning the reception hall of the former Department of Worship and Education in Zagreb. Dabac Studio, Zagreb.

Engraving by courtesy of Croatian Catholic Union.

Plate 57.

Artist's conception of the betrothal of the Hungarian princess Helen to the Croatian king Zvonimir, an appointee of Pope Gregory VII. A mural in the reception hall of the former Department of Worship and Education in Zagreb. Dabac Studio, Zagreb.

Engraving by courtesy of Mrs. Augusta Mertz.

Plate 58.

Artist's conception of a conference between King Kálmán of Hungary and the leaders of Croatian nobility. An historical episode, commonly called "Pacta Conventa," or establishment of a constitutional union between Hungary and Croatia, which continued for over eight hundred years. Dabac Studio, Zagreb.

Engraving by courtesy of the Croatian Peasant Party of Canada.

Plate 59. Croatian peasants from the region of Verlika in Dalmatia. Dinaric race as apparent in the man at the extreme left. Here we see the Mediterranean type with traces of the

(George Kufrin Studio, Chicago, Ill.)

Engraving by courtesy of Mr. John A. Layevich.

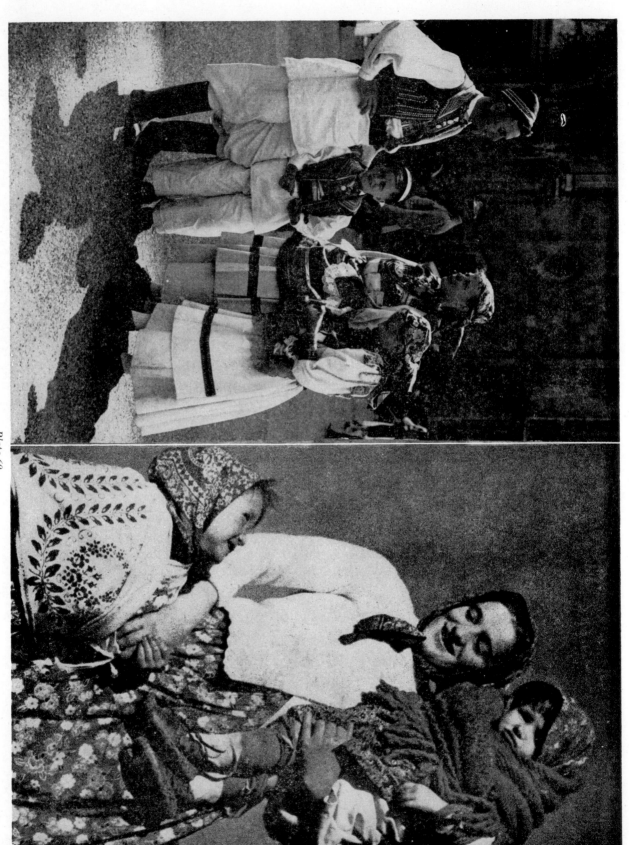

Plate 60.

Croatian peasants from the area of Zagreb, capital of those observed on the seashore. (George Kufrin Studio,
Croatia. Here the racial type is mesocephalic Slavic. Chicago, Ill.)
Emotionally and temperamentally the people differ from *Engraving by courtesy of the Chicago Branch of the
"Croatian Woman" Society.*

Plate 61.

1) Peasant girls from Polvitse (Poljice), a diminutive ornate headgear called "kinchaw." (George Kufrin Studio, republic along the seacoast, not unlike San Marino of Chicago, Ill.) Italy or Andorra of the Pyrenees. *Engraving by courtesy of Mr. Matthew Kovachevich.*

2) Another peasant beauty in her Sunday best with an

Plate 62.
Croatian peasants from Bosnia in local oriental dress.
They represent both the mesocephalic and dolichoce-
phalic type. (George Kufrin Studio, Chicago, Ill.)
*Engraving by courtesy of the Croatian Peasant Party of
Canada.*

Plate 63.
Peasant women from the Sava valley in Slavonia. Note the Greek profile of the girl at left. (George Kufrin Studio, Chicago, Ill.)
Engraving by courtesy of Mrs. Anna Matoshich.

Plate 64.

Native girls of Zlarin, a town near Split, in their Sunday best. The population of the town engages in coastal shipping, fisheries and sponge fishing, a profitable occupation in that area. Interesting is the trace of Mongoloid ancestry in the girl on the left. The Mongols not only swept through Pannonia in 1240, but sent an army down along the Adriatic coast in pursuit of the Hungarian king.

(Anton Schroll & Co., Vienna.)

Engraving by courtesy of Mr. William M. Boyd.